Last Rights

Financial Management Association Survey and Synthesis Series

The Search for Value: Measuring the Company's Cost of Capital
Michael C. Ehrhardt

Managing Pension Plans: A Comprehensive Guide to Improving Plan Performance
Dennis E. Logue and Jack S. Radar

Efficient Asset Management: A Practical Guide to Stock Portfolio Optimization and Asset Allocation
Richard O. Michaud

Real Options: Managing Strategic Investment in an Uncertain World
Martha Amram and Nalin Kulatilaka

Beyond Greed and Fear: Understanding Behavioral Finance and the Psychology of Investing
Hersh Shefrin

Dividend Policy: Its Impact on Firm Value
Ronald C. Lease, Kose John, Avner Kalay, Uri Loewenstein, and Oded H. Sarig

Value Based Management: The Corporate Response to Shareholder Revolution
John D. Martin and J. William Petty

Debt Management: A Practitioner's Guide
John D. Finnerty and Douglas R. Emery

Real Estate Investment Trusts: Structure, Performance, and Investment Opportunities
Su Han Chan, John Erickson, and Ko Wang

Trading and Exchanges: Market Microstructure for Practitioners
Larry Harris

Valuing the Closely Held Firm
Michael S. Long and Thomas A. Bryant

Last Rights: Liquidating a Company
Ben S. Branch, Hugh M. Ray, Robin Russell

Last Rights

Liquidating a Company

Ben S. Branch   Hugh M. Ray   Robin Russell

OXFORD
UNIVERSITY PRESS

2007

OXFORD
UNIVERSITY PRESS

Oxford University Press, Inc., publishes works that further
Oxford University's objective of excellence
in research, scholarship, and education.

Oxford New York
Auckland Cape Town Dar es Salaam Hong Kong Karachi
Kuala Lumpur Madrid Melbourne Mexico City Nairobi
New Delhi Shanghai Taipei Toronto

With offices in
Argentina Austria Brazil Chile Czech Republic France Greece
Guatemala Hungary Italy Japan Poland Portugal Singapore
South Korea Switzerland Thailand Turkey Ukraine Vietnam

Published by Oxford University Press, Inc.
198 Madison Avenue, New York, New York 10016

www.oup.com

Library of Congress Cataloging-in-Publication Data
Branch, Ben, 1943–
Last rights: liquidating a company / Ben S. Branch, Hugh M. Ray,
Robin Russell.
p. cm.—(Financial Management Association survey and synthesis series)
Includes index.
ISBN-13 978-0-19-530698-9
ISBN 0-19-530698-8
1. Liquidation—United States. I. Ray, Hugh. II. Russell, Robin,
1960– III. Title. IV. Series.
KF1475.B73 2007
346.73′0662—dc22 2006011611

9 8 7 6 5 4 3 2 1

Printed in the United States of America
on acid-free paper

Acknowledgments

The authors gratefully acknowledge permission granted by Leslie Horowitz and John A. Lapinski to reprint portions of their article "Assignment for the Benefit of Creditors," published in the May 1993 edition of the *Los Angeles Lawyer* (Los Angeles County Bar Association); and permission granted by D. Michael Lynn and Thomas E. Lauria the authors of a CLE article "Liquidating Plans of Reorganization," published in April 1990. D. Michael Lynn currently sits as a bankruptcy judge for the Northern District of Texas, Fort Worth Division. Part of chapter 5 was adapted, with permission, from "Managing a Pension Shutdown in Chapter 7," by Dr. Ben Branch and Gary Tameo, which appeared in the *Journal of Corporate Renewal,* volume 18, no. 7 (July 2005): 8–13. Part of chapter 8 was adapted, with permission, from "Maximizing Estate Value Through Effective Economic Litigation Analysis," by Ben Branch, Hugh Ray, and Robin Russell, which was published by West Group in *Norton's 1998 Annual Survey of Bankruptcy Law at 21.*

This guide owes much to the valuable input of Andrews Kurth, LLP, attorneys Douglas Walter, John Sparacino, John C. Melissinos, Christy Milner, and Lidell Page, and to the production assistance of Elisa Cabrales, Nancy Ediger, Patricia Curtis, Joe Charles, and Cheryl Bownds. To the degree this book succeeds in its purpose, it is in large measure a result of their efforts and expertise. Despite the fact that this book has benefited from the suggestions, comments, and support of other individuals and organizations, the authors bear sole responsibility for any errors or omissions. Robin Russell also wishes to thank her children, Sterling and Diana, for enduring the hours required to prepare this book. It is dedicated in loving memory of her mother, Helen Owen Filson Russell (1917–2006), a gifted teacher and writer.

Preface

Justice is costly. Life is short. You have to learn how to
make difficult decisions and move on.
—Professor Louis S. Muldrow, Baylor University School of Law

Liquidation of a company requires good business judgment and common sense. Successful liquidators are able to gather relevant information as quickly and economically as possible and then make difficult decisions based on that information. The authors have been involved in numerous liquidations and the litigation resulting from those failed businesses. This book provides an overview and summary of the liquidation process for those brave souls who wish to understand and perhaps participate in that process. It does not provide legal advice and should not be used as a substitute for legal advice. Accordingly, readers should always consult their attorneys with respect to these issues.

Contents

Last Rights

1

The Basics of Liquidation

Liquidate: to convert assets into cash
—*Black's Law Dictionary*, Sixth Edition

No one lives forever. Nor does any business operate forever. At death, an individual's survivors and society at large must take appropriate action to dispose of that person's body and assets. Much the same can be said of a dead business. Yet while hundreds of books have been written about death and the disposition of personal estates, from internment through final probate distributions, not one book has been written about the liquidation of a business. Fortunately, if approached properly the business liquidation process is not all that difficult to understand—certainly no more so than initial public offerings, spin-offs, or mergers. Our purpose is to explain how one goes about liquidating a company, from start to finish.

Chapter 2 outlines the liquidator's specific role in a Chapter 7 bankruptcy.

Chapter 3 discusses the Chapter 11 plan process leading to the formulation and implementation of a Chapter 11 liquidating plan of reorganization and a liquidating trust.

Chapter 4 tells a tale of two liquidations, one a Chapter 7, one a Chapter 11, which will provide a framework for the discussion in the remaining chapters.

Chapter 5 addresses the management of the employees of the business and their benefit plans until those employees are terminated or transferred to the buyer of the business unit that employs them.

Chapter 6 covers the day-to-day management issues, including the liquidator's management of records, accounting, tax and SEC issues.

Chapter 7 explores methods for evaluating and disposing of assets in a manner designed to maximize their value and the legal procedures for disposing of such assets.

Chapter 8 discusses the pursuit of the estate's causes of action through litigation, together with a method for assessing the economic value of potential actions.

Chapter 9 deals with the liquidator's role in the investigation and allowance or disallowance of claims. The priority, calculation and timing of distributions on allowed claims is also reviewed.

Chapter 10 provides an overview of state and federal equity receiverships and the state law liquidation procedure of assignment for the benefit of creditors.

Chapter 11 outlines the procedure for closing down the business entity once the liquidation is complete, disposing of business records and ultimate dissolution.

The authors bring a variety of life experiences to this task, but all approach this work from the perspective of a professional charged with the duty of closing down a business efficiently, maximizing the assets available for distribution to those legally entitled to receive them. One is an academician who has also overseen the successful liquidation of a billion-dollar business. The others are practicing attorneys with substantial hands-on experience in the liquidation of businesses, large and small.

That said, we hope to avoid being either too legalistic or too academic. A liquidator, even one with a law degree, typically employs legal specialists for the various details of liquidation—bankruptcy proceedings, associated litigation, real estate transactions, labor agreements, and so forth. Likewise, while an academic background in business management is useful and sometimes even vital to success, liquidation is at its core an immensely practical and often bare-knuckle environment. A nose for fraud may be just as useful as a master's degree in business.

In this book, we explain the task of winding up the affairs of a company that has either decided voluntarily to liquidate or been forced to liquidate by its creditors. Step by step, we provide a methodology for maximizing and creating value, particularly in the deteriorated and chaotic business environment that so often leads to a liquidation. Working from our experience with a number of large-firm liquidations, we examine the liquidation process from start to finish. And though we have changed names to protect the guilty, we do not hesitate to relate lessons learned from our failures, as well as from the successes and failures of others. We intend this book to prove useful to a variety of readers: prospective liquidators, professionals who work with liquidators, students of business organization and practice, and business people who need to work with liquidators (preferably as secured creditors)—in short, anyone who needs to know how liquidators think and what they do. The disposition of a large company is a major undertaking, but not one beyond the grasp of most people, once given the opportunity to understand the methods and basic rules. The rest is experience.

The General Liquidation Environment

Businesses close for many reasons, and in many ways: in and out of court, under either state or federal law. The great majority of significant business liquidations take place in federal Bankruptcy court, and for good reason. As we explain in some detail, federal law usually grants enormous advantages in the liquidation process. Those businesses that are willing and able to file or that might be forced into bankruptcy liquidation against their will by disgruntled creditors are likely to prefer the federal bankruptcy court to the various alternatives. Thus, most of the book and the case study focus on the bankruptcy environment.

One should however, realize that many business liquidations never darken the courthouse door, for reasons both happy and sad. Sometimes a business is solvent and thriving or is, for other reasons, a desirable candidate for merger or acquisition. One company may cease to exist because its owners have chosen to sell at a good price, and assets then may change hands in the process. Since this form of liquidation poses few problems of interest to us and is much written about, it is not discussed in this book.

A business may have given up the ghost long before its formal dissolution. Secured creditors have exercised their foreclosure rights, and unsecured creditors are unwilling to spend the money necessary to secure an uncollectible judgment. Even its owners cannot justify the expense of a bankruptcy filing or the filing of documents of dissolution. There is simply nothing left to liquidate. Its assets and employees are gone, so the business continues to exist only as a few sheets of paper moldering in a government filings office. Sometimes the value remaining in the company is so small that a fire sale, or forced liquidation—typically, a brief inspection, followed by a half-hour auction at dramatically reduced prices—is the only cost-effective option. For obvious reasons, these sorts of liquidation also are outside the scope of our work.

Our area of interest is the broad middle ground: A company that may still be operating and that may have some theoretical or real value when viewed as a going concern, but is insolvent—that is, has assets worth less than its liabilities—most often because of unmanageable debt. Here, one often finds wishful thinking blurring recognition of economic realities. Most companies that file for bankruptcy actually do so with reorganization in mind. Sometimes, this is not a false hope. Some companies in Chapter 11 can rehabilitate. A company may be able to use bankruptcy to give it breathing room, to restructure debt, renegotiate contracts, and develop a rational court-approved business plan. In some high-profile cases, this sort of reorganization effort has succeeded. This book is not about those rehabilitations.

Most businesses that find themselves teetering on the brink of failure are there for good reason. They will die as a natural part of the business cycle or in consequence of irretrievably flawed management decisions made years earlier. It is not surprising, however, that those closest to the business may be the least able to face reality. All too often people throw good money after bad, doggedly pursuing failed concepts when their time and talent would be better spent elsewhere. Sooner or later, though, management will reach a decision to terminate the business, or dissatisfied creditors and a court will make the decision for them. When liquidation begins, the value that remains is best extracted through a methodical disposal of all the failed firm's assets. Doing this right—maximizing what assets remain—is what this book *is* about. Sometimes this disposal is accomplished under state-court receiverships, assignments for the benefit of creditors, or similar remedies. Most often, the venue of choice or necessity is federal Bankruptcy Court. For that reason, some introduction to bankruptcy law and practice is helpful.

An Overview of Liquidation under the Bankruptcy Code

Bankruptcy is foreign territory, even to most lawyers, for very good reason. Unlike most areas of law, in which state court practice predominates or state and federal courts share the turf, the United States Constitution reserves the subject of bankruptcy solely to federal courts. Even within the federal system, bankruptcy is a highly specialized area governed by its own set of rules—the Bankruptcy Code—and administered by its own set of judges.

Fortunately for the average businessperson, some of the same qualities that make bankruptcy practice arcane and vaguely forbidding to many lawyers make it more accessible and friendly to nonlawyer business professionals. Historically speaking, bankruptcy courts are courts of equity. Bankruptcy practice is characterized by common sense and expediency; bankruptcy judges are more concerned with efficiency and results than with legal detail. For business liquidations, this means that both an effective bankruptcy judge and a successful business professional are always looking at the bottom line—the efficient resolution of problems in a way that best maximizes the ultimate payout.

The liquidator's bible is the Bankruptcy Code, that is, the Bankruptcy Reform Act of 1978, (codified at Title 11 of the United States Code, beginning at section 101). Like a book, the Bankruptcy Code divides the law and practice of bankruptcy into different chapters (see table 1.1). Chapters 1, 3, and 5 establish the structure usually applicable to all bankruptcy cases. The remaining chapters

Table 1.1

Generally applicable	Chapter 1	General provisions and definitions
	Chapter 3	Case administration
	Chapter 5	Relationship between creditors, the debtor, and the estate in certain situations
Specific treatments	Chapter 7	Liquidations
	Chapter 9	Municipalities
	Chapter 11	Reorganizations
	Chapter 12	Family farmers with regular annual income
	Chapter 13	Individuals with regular income
	Chapter 15	International bankruptcies

cover specific types of bankruptcy cases, from municipal insolvency (9) and international bankruptcies (15) to individuals (13) and family farmers (15). For liquidators, Chapters 7 and 11 (liquidation and reorganization, respectively) are the "big" chapters.

Chapter 7

Chapter 7 of the Bankruptcy Code is specifically designed for liquidations. The debtor that files under Chapter 7 has its assets placed in the hands of the appointed (or occasionally elected) bankruptcy trustee (different from the United States Trustee, described below). This Chapter 7 trustee is charged with liquidating the assets for the best price available, distributing the net proceeds to the claimants, and administering the estate as the liquidation proceeds. The trustee performs the duties that the debtor would have performed had the estate remained outside of bankruptcy. While operating the business of the debtor for a limited period, the trustee's primary responsibility is to sell the assets. Frequently, no equity remains for property of the debtor on which a lien has been placed. Accordingly, the lien holder (secured creditor) may be permitted to take the property back. The trustee may be elected by the creditors and must be a qualified disinterested person. This individual is awarded a fee from the proceeds recovered by the estate for his or her services. These are the burial costs for a failed business.

Chapter 11

Rehabilitation is the articulated theme in Chapter 11. Chapter 11 was adopted in order to provide an opportunity for the reorganization of a debtor, rather than a liquidation of its assets. In Chapter 11, the debtor retains control of its assets and continues its operations while various parties attempt to draft a feasible plan of reorganization. Statistically, however, only one out of every eight cases that file for Chapter 11 is able to reorganize successfully, according to the

Administrative Office of U.S. Courts. A hugely popular vehicle for implementing a liquidation has become what is known as a Chapter 11 liquidating plan. The basic concept is that a plan of reorganization is confirmed in which the creditors select a party to liquidate the assets of a debtor. A liquidating trustee is selected to sell off the assets and pay out the proceeds to the creditors pursuant to the agreed upon distributions. This liquidating trustee has the full opportunity to utilize the protections of the bankruptcy court, should the plan so provide. It is frequently less expensive and more efficient to liquidate in Chapter 11 than Chapter 7. The greater flexibility of the Chapter 11 process provides some practical legal advantages in a complicated liquidation process.

The Automatic Stay

The prime immediate benefit that companies receive by filing either Chapter 11 or 7 is the imposition by federal law of an automatic stay of the actions of creditors to collect from the debtor. Immediately upon filing, the stay goes into effect and an estate is created. Much like a probate estate, all of the debtor's property passes into the bankruptcy estate. The stay allows an orderly liquidation (rather than a fire sale) to proceed, and the use and sale of the estate's property is subject to careful court supervision. This very broad stay cannot be taken lightly. For example, creditors cannot, once the stay is in place, proceed to enforce their liens and cannot take steps to seize assets. In other words, repossession and the sale of collateral securing loans is stopped cold.

Liquidation outside Bankruptcy

Most liquidations outside bankruptcy fall into two extremes. The *solvent* company sells itself or its assets and, after paying off its liabilities, distributes the remaining funds to its equity owners. It has no need for the bankruptcy process. The business with *no equity*, after defaulting on its secured obligations, allows its secured lender to repossess the collateral/assets and sell the assets in a foreclosure sale. Infrequently, state court procedures of receiverships and assignments are used for the benefit of creditors and federal-court equity receiverships in which orderly liquidations of the assets of insolvent companies take place outside of bankruptcy (see chapter 9).

The Liquidator

The term "liquidator" refers to the senior manager of the liquidating estate, whether that liquidation is occurring in or out of bankruptcy. Actually, numerous titles are given to individuals performing liquidations (see table 1.2).

Table 1.2

Title	Definition
Trustee	A trustee appointed under Chapter 7 or 11 of the Bankruptcy Code. (Does not include the United States Trustee or an indenture trustee.)
Liquidating trustee	The trustee selected under a plan of reorganization to liquidate the estate after a plan of reorganization setting up the liquidation has been confirmed.
Estate representative	Any and all individuals that have been selected under the terms of the Bankruptcy Code or a plan of reorganization to liquidate the assets of an estate.
Receiver	An individual selected by a state or federal court to liquidate a business.
Assignee	An individual selected by the assignor to liquidate its business under state law.
Liquidator	Applies to all of the above.
Indenture trustee	The trustee for an issue of corporate bonds.

The term "trustee" usually means a trustee appointed under Chapter 7 or 11 of the Bankruptcy Code. It does not include the United States Trustee. The term "trustee" refers specifically to the Chapter 7 or Chapter 11 bankruptcy trustee. The term "liquidating trustee" refers to the trustee selected under a plan of reorganization to liquidate the estate after a Chapter 11 plan of reorganization has been confirmed. The term "estate representative" refers to any and all of the individuals mentioned above that have been selected under the terms of the Bankruptcy Code or a plan of reorganization to liquidate the assets of an estate. The term "receiver" is an individual selected by a state or federal court to liquidate a business in the rare instances when that occurs. The term "assignee" is an individual to whom an assignor (debtor) under state law makes an assignment for the benefit of creditors. The assignment or transfer of assets to an assignee is also rare. The term "liquidator" applies to all of the above. Another type of trustee that frequently appears in a bankruptcy proceeding but is *not* a liquidator is an indenture trustee. The indenture trustee is a financial institution that serves as the trustee under the Trust Indenture Act for an issue of corporate bonds.

Managing the Players in the Liquidation Process

The liquidator ultimately manages the process, the assets, and, most importantly, the people involved in a liquidation. This person must understand peoples' roles, power, alliances, and motivations. Who is powerful and who is not? Whom do you have to be nice to? Whom can you ignore? In the bankruptcy arena, this task is particularly important.

The Judge

The presiding judge is assigned or "referred" the case by the relevant United States District Court and is a judicial officer operating under that referred authority. Often, the debtor's counsel carefully analyzes (prior to filing) the judges in the potential filing locations. From the moment the case is filed, no decision is made by the trustee or by the creditors without considering how the bankruptcy judge will respond. Some judges are viewed as notoriously lenient or pro-debtor while others have reputations as being pro-creditor. Some judges are pro-active and rule quickly on matters brought before them. Others do not.

Most experienced bankruptcy lawyers agree that bankruptcies do not improve with age. If a bankruptcy judge allows his or her court to be used as a parking lot, you should beware. Asset values tend to deteriorate in bankruptcy. In addition, administrative (mainly legal) costs mount as time passes.

The Debtor

This is the entity seeking relief in the bankruptcy court. This unlucky entity use to be referred to as "the Bankrupt." As a part of the Bankruptcy Reform Act that became effective in 1979, that phrase was expunged from the statute because of negative connotations. The cognomination lives on, however.

The Debtor-in-Possession

The debtor in a Chapter 11 case that is still in possession of the company's property (no trustee has been appointed) is called a debtor-in-possession. This debtor-in-possession has certain fiduciary duties, similar to those of a trustee, requiring it to operate its business in an equitable and fair manner. In a liquidating Chapter 11, the debtor-in-possession often stays in control until the assets are turned over to the liquidating trustee.

The United States Trustee

The Bankruptcy Code provides for United States Trustees. Each state contains at least one federal court district; some have as many as four. Each federal court district has a United States Trustee, an employee of the Department of Justice who appoints bankruptcy trustees, creditors' committees, and performs other administrative tasks that are intended to help bankruptcy cases run smoothly.

Secured Creditors

A creditor that holds a valid, perfected lien on property that belongs to the debtor or has right of setoff against property of the debtor holds a secured claim, and the creditors who hold such claims are called secured creditors. These creditors often are the most powerful force with which to be dealt. If a creditor has a lien on the debtor's accounts receivable (which when collected become cash), the secured creditor can try to control the debtor's use of that cash following bankruptcy. The cash is referred to as "cash collateral." A debtor without cash to operate does not last long.

Unsecured Creditors

A creditor who does not hold a lien on any of the debtor's property has an unsecured claim. If property owned by the debtor on which a secured creditor holds a lien is not at least equal in value to the amount of the claim, then the claim can be partially secured (the value of the collateral) and partially unsecured (the difference between the value of the collateral and the amount of the claim). An unsecured creditor may be either senior or subordinated to other creditors. Indeed, several layers of subordination may exist.

Debt Holders

Debt holders, particularly public bondholders, often hold a controlling interest in a liquidating bankruptcy. They may hold a large amount of debt in the form of high-coupon, or junk, bonds. In order to understand their motivations, the following questions become important: Who bought their bonds at par? Have any large investors recently entered the picture? Who is accumulating and who is selling? At what prices? Are the large creditors mainly insiders or affiliates of the debtor or is only one large institutional creditor involved? The principal categories of major creditors are institutional investors (e.g., banks, insurance companies, mutual funds, college endowments, etc.), distressed debt funds and large individual investors (e.g., arbitragers, vulture investors). The institutional investors generally purchased their bonds (earlier) at or near par, while the distressed debt funds and large individual investors are more likely to have acquired their holdings (recently) at a steep discount from par. As a rule, the distressed debt funds and large individual holders tend to be more aggressive and more interested in a quick resolution and payout. They would like to turn their money over at a nice profit and then go on to something else. The institutional investors are likely to be more patient and more inclined to work through the situation for a higher ultimate payout, even if it takes a bit longer to achieve.

Indenture Trustees The indenture trustee, typically the corporate trust department of a large financial institution, acts for the benefit of the holders of the debt represented by the indenture. The indenture is the contract between the company and the trustee under the Trust Indenture Act, pursuant to which the company issues bonds. The indenture trustee is authorized to take action on behalf of the bondholders. In particular, the indenture trustee is responsible for filing a proof of claim on behalf of the creditor group that they represent in a bankruptcy case. The indenture trustee is often also a member of the creditors committee.

Agent Banks A large credit facility typically has multiple lenders. One lender acts as the agent under the credit agreement and coordinates the lender group. The agent bank is typically a power player in the bankruptcy process and often controls selection of the liquidator. The agent bank also is often a secured creditor with a lien on the asset securing the debtor's obligations to the lender group. The debtor's cash is often in a deposit account with the agent bank.

Trade Vendors

Trade vendors provided goods or services to the debtor prior to bankruptcy for which they were not paid. As a result they have claims against the debtor. Vendors with whom the debtor or liquidator have a continuing relationship typically are given more deference than those that are irrelevant to the continued operation of the estate.

Employees

If the business is still operating, the employees are often the single most important constituency. The going concern value of a business can quickly disappear if the employees' institutional knowledge walks out the door (see chapter 4).

The Creditors' Committee

The creditors' committee consists of the representatives of the creditors in Chapter 11 cases. The United States Trustee or the bankruptcy judge appoints the committee to oversee the debtor-in-possession and assist in the formulation and confirmation of a plan. A creditors' committee may also be appointed in a Chapter 7 case, but its role is likely to be much smaller, as they are unable to hire counsel that is compensated from the estate.

The United States Trustee usually selects the major unsecured creditors to become members of the official unsecured creditors' committee, although the committee is suppose to represent the unsecured creditor group as a whole. For this reason, at least one landlord and one trade creditor typically are asked by the United States Trustee to serve on the committee. In certain large cases, trade creditors may have their own committee. Equity committees are rare but are formed in cases in which the judge and United States Trustee are convinced that some residual value in the debtor may exist for equity.

The Professionals

The bankruptcy trustee typically retains counsel to represent the estate in the proceedings before the court. Similarly, the debtor and creditors' committee in a Chapter 11 case retain separate counsel. Other professionals, such as accountants and investment bankers, may also be retained (see appendix 1). The professional fees are one of the costs that make bankruptcies so expensive. One interested party (e.g., the indenture trustee for the senior creditor bondholders) may retain one law firm to achieve one objective (maximum recovery for the seniors) while a second group (e.g., the indenture trustee for junior bondholders) may retain lawyers to pursue a conflicting objective (e.g., maximum recovery for the juniors). In a Chapter 11 case (but not Chapter 7), the estate picks up the costs of both lawyers' work (subject to approval by the bankruptcy judge). Moreover, as administrative claims, the claims for fees have the highest priority in settling the affairs of the estate.

Chapter 11 cases tend to revolve around the professionals, their fees and the expensive squabbling between the various groups of creditors. In a Chapter 7 case, this type of conflict is markedly reduced. Frequently, the high cost of the professionals in Chapter 11 is given as a prime reason for operating a case in liquidation through Chapter 7. Understanding how the professionals operate is one of the keys to any successful liquidation. A reading of the laws, rules, and treatises on bankruptcy will not give the uninitiated the "feel" necessary for understanding their importance. Frequently, the creditors get carried away with the idea of communal lawyers, investment bankers, and accountants and end up overutilizing them. Spending the estate's funds in an effort to bring in additional funds is one thing. Spending the estate's funds to fight over how to divide up the estate's limited resources is quite another.

What Is There to Liquidate?

The liquidation of a company obviously requires selling all its assets. These assets may be thought of in terms of their commercial classification. When a commercial lender secures a loan with all assets of the company, it relies on the categories of assets established under the Uniform Commercial Code (UCC), a uniform state law governing commercial transactions (appendix 3). All assets of a business would include the following:

- Real estate
- Leasehold interests
- Oil, gas, and mineral interests
- Fixtures
- Leasehold improvements

- Inventory
- Accounts receivable
- Equipment
  * Investment property (e.g., investments in subsidiary corporations, limited liability companies, limited partnerships and joint ventures), which may or may not be evidenced by stock certificates
- Bonds
- General intangibles (e.g., tax refunds, patents, copyright, trademarks)
- Instruments such as negotiable instruments and promissory notes
- Deposit accounts
- Documents that include bills of lading, dock warrants, and warehouse receipts
- Motor vehicles
- Boats and vessels
- Aircraft
- Rolling stock
- Tort claims and other causes of action
- Letter of credit rights

Many assets held in a business function together and create going concern value. Other assets stand alone and are not intertwined in the business' day-to-day operations. Logic dictates that the highest value is to be obtained by selling the assets that function together as a business unit. In most instances, that is the preferred method of sale in bankruptcy.

Conclusion

The process of liquidating is fairly simple: The liquidator disposes of assets, pursues litigation, resolves claims, and ultimately distributes funds to creditors. At the same time, the liquidator manages the players involved in the liquidation and fulfills reporting obligations and other requirements. If the liquidator is doing all of this in the context of a bankruptcy, additional requirements must be met. Bear in mind that common sense, good business judgment, and perseverance are key to a successful liquidation. This book simply provides a framework in which to use these talents.

2

Chapter 7 Liquidations

Compared to the complexities of Chapter 11, Chapter 7 is quite simple and straightforward. A trustee is appointed. The trustee must liquidate to achieve the best recovery for the estate and distribute the money to the parties entitled to receive the money. The trustee has a fiduciary obligation to the claimants.

The Chapter 7 Trustee

Appointment and Qualification of an Interim Trustee

The Bankruptcy Code mandates that the United States Trustee appoint a disinterested panel member to serve as interim trustee in a Chapter 7 case immediately after the petition is filed and the order for relief entered. The interim trustee serves until a permanent trustee is elected by the creditors and qualified. If no trustee is elected at the first meeting of creditors, the interim trustee becomes the permanent trustee. The interim trustee has all the duties and powers of a permanent trustee. Usually the trustee's assignment begins at this point.

Election of a Trustee

Creditors in a Chapter 7 case may request the opportunity to elect a trustee at the first meeting of creditors (also called the Section 341 meeting). The election is properly requested if creditors having 20% of the eligible claims request the election. To request an election and to vote in an election, a creditor must:

- hold an allowable, undisputed, fixed, liquidated, nonpriority *unsecured* claim of a kind entitled to distribution;
- not have an interest materially adverse, other than an equity interest that is not substantial in relation to the creditor's interest as a creditor, to the interest of creditors entitled to distribution;
- not be an insider; and
- have fiied a proof of claim or a writing setting forth facts evidencing a right to vote, that has not been objected to and that is not insufficient on its face.

To be elected, the candidate must receive the votes of creditors holding the dollar majority of those claims voted (which must total at least 20% in amount). A group of bondholders frequently are in a position to elect a Chapter 7 trustee.

How to Become a Trustee

A frequently asked question is how does one become employed as a Chapter 7 trustee? The selection and qualification of Chapter 7 trustees is largely controlled by the Office of the United States Trustee in each of the various districts around the country. Each district selects a group of trustees called a panel. A panel trustee is appointed as the interim trustee. While the trustee elected by the creditors is not necessarily a panel trustee, many are selected in this manner. The Office of the United States Trustee in each of the federal districts is listed in the telephone book. An application for approval to serve as a Chapter 7 trustee can be requested with a telephone call. There are basically two routes to become employed as a trustee. One is election by the creditors, the second is application to the Office of the United States Trustee. Both require Federal Bureau of Investigation (FBI) background checks.

Duties of a Trustee

One of the primary responsibilities of the Office of the United States Trustee is to supervise the actions of Chapter 7 trustees, who in turn must make sure that the Chapter 7 case is administered to maximize and expedite dividends to creditors. This individual is a fiduciary charged with protecting the interests of the various parties in the estate. The specific statutory duties of a trustee are as follows:

- Investigate the financial affairs of the debtor.
- Collect and reduce to money the property of the estate and close the estate as expeditiously as is compatible with the best interests of parties in having an interest in the estate.
- Be accountable for all property received.
- Examine proofs of claims and object to the allowance of any claim that is improper.

- Unless the court orders otherwise, furnish such information concerning the estate and the estate's administration as requested by a party in interest.
- If the ongoing operation of the debtor's business is authorized, file with the court—and with any governmental unit charged with the responsibility to collect or determine any tax arising out of such operations—periodic reports and summaries of the operation of such business, including a statement of receipts and disbursements, and such other information as the court or the United States Trustee requires.
- Make a final report and file a final account of the administration of the estate with the United States Trustee and the court.

The Chapter 7 trustee represents the estate in every respect. As such, the trustee is a fiduciary charged with protecting the interests of *all* estate beneficiaries—namely, all classes of creditors, including those holding secured, administrative, priority, and nonpriority unsecured claims. Specifically, the Chapter 7 trustee must secure for the estate all assets properly obtainable under applicable provisions of the Bankruptcy Code, defend the estate against improper claims or other adverse interests, and liquidate the estate for distribution to creditors as expeditiously as possible.

Exigencies of the circumstances might sometimes require a Chapter 7 trustee to jump ahead into a firefight with a specific creditor who is seeking to take some action in violation of the automatic stay, or an emergency with a taxing authority might cause a particular problem. In the ordinary course of affairs, however, a calm methodological approach is most productive. The trustee should use a definite methodology in a step-by-step process to fulfill these duties. By taking it one step at a time, the task becomes much simpler.

Investigation of Debtor

As the first order of business, the Chapter 7 trustee must investigate the debtor's financial affairs. This investigation should be approached in an uncritical way. Finding fault with the way a business has been run is the norm. An effective trustee keeps these criticisms private. They can be acted on later in the process, if the trustee determines these mistakes rose to the level of gross negligence or willful misconduct on the part of management.

Preliminary Fraud Investigation

Criminal acts and hiding assets is not to be tolerated and certainly not excused. All too often, money has been siphoned off or set aside and/or insiders have been preferred. This possibility requires a careful investigation. The investigation is typically accomplished by (i) reviewing the debtor's schedules of assets and liabilities, statement of financial affairs, and schedules of current income and expenditures, which the debtor *must* file; (ii) questioning the debtor at the first creditors' meeting shortly after the case is filed; and (iii) conducting such other investigation as necessary, including hiring forensic accountants and certified fraud examiners and conducting depositions of persons with knowledge of the debtor's business affairs. These are known as Rule 2004 examinations. If a crime has occurred, the Chapter 7 trustee must report it.

Identifying Assets

A Chapter 7 trustee also has a duty to ensure (and can require) that a debtor files all the mandated schedules and statements. Next, the trustee must review the sufficiency of the petition, mailing matrix (list of creditors' names and addresses), statements, and schedules. What should these forms reveal? Both a Chapter 7 and Chapter 11 debtor's petition must include the debtor's name, employer's tax identification number, and all other names used by the debtor within six years prior to the filing. In addition to the petition, the following schedules and statements must be filed:

Schedule A—Real Property

Schedule B—Personal Property

Schedule D—Creditors Holding Secured Claims

Schedule E—Creditors Holding Unsecured Priority Claims

Schedule F—Creditors Holding Unsecured Non-priority Claims

Schedule G—Executory Contracts and Unexpired Leases

Schedule H—Co-Debtors

These schedules are official printed forms that ask for specific financial information, and they must be answered completely. Among other things, they require the debtor to give its estimate of the fair market value of each asset. If the schedules and statements did not accompany the petition when it was filed, the debtor should have filed the petition with a list containing the names and addresses of all the debtor's known creditors. This is the minimum requirement for filing. The debtor might ask for additional time to file. If such a list is filed, the debtor is granted 15 days from the filing to supply completed schedules and statement(s) of affairs. The trustee must receive notice of any request for an extension of time to file these documents. The trustee cannot be ignored or trifled with on this score.

The Chapter 7 trustee must verify submission of the schedules and take action in the event of noncompliance. The lawyer for the trustee should be prepared to go to court, if necessary, to force compliance.

Finding a Responsible Party

If no individual is performing the duties of the corporate or partnership debtor, the Chapter 7 trustee requests the bankruptcy court to designate a responsible party (i.e., officer, director, partner, or person in control) to perform the duties of the debtor. Frequently, on the way into a Chapter 7, many of the people who have been responsible for managing the company toss the keys onto the table and walk out the door. The Bankruptcy Code provides a remedy for that type of activity. Chapter 7 trustees can tap someone to answer for the debtor. The task of bringing order out of chaos seems difficult, as can be seen thus far. Nevertheless, working with a lawyer, the trustee generally has ready recourse to the court at every step of the way whenever problems arise.

Control over Assets

All legal and equitable interests of the debtor, wherever located and by whomever held, are property of the estate. A trustee must ensure that a debtor surrenders to the trustee all of the estate's property held by the debtor as well as the estate's books and records. The trustee must ensure, through interviews with or depositions of the debtor, that the debtor reveals information about any estate asset that is in the possession of third parties as well as any asset in which the estate holds a contingent interest. The Chapter 7 trustee must obtain control over this property. The trustee can also compel the debtor and third parties to turn over property to the trustee. Turn-over motions are frequently filed by Chapter 7 trustees. The trustee can change the locks on the debtor's places of business, warehouses, and storage facilities. Locksmiths and security guards can be hired, if necessary.

Preservation of Assets

The trustee has the duty and responsibility to insure and safeguard all estate property and property that comes into the trustee's hands. The trustee should request proof of insurance from the debtor and ensure its continuance for the benefit of the estate. If none exists, the trustee should immediately obtain insurance in an amount sufficient to protect the estate's property (which may include insurance against fire, theft, vandalism, liability, and other possible hazards) and take any other steps which may be reasonably necessary to preserve the assets. Insurance agencies can readily write the policies needed to protect the business. Who pays for this?

If no insurance is in place and no estate funds are readily available, the trustee should contact secured creditors immediately, so that the secured creditor can obtain insurance or otherwise protect its own interest in the property. Usually, a bank officer is assigned to this task and the funds come quickly. When the uninsured property has value, the trustee may consider seeking (i) an agreement with the secured creditor to fund the expense of insurance and provide proper safeguarding under the Bankruptcy Code or (ii) a court order allowing the trustee to insure or safeguard the property involuntarily at the expense of the secured creditor. When the property cannot be insured, the trustee should liquidate the property as quickly as possible in a reasonable manner. Under these circumstances, the trustee is strongly encouraged to file motions to shorten the time within which objections may be filed to the proposed sale. Usually these distress sales occur within days. The trustee should immediately abandon to the lienholder any fully secured property or uninsured property that has no value to the estate and attempt to negotiate a release or compromise with the creditor of the amount of its deficiency claim.

If a loss occurs as a result of the trustee's failure to insure or protect estate property, the trustee could be subject to liability including a surcharge. In summary, move quickly. Does this make the trustee some sort of guarantor or insurer? Of course not. The trustee should, however, move as quickly as possible and make judgments based on the best information available. No one expects the trustee to be an expert appraiser or security guard. If the trustee has obtained the best information available and has acted in good faith based on that information, the trustee is well protected against any charge of negligence. On the other hand, if a long period of time has passed and the trustee has done nothing to insure and protect the property, the court can be expected to hold the trustee responsible.

Inventorying Property

A Chapter 7 trustee must file a complete inventory of the debtor's property within 30 days after qualifying as a trustee, unless an inventory has already been filed. The nature and extent of the inventory depends upon the type and value of the debtor's assets. The inventory should be sufficient to enable the trustee to verify later whether an auctioneer or other liquidator has accounted for all property turned over for sale.

Generally, the debtor's schedules will satisfy the inventory requirements as long as the trustee is able to verify at the creditors' meeting that the debtor's inventory, as shown on the schedules, is complete and satisfactory. On occasion, the trustee obtains a more detailed inventory in order to administer the assets properly. In addition to the written list, the trustee should consider using other methods, such as videotaping, to document the assets.

Investment of Funds

The Bankruptcy Code governs the trustee's investment of funds (see appendix 2).

Administration of Claims

A trustee is required to examine proofs of claim and object to the allowance of any improper claim, if a purpose would be served by doing so. For example, if assets are only sufficient to pay priority creditors, then no purpose would be served by examining or objecting to general unsecured claims (see chapter 9).

Reporting to Stakeholders

The trustee should reply in an expeditious manner to inquiries from creditors and other parties in interest. This is probably the most onerous part of a trustee's duties. Getting one's arms around the assets, locating the combination to the safe, and the like, are interesting and worthwhile tasks. Responding to telephone calls from misinformed and angry creditors is not. The trustee has a duty to be polite and to respond to their questions, however venal and insensitive they may seem. Many claimants seem to think the trustee is somehow responsible for their losses and their own impending business failures as a result of being unpaid. They often use vitriol and profanity. These calls can consume hours of a trustee's time and can continue for days and even weeks. However, it is important to respond to all telephone calls. When there is a large estate, a trustee may deputize someone to handle telephone calls. Paralegals and assistants can be trained to respond properly to these calls in a few hours, as the answer to virtually all of the questions is "We simply don't know yet." The creditors always want to know when they can expect to receive payment. The taxing authorities will have many of the same questions, and the secured creditors will want to know when they can come and pick up their collateral. Training someone to answer these questions and forward to the trustee those that really do need more detailed answers is important. After a period of weeks, these calls, even in major situations, dwindle to nothing, at least for a while. In a large liquidation, the trustee should consider establishing a Web site where creditors can find court pleadings, United States Trustee reports, and answers to frequently asked questions.

Operating Reports

The trustee must meet report-filing requirements, as described in chapter 6.

Final Report and Final Account of the Estate

The last step is preparing a final report and filing a final account of the administration of the estate with the United States Trustee and the court (see chapter 11 of this book).

Operating the Debtor's Business

Once the trustee has gathered the information, protected the property, and taken an inventory, what needs to be done if the debtor's business is still operating? The court may authorize a Chapter 7 trustee to operate the business of a debtor for a limited period of time. In order for the court to grant such a request, two requirements must be met: First, operation of the debtor's business must be in the best interest of the estate. Second, such operation must be consistent with the liquidation of the estate.

A trustee is allowed to sell the business as a going concern. Unlike a Chapter 11 case, in a Chapter 7, only the trustee and *not* the debtor may be authorized to operate the debtor's business. Authorization might be appropriate, for example, for the interim operation of the debtor's business to complete work in process, if the final product will realize a net return greater than would be the value of the parts sold individually. Similarly, continued operation of the debtor's business may be authorized when either the debtor's business appears likely to be sold for a greater price as a going concern or sudden termination of the business would cause great hardship to the general public or innocent third parties (e.g., patients in a nursing home).

The Chapter 7 trustee should consider the following factors in determining whether continued operation is in the best interests of the estate.

- cost of shutting the business down
- whether operating the business would result in an operating loss
- tax consequences of operating the business
- costs necessary to bring the business within compliance of local laws, to the extent local laws do not conflict with the Bankruptcy Code
- potential liabilities and claims against the estate and the trustee which may arise from the operation of the business
- length of time the business would be operated

Even when the court finds that operating a business would increase the estate's value without endangering the estate assets, the trustee should seek to operate the business for the shortest practical period.

Prior to obtaining a court order approving and authorizing operation of the debtor's business, the Chapter 7 trustee must consult with the United States Trustee to discuss the nature of the operation and cash management controls, and to obtain the appropriate monthly operating business report form. The format of the operating report may vary from district to district. If the blanket bond does not cover the trustee's operation of a business in a Chapter 7 case, the trustee may be required to obtain a separate bond.

The Trustee's Bond

Trustees are required to be bonded. The amount of the bond is set by the United States Trustee. The required amount may be increased or decreased during the liquidation, based on cash balances in the estate. Since bond premiums are based on the amount of the bond, the Chapter 7 trustee should ask to reduce the bond after large distributions are made to creditors and cash balances in the estate have decreased. This will reduce the estate's costs.

A Chapter 7 trustee's bond is a fidelity bond and is fairly easy to obtain. The Office of the United States Trustee furnishes the particular requirements for each district. The names of bonding companies are usually available from the United States Trustee or any large insurance agent. The Chapter 7 trustee fills out an application form and submits it to the bonding company, which works with the United States Trustee to post the bond. The fees to cover the premiums for the bond are paid from the estate.

Maintenance of Insurance on an Operating Business

In addition to having a general duty to maintain and preserve property of the estate, the Chapter 7 trustee of an operating business should insure the estate's assets against all normal business risks, including general liability, property damage, and worker's compensation, as well as all other types of insurance that may be required for a particular operation. A trustee who either exceeds his or her granted authority or is guilty of a breach of a fiduciary duty may be personally liable for any loss to the estate. As such, the added cost of these types of insurance may render the operational concept infeasible.

Use of Cash Collateral

When a Chapter 7 trustee operates the debtor's business, the ability of the trustee to use, sell, or lease property of the estate or to obtain credit or incur debt is governed by strict restrictions of the Bankruptcy Code. The trustee may sell, use, or lease property in the ordinary course of the business but *may not* use the cash collateral of a secured creditor to continue the operation without first obtaining either an order of the court or the secured creditor's consent.

Borrowing Money

The trustee who has been authorized to operate a business may obtain unsecured credit and incur unsecured debt in the ordinary course of the business without court approval. Note that the debts incurred become an administrative expense, thereby placing the trustee's compensation at risk. The trustee may not borrow money or incur unsecured credit *other than* in the ordinary course of business without court approval. This is a perilous area. Unless the trustee is confident that the debts incurred while operating a business can be repaid, he or she should proceed with extreme caution. Absent an operating business, Chapter 7 trustees are highly unlikely to borrow money.

Employee Issues

If the business has employees, the Chapter 7 trustee must, of course, withhold income, social security, and other applicable taxes from any wages paid, as well as file employment tax returns and remit the amounts withheld, plus the employer's portion of the taxes, to the appropriate taxing authority (see chapter 6).

The trustee also must comply with other laws applicable in the state(s) in which the business operates. Here again, operating a business in Chapter 7 creates risks for the trustee.

Conversion from Chapter 7 to Chapter 11

If the estate is likely to benefit from an extended period of operation, the Chapter 7 trustee should consider filing a motion seeking conversion of the case to Chapter 11. After the brief operation of a business in Chapter 7, the trustee (and almost invariably the creditors whose money is at risk) may decide that, due to changed business climate or improved management, the company could be rehabilitated because the creditors would recover substantially more on their claims through the ongoing operations of the business. This phenomenon occurs when a company goes into liquidation because it simply missed its market. In other words, the entrepreneurs studying and running the business had a great idea but brought it to market before the public was ready to buy their product or service. A lack of capital frequently causes these entities to file bankruptcy. In these rare instances, during the Chapter 7 operations of the business (and remember, that in itself is unusual), the positive going concern value of the business will emerge. The Chapter 7 trustee should consult with the major creditors when this operational miracle occurs. The trustee should expect to be questioned concerning whether a proposed plan to be crafted would satisfy the requirements of plan confirmation (see chapter 3). If the decision is made to convert to Chapter 11, the trustee should request to be appointed as the Chapter 11 trustee. If the creditors feel that such a conversion is warranted and the Chapter 7 trustee fails to request conversion of the case and the appointment of a Chapter 11 trustee, they can ask the United States Trustee to do so. As a last resort, the creditors can request conversion to Chapter 11.

Compensation of a Chapter 7 Trustee

As indicated, the compensation of Chapter 7 trustees can be quite remunerative, particularly in large estates. The U.S. Congress created the United States Trustee system in large part so that the government would have input on the compensation of trustees. Applications for compensation and reimbursement of expenses filed by Chapter 7 trustees must be prepared in accordance with the procedural guidelines adopted by the Executive Office for United States Trustees. The trustee should be familiar with the fee guidelines. Fee applications submitted by Chapter 7 trustees are subject to the same standard of review as are applications of other professionals. The United States Trustee carefully reviews Chapter 7 trustee fee applications and objects to inappropriate fees and expenses.

Compensation Rules

Trustee compensation rules and procedures are spelled out in the Bankruptcy Code. The maximum compensation allowable consists of varying percentages of all moneys disbursed or turned over by the trustee to parties in interest, excluding the debtor but including holders of secured claims. A court may award a trustee *less than* the statutory maximum but may *not* exceed the 3% compensation ceiling. The trustee also receives a portion of the filing fee when administration of the case has been completed. The trustee should keep time records in every case as evidence of the services performed. However, local rules and practices sometimes provide that time records need not be submitted, when the compensation request is under a specified amount. Trustee duties performed by a paraprofessional employed by the trustee are also subject to the limit on trustee compensation.

Interim Compensation of Trustees

A trustee is permitted to apply to the court for interim compensation or reimbursement of expenses. While a literal reading of the law requires that a trustee receive compensation only after a disbursement to parties in interest, in a number of cases, interim reasonable compensation to trustees has been allowed in certain circumstances, although distribution had not been made to any creditor. The United States Trustee carefully examines a trustee's request for interim compensation and objects as warranted. In at least one very large case, the bankruptcy judge periodically awarded the trustee compensation, on an interim basis, half (1.5%) of the statutorily allowed 3%, as funds were brought into the estate. In his original order, the judge indicated that an additional award remained available at the end of the case to bring the total to 3%, when the final calculation of disbursed funds could be made.

Conclusion

Chapter 7 provides the standard vehicle for bankruptcy liquidations. An interim Chapter 7 trustee is appointed by the United States Trustee and then generally becomes the permanent trustee, unless the creditors elect a replacement. The Chapter 7 trustee has broad powers to manage the estate and its liquidation subject to the supervision of the Bankruptcy court. The role of the estate's creditors is very limited in a Chapter 7 liquidation. The explicit instructions provided by the statute make the job description for a Chapter 7 trustee quite clear and specific. It's like most government work, except it sometimes pays a whole lot better.

3

Liquidating in Chapter 11

A majority of confirmed Chapter 11 plans of reorganization are not reorganizations at all; rather, they are liquidating plans that provide for the dismantling of a business entity. Such a plan could involve a third party's acquiring the going concern business of the debtor and placing the remaining assets (often consisting largely of causes of action) in a trust or similar vehicle to be sold, pursued, or otherwise collected upon for the benefit of creditors, or it could place all of the assets in a liquidating trust to be sold by a liquidating trustee (see table 1.2). In either case, creditors do not look to the going concern value of the business for a return on their claims, because there is no business. The distribution to claimants depends on maximizing the proceeds from asset sales and litigation and the proper administration of claims. Flexibility and reduced costs have led to a huge upsurge in liquidating plans implemented by liquidating trustees.

The Road to a Chapter 11 Liquidating Plan

While in a pending Chapter 11, some companies liquidate in a "creeping" liquidation process; that is, the debtor-in-possession simply bleeds itself of most of its assets before a plan is confirmed. After the liquidating sales, what typically remains is cash subject to a plan that simply decides how to divide it up. These creeping Chapter 11 liquidations tend to be expensive because the professionals for the creditors' committee, banks, debtor's counsel, and the like continue to accrue fees. The Friede Goldman Halter case was such a creeping liquidation (see chapter 4).

In the typical postbankruptcy plan liquidating trust, only the liquidating trustee and the trustee's own set of professionals are compensated. Usually, this approach reduces costs. For this reason, postconfirmation liquidations are favored over preconfirmation liquidations. In either situation, the company must proceed through the Chapter 11 plan process.

Exclusivity

In the early stages of a Chapter 11 case the preparation and approval of the reorganization plan is under the absolute control of the debtor. Initially, the Bankruptcy Code provides the debtor with an exclusivity period of several months, during which it and it alone can propose a plan of reorganization. At the end of the initial exclusivity period, any party in interest can file and seek to obtain approval of its plan. The debtor is typically in negotiations with its creditors during the exclusivity period.

Negotiating the Plan

Because the claims against an insolvent entity substantially exceed the value to distribute, negotiating a plan can be protracted and frustrating. This situation creates tensions between the various classes of creditors. Negotiations between the secured and unsecured groups are intense and frequently acrimonious. If secured creditors believe they will be paid in full in a liquidation, they may support a liquidating plan. If unsecured creditors believe their only hope of a meaningful recovery is the reorganization and restructuring of debt, they will oppose a liquidating plan. Debtor's management may see a reorganization as job security or there may be no managers left to push a reorganization.

Most large businesses in Chapter 11 have various levels of outstanding unsecured indebtedness. Each level seeks the most advantageous treatment for its class. Alliances form and dissipate and reform among different groups. This balkanization can be tedious and torturous but eventually may reach a successful conclusion that no one really likes. As with a Chapter 7, the ultimate return to unsecured creditors depends on a fraction in which the numerator is equal to gross proceeds less the cost of liquidation, secured claims satisfied, and priority claims. The denominator of the fraction is equal to the total of unsecured claims participating in the liquidation proceeds. Ordinarily, all unsecured creditors participate equally in the proceeds of a liquidation. However, a liquidating plan could provide for multiple classes of creditors participating in the fixed fund, with the participation weighted depending upon the preconfirmation posture of each class. In other words, how much creditors actually receive can vary wildly.

Voting and Solicitation

Parties whose legal, equitable, and contractual rights are unaltered, do not need to vote in favor of a plan for it to be approved. Each class of impaired parties, that is, those whose legal rights are altered, must vote two-thirds in an amount of their claims and more than one-half in number of claims voting in favor of the plan, in order for that class to be classified as approving the plan.

Confirmation Hearing

After a favorable vote, the court holds a confirmation hearing. At this hearing, the court considers the tally of votes and hears evidence on a variety of issues: (i) that the plan has been proposed in good faith; (ii) that the claims have been classified properly; (iii) that the plan is feasible; (iv) that its acceptance has not been procured by any means prohibited by law; and (v) that certain other technical requirements have been met, as specified in the Bankruptcy Code. The prime area of concern is frequently whether or not the plan is in the best interests of creditors. This best-interest test requires that each impaired creditor receive a larger distribution under the plan than the creditor would receive in a Chapter 7 liquidation.

Cram Down

Even if a class of claims does not accept the plan, the law permits the plan to be approved over the vote of the dissenting class. An override is accomplished through what is commonly called the "cram down." To overrule the dissenting class, the plan must be found not to discriminate unfairly and must be found to be fair and equitable with respect to impaired nonaccepting classes. By not discriminating, the law generally means only that the holders of claims or interests with similar legal rights cannot be treated differently. To be fair and equitable as to a class of dissenting secured creditors, the secured creditors must receive the indubitable value equivalent to their claims or retain their liens and receive deferred cash payments of a value equal to their interest in the estate's interest in the property.

For a plan to be judged fair and equitable as to a class of dissenting unsecured creditors, the plan must provide either that the unsecured creditors receive property of a value equal to the allowed amount of the claim or that the holder of any claim or interest junior to the dissenting class will not receive or retain any property on account of the junior claim. In other words, the classes below the dissenting unsecured class must receive nothing if the dissenting class is to be crammed down. This requirement is called the absolute priority rule.

Consummation

After approval in a confirmation hearing, the plan is consummated by transferring the remaining assets to the liquidator, as described in the liquidating plan of reorganization. Ultimately, a report is made to the judge that the liquidation is complete and the pending legal issues have been wrapped up, at which point the case is closed.

Why Liquidate under a Chapter 11 Plan?

Liquidating under a plan confirmed in Chapter 11 has substantial, practical advantages. Creditors have more control over the process and it is less expensive than Chapter 7. The pressure to sell assets prematurely is reduced, and the investment options for the sales and litigation proceeds, once they are received, are increased. Overall, a Chapter 11 liquidation provides greater flexibility.

More Creditor Control

Creditors are able to exert more control over their destiny. In Chapter 7, a creditors' committee (if one exists at all) provides only an advisory function in the liquidation process. A liquidation conducted pursuant to a plan of reorganization is typically conducted in accordance with a structure negotiated and even formulated by creditors. The trustee supervising the liquidation under a plan of reorganization is usually selected by the creditors and is very likely subject to control and even replacement by creditors. By controlling the identity of the trustee and designing the function of the creditor overseers under the plan, creditor groups can ensure that liquidation under a Chapter 11 plan follows the course deemed appropriate by creditors. This may not be true of the totally independent fiduciary, the Chapter 7 trustee.

Less Pressure to Sell Assets Prematurely

Liquidation under a plan of reorganization reduces the pressure to sell assets prematurely. The creditors can usually take as much time as they desire. Liquidations under a plan of reorganization need only resemble a forced sale to the extent deemed appropriate by creditors. In Chapter 7, a trustee is likely to feel greater pressure to dispose of property quickly and thereby not necessarily obtain the best price possible. This problem is aggravated by the limited ability of the Chapter 7 trustee to maintain property and to conduct the business affairs of the debtors. By comparison, the trustee under the terms of a liquidating plan of reorganization is likely to have broader authority both to operate business segments pending their sale and to take actions deemed necessary to preserve and maintain property of the estate.

More Investment Options

A Chapter 7 trustee is severely limited in the way he or she may handle funds. A trustee under a plan of reorganization, on the other hand, is required to handle funds in whatever fashion the plan provides. This added flexibility may permit investments at better interest rates, to the ultimate benefit of creditors. By having greater freedom in the handling of funds, the onerous consequences of a long liquidation process may be to some extent ameliorated.

Reduced Cost

The expense in maintaining a Chapter 11 prior to confirmation with all the various creditors' committees, professionals, and debtors-in-possession is enormous. This situation provides too much overhead on what may simply be a liquidation better accomplished by an independent trustee under creditor supervision. In a liquidating plan of reorganization, access to professionals is simpler and less expensive. The hiring of a professional usually does not require court approval, and normally the creditors, not the court, exercise control over the payment of the professionals. Liquidating under a plan is cheaper than under an operational Chapter 11 with liquidation occurring as the case goes on.

To place the case in Chapter 7 creates the fee structure discussed in chapter 2, which might lead to as much as 3% of the estate's value being paid to a Chapter 7 trustee. With a huge business, setting up a liquidating trust with a trustee compensated on an hourly or success-based formula lower than 3% may be much cheaper. Under Chapter 11, these formulas are a matter of pure negotiation between the proposed liquidating trustee and the plan of reorganization proponents. Compensation can be more flexible and better suited to the circumstances.

More Overall Flexibility

The primary reason why creditors often prefer a Chapter 11 liquidation is overall increased flexibility. Liquidating plans of reorganization provide the necessary leeway to mix the benefits and protections of the Bankruptcy Code with tailored contractual provisions governing the liquidation process in a way that favors the specific legitimate needs of creditors. Creditors usually articulate certain identifiable goals in the formulation of a liquidating plan of reorganization. The principal creditor objective in any liquidating plan is to obtain maximum distributions to creditors in the minimum amount of time (more precisely, to maximize the present value of the distributions).

The Estate Representative as Liquidator

The liquidating plan of reorganization creates a structure for the conduct of the liquidation. This plan is the seminal authority for the governance and management of the liquidation process. Usually, an estate representative of some sort is designated to act as the liquidator. This person acts in court and otherwise (e.g., execution of transfer instruments) on behalf of the estate. Typically, the estate representative answers to a committee selected by the creditors.

Types of Estate Representatives

The term "estate representative" may be applied to any of the following four situations: (i) a formal Chapter 11 trustee appointed under the Bankruptcy Code; (ii) a trustee picked by the creditors for a liquidating trust; (iii) the debtor or debtor-in-possession; and (iv) the manager of an entirely new business entity, such as a limited liability company, owned or controlled by creditors and created to liquidate the estate.

Chapter 11 Trustee

A Chapter 11 trustee appointed under the Bankruptcy Code has the advantage of having his or her powers and responsibilities more clearly laid out. This type of trustee is appointed during the case, prior to confirmation of the plan. Because this trustee function is created by statute, and because the Bankruptcy Code and case law have clarified the scope of a trustee's authority, power, and responsibilities, the likelihood of a dispute over the trustee's role is greatly reduced. Everyone knows where to look for the authority of the Chapter 11 trustee—the Bankruptcy Code.

Additional advantages arise from the fact that the Chapter 11 trustee is appointed while the case is still active in Chapter 11 and prior to the implementation of the liquidating plan. These advantages include continuity and protection from collateral actions. Presumably, a Chapter 11 trustee is also knowledgeable regarding both the assets he or she has been administering and the history of the case. This knowledge facilitates liquidation and, perhaps, accelerates the disposition of assets.

A Chapter 11 trustee has a degree of immunity to attack by creditors, the debtor, and others. This protection should avoid or limit indemnification requirements for the trustee. Clearly, the trustee does not face potential liability for government penalty or forfeiture claims, if he or she is appointed pursuant to the Bankruptcy Code. The fact that the trustee is not susceptible to attack personally for such claims and the clarity with which a statutory trustee's role is perceived, decreases the need for reserves in connection with distributions to creditors and, therefore, facilitates prompt payout. Finally, bonding a Chapter 11 trustee is typically easier than bonding one appointed pursuant to a plan.

On the other hand, having a Chapter 11 trustee conduct the postconfirmation liquidation of the debtor has several disadvantages. First, the statutory trustee's cumbersome and often expensive connection with the court is maintained. Employment of professionals must continue to occur only upon order of the court and their payment continues to be governed by normal court procedures. Reporting is required by applicable Bankruptcy Rules. Most importantly, the investment of estate funds is governed by the extremely conservative strictures of the Bankruptcy Code.

A Chapter 11 trustee has an independent fiduciary duty to the estate and its creditors. That independent duty is likely to limit—if not eliminate totally—creditor control of the liquidation process. In addition, the statutory trustee must continue to fulfill disinterested roles even after confirmation of the plan. Because the party liquidating an estate postconfirmation is frequently involved in the control of subsidiaries of the debtor and may even serve as an officer or director of those subsidiaries, remaining disinterested is a problem for a Chapter 11 trustee attempting to wear more than one hat.

In a business liquidation, more than one corporate entity often needs to be liquidated. Most corporations have officers and directors that are common to all the affiliate corporations. This overlap can create a huge problem for a trustee appointed under the provisions of Chapter 11, which require trustees to be totally disinterested. Such a trustee must avoid any hint of impropriety. Functioning as the CEO of several companies in a corporate structure involving intercompany debts and different creditors for each of the separate corporate entities creates that hint. In a liquidating plan with a plan trustee selected by the creditors, these problems can be avoided simply by having the plan state that a liquidating trustee can serve in multiple capacities. A trustee appointed by the court is much more limited.

Plan Trustee

The advantages of utilizing a liquidating trustee, whose position is created by the plan and whose duties and powers are tailored by the plan, are almost a mirror image of the disadvantages of a Chapter 11 trustee. Creditor control of the duties of a plan trustee may be tailored to the unique needs of each case. Because the plan is the instrument creating the role of the liquidating trustee, that role may include whatever opportunities for creditor input and control creditor representatives deem appropriate. While the trustee almost certainly is granted the powers of a Chapter 11 trustee, he or she may receive contractual powers beyond those afforded a Chapter 11 trustee, if deemed appropriate by the creditors. For example, the trustee appointed pursuant to a plan of reorganization may have the power to compromise controversies or sell property on limited notice or on no notice at all, and to invest funds in ways other than those permitted by the Bankruptcy Code or the United States Trustee. These powers, which may be exercised without seeking authority from the court, allow a faster, smoother liquidation. By eliminating the need to go to court at each step of the liquidation, costs are reduced. Additionally, the trustee appointed pursuant to a plan, is not subject to the same disinterestedness requirements of the Bankruptcy Code and can serve in any situations and capacities approved by the creditors.

Because of the relative absence of a statutory law basis for the plan trustee role, the plan trustee may require extensive indemnification. Similarly the trustee appointed pursuant to the plan of reorganization may be concerned about his or her potential personal exposure. These factors can cause delays in distribution and maintenance of large reserves to ensure against what are, in fact, remote contingencies.

Debtor as Estate Representative

The debtor can serve as estate representative, but this choice is usually ill advised. Retaining the debtor as the postconfirmation estate representative has clear drawbacks. While the debtor's ownership may bc altered to reflect creditor control of the equity in the debtor, implementing that control may have practical difficulties. For example, if ownership of the debtor is transferred to creditors, the number of creditor-shareholder entities may be required to report under the Securities Exchange Act. Income may be taxed twice, taxation on income to the corporation as well as taxation on dividends to creditor-shareholders. Finally, a Chapter 11 debtor that is a business entity whose assets were acquired pursuant to a plan may not survive in a form suitable to conduct the rest of the liquidation. In practice, the creditors want to choose a liquidator who is answerable to them.

New Business Entity

The remaining alternative available in a postconfirmation liquidation is the creation of an entirely new entity to serve as the estate representative and conduct the liquidation. Limited liability companies (LLCs) in particular have been popular postconfirmation entities. LLCs are taxed as partnerships for federal tax purposes. On the plus side, partnership classification for tax purposes removes the two tiers of tax (corporate and shareholder). Because it is a flow-through entity, only one tier (the beneficial owner) remains. On the minus side, however, LLCs that are taxed as a partnership for federal tax purposes are deemed to be in an active trade or business in some states. Therefore, such entities may be subject to other state business taxes such as franchise taxes and gross receipt taxes. The transfer of the assets to the partnership further removes any lawsuits from the original parties at interest and may impact the tax character of certain recoveries.

Governing the Estate Representative

In formulating a liquidating plan of reorganization the creditors must determine both who will control the estate representative and the extent of that control. While control of the liquidation process is one of the key goals in most liquidating Chapter 11 cases, a variety of concerns contribute to whether and how to exercise that control. Essentially, creditors have three ways to exercise control.

Minimum Oversight

First, creditors may elect to exercise little or no control. Sometimes, particularly if the liquidator is a Chapter 11 trustee or is the continuing debtor, the creditors want the liquidator to be subject to supervision and control by the bankruptcy court. These cases are not the norm. While a liquidator under a creditors' trust may be made independent, normally creditors want to exercise control postconfirmation.

Committee Control—The New "Board of Directors"

Creditors typically exercise control through a committee named in the plan. This committee may be the statutory creditors' committee, or it may be a new committee created pursuant to the plan. The creditors decide. A number of practical problems arise in attempting to control the liquidation process through a committee.

First, the committee does not have the in-depth knowledge that the liquidator has and therefore must defer in large part to the liquidator on various issues, many of which are critical to the liquidation process. If the committee has confidence in the liquidator, this lack of detailed knowledge is no problem. However, a great deal rests on trust.

Second, committee members usually are not compensated for overseeing the liquidation process. A complex liquidation may require numerous decisions and a substantial time commitment. They are likely to receive nothing other than the same pro rata share of the estate that creditors who do not serve on the committee receive.

Finally, members of a creditors' committee must be extremely cautious not to exercise their powers for their own benefit. They are fiduciaries. Fiduciaries acting for the benefit of the creditor group may be held liable to the creditor group, if they put their own interests first.

The role of a committee that oversees the liquidator should be spelled out clearly. While the plan may define the committee's role in general terms, the committee should also establish a set of rules of operation covering its powers, duties, and interaction with the liquidator. In general, the control exercised by a creditors' committee is similar to the control exercised by a board of directors.

The committee should have an operative document (i.e., bylaws, LLC agreement, etc.) that ensures that it (i) approves or rejects major transactions proposed by the liquidator, (ii) oversees the compensation of any professionals, (iii) receives regular reports on the status of the liquidation process and the manner in which funds are being handled, and (iv) meets often enough to provide meaningful supervision to the liquidator. Yet, the liquidation process must be turned over to the liquidator. As a practical matter, the liquidator must have a degree of freedom in areas such as marketing, negotiating, litigation, and the like. The analogy of a board of directors working with a chief executive officer (CEO) is apt.

Independent Officers and Directors

The appointment of independent directors and officers, a third approach for governance of the liquidator, only makes sense when the entity conducting the liquidation is a corporation. Providing for independent directors and officers has the advantage of reducing the possibility of self-dealing that exists with any committee made up from among the largest creditors in the case. However, finding persons willing to serve as officers or directors of a debtor engaged in a relatively short-term liquidation is difficult, especially if the reorganized debtor is a publicly reporting company. The debtor's recent time in bankruptcy court increases the difficulty of finding insurance for officers and directors in a liquidation scenario. This creates indemnity problems beyond those that might be expected with a trustee appointed pursuant to a plan of reorganization. The corporate vehicle is usually considered and then dropped for these reasons.

Which Structure Is Best?

How best to supervise the liquidator depends on the facts of the case. A smaller case is likely to require less sophisticated supervision than a large one. A case in which the liquidation process is complex and multifaceted requires more supervision than one involving a small number of assets or just one or two items of litigation. If the debtor conducts a business preconfirmation, which is consistent with postconfirmation liquidation (e.g., sales of land in a discreet development), less supervision is required than if liquidation were not within the debtor's ordinary business activities.

Protection of the Liquidator

One of the liquidator's first responsibilities is to ensure that the liquidation process and the representatives of creditors who conduct it are protected from unwarranted lawsuits. This requires a balancing of goals. On the one hand, lawsuit insulation is needed to provide assurance to the liquidator and the creditors that actions taken in good faith and furtherance of the liquidation process will not result in personal liability. On the other hand, creditors must, of course, have some recourse against a dishonest or incompetent liquidator. Finally, in certain situations protecting the estate and its representative from parties outside the liquidation process is more important than protecting parties within the process from each other.

The first problem area is the potential for litigation involving the liquidator's conduct of the business, either pending or during the liquidation. The plaintiff may be either outside or within the process. A liquidator operating a business after confirmation of a plan of reorganization is susceptible to suit if he or she commits a tortuous or contractual wrong in connection with the operation of that business. A liquidator might also be attacked for his or her wrongful conduct of the business by one of the beneficiaries of the trust.

The liquidator might also inherit problems from the Chapter 11 case itself. For example, the liquidator may be responsible for holding assets with environmental problems. If the liquidator fails to handle these matters properly, he or she could be held personally liable for violations of environmental laws. Similarly, the liquidator who is not the Chapter 11 Trustee may be held liable for a failure to pay taxes or other governmental claims.

The plan of reorganization and other enabling documents should limit the liquidator's liability to wrongful conduct that is willful, reckless, or grossly negligent. This type of provision is customary and the only practical protection available. The plan and other enabling documents should also provide for indemnification of the liquidator and others who may be vulnerable to suit for his or her conduct after confirmation of the plan.

Directors' and officers' (D&O) liability insurance may be available to the liquidator and the group governing the liquidator's conduct. Ordinarily, D&O liability insurance is expensive to obtain for a debtor who is fresh out of Chapter 11 and undergoing liquidation.

To the extent that money or property come into the liquidator's possession, he or she should be bonded. While these bonds are expensive, a creditors' committee that fails to require a bond for a liquidator may find itself subject to criticism (and perhaps a lawsuit), if that liquidator breaches his or her trust.

Liquidator's Attorney-Client Privilege

The liquidator has the ability to assert or waive the attorney-client privilege on behalf of the debtor. Problems arise when one or more members of a creditors' committee does not fully understand the importance keeping matters discussed within the committee confidential. In the early stages of the liquidation, a liquidator and supervisory creditor group should determine what information will be disseminated to committee members and when it will be disseminated. The committee may want to restrict certain areas of confidential information to a subcommittee. Other than that, little can be done except to impress upon committee members the importance of maintaining the confidentiality of discussions within the committee.

Avoiding the Appearance of Impropriety

Liquidators must strive to avoid the appearance of impropriety. Typically, the liquidator is overseen by a group of creditor representatives. Usually, the largest creditors are on the supervising creditors' committee. Frequently, one of these creditors has a substantial issue regarding the validity or enforceability of part or all of its claim. This individual creditor may well have both the ability and desire to intimidate the liquidator in order to discourage an objection or to receive other favorable treatment for its claim. A liquidator in this situation clearly has a problem. Certainly, the governing documents need to be drafted in such a way that the liquidator will not be discouraged from objecting to any particular claim, especially the claim of a creditor sitting in oversight. This issue can be dealt with in one of several ways. If necessary, court intervention can be requested. A less expensive solution is to require a substantial plurality of the oversight committee members to object to compensation. In the event that plurality is achieved, the governing documents can also require that court advice be sought.

A practical and efficient way for the liquidator to handle this situation is to be very open and thorough in communicating with the members of the committee. Communication is the key here. All of the objections to the large claims should be communicated to the full committee in order to head off this issue in advance. The liquidator should communicate equally and completely with each one of the members of the governing body of creditors. This approach should help avoid a confrontation with one of the substantial creditors sitting in judgment of the liquidating trustee's fees.

Funding the Liquidating Trust

The liquidator and the creditors frequently discuss how much money to hold and how long to hold it. Taxes can be an important issue. The first amount is set aside, after consulting with the trustee's tax advisors, to cover any potentially conceivable tax liabilities until the liquidator is ready to close the estate and all the returns due to be filed have been blessed by the IRS. A delay of several years in closing the estate is not unusual for this reason. The liquidator must also hold back enough to cover all professional and trustee's fees and maintain reserves sufficient to cover other liabilities that might be assessed against the liquidator. While maintaining this reserve may temporarily diminish the return to creditors, this approach is preferable to the liquidator facing large, personal liability for distributing money to the wrong recipients. In a liquidating trust established for the sole purpose of pursuing litigation, the trust must be funded at its inception with seed money. This amount is set aside at confirmation out of cash in the estate funds and used to fund the ongoing litigation. The fund may thereafter be increased with litigation proceeds as cases are settled or otherwise resolved. The liquidator often negotiates with his or her professionals for contingency fee arrangements or fee caps in order to avoid running out of money prior to the conclusion of litigation (see chapter 8).

Compensation of the Liquidator under a Liquidating Plan

Compensation of the liquidator is negotiated in each case. The liquidator is typically identified in advance of plan confirmation. Compensation is addressed in the plan and disclosed in connection with solicitation of acceptances. If the name of the liquidator is not known until after confirmation, the plan should make provision for the negotiation of a compensation arrangement. In this instance, the plan should be flexible so that the committee or other entity empowered to oversee the liquidator can strike the best possible bargain.

The liquidator is commonly compensated on the basis of an hourly rate, an annual fee, a percentage of recovery, or some contingency or progress standard. Which of these ways of compensating a liquidator is best varies from case to case. In general, the larger estates tend to compensate the liquidator on more of an hourly rate, and the smaller estates tend to compensate the liquidator on a success-based formula. Typically, compensation plans provide for a minimum hourly rate. With all but the very largest billion-dollar estates, an incentive, or "kicker," is used to motivate the liquidator to maximize the assets available for distribution. The incentive may be based on a percentage of the amount of money distributed in the estate or on the percentage of recoveries of the creditors under the plan. Obviously, the facts of each particular case control the weightings of compensation between hourly and contingency formulas. A prospective liquidator may decline the appointment if the method of compensation is not satisfactory. Flexibility on this particular issue is important. Without flexibility, persons who would otherwise be well suited to perform the role of liquidator may be unobtainable, resulting ultimately in detriment to the estate. The most effective liquidation is not necessarily the cheapest.

Compensation of the liquidator should be subject to some controls. Chapter 7 and Chapter 11 trustees are clearly subject to court control of compensation. The compensation of any other type of liquidator is subject to court scrutiny only when provided in the plan. The liquidating plan of reorganization should include a mechanism for review of the liquidator's compensation under certain circumstances. Usually that mechanism relies only on the participation of the creditors' committee or other oversight body. Court supervision is not usually required.

Duties of the Liquidator under a Liquidating Plan

The liquidating plan of reorganization should clearly define the liquidator's functions. These functions are similar to those duties of a Chapter 7 trustee.

While the functions may vary from case to case, the liquidator is expected to perform six general categories of duties: (i) protection of assets, (ii) operation of assets (to the extent appropriate), (iii) liquidation of assets, (iv) investment of funds, (v) administration of claims, and (vi) reporting to stakeholders. But much more flexibility is provided to the liquidator for performing these duties under a postconfirmation liquidation.

Protection of Assets

The goal is to maximize the present value of the cash proceeds of the estate which will ultimately be available for distribution to creditors. The liquidator must take whatever steps are necessary to protect assets of the estate. As in Chapter 7, the first task of a liquidator is to review the property of the estate and determine what steps need to be taken regarding maintenance, protection, and insurance. To the extent that such issues can be foreseen, the plan should provide the liquidator with general guidance in this area, as well as establish a procedure for making extraordinary decisions, such as the discontinuation of security or insurance.

Operation of Assets

Second, the liquidator may need to operate assets of the estate. Operations should not occur at a loss except under the most peculiar circumstances. One such circumstance arises when the operation of an asset preserves a "going concern" value that greatly exceeds the liquidation value. Another is when large noncash charges cause the operation to show losses for accounting purposes but nonetheless to generate positive cash flow. On the other hand, to the extent that the cost of maintaining assets may be offset by their operation, the liquidator has a clear duty to undertake that operation. The liquidator should have some leeway in overseeing operational assets that are part of the estate.

The plan of reorganization, while obligating the liquidator to obtain the maximum return from an operational asset, should provide for continued operation only after the evaluation of the cost of operation and the appurtenant risks to the estate. For example, the liquidator probably should not operate an asset that exposes the estate to substantial tort risks, even though such operation might appear to be profitable.

The liquidator must gather the facts that support the economic viability of the continued operations and weigh these against the potential liabilities of maintaining those operations. The methodology for making this decision is ultimately a business judgment. The liquidator should be in a position to make such judgments after advising the supervising creditors of the business facts. The business acumen of the liquidator is important to this process. Each situation is somewhat different and intriguing and presents an excellent opportunity for an energetic business executive to display his or her business skills.

Liquidation of Assets

While the liquidator should have the authority to operate businesses owned by the estate, his or her true role is to liquidate those businesses sooner or later for the benefit of the estate. The liquidator should have the clear obligation to take appropriate steps to liquidate the estate. The mechanics of liquidation should be clearly set out in the plan. Liquidation by the liquidator without involvement of the bankruptcy court is often preferable. Nonetheless, some buyers, especially in connection with large asset dispositions, want an order from the bankruptcy court ("comfort orders") approving the sale.

Investment of Funds

The liquidator has the duty to invest the estate's funds. As a fundamental matter, the plan should provide that the liquidator invest the funds safely. Postconfirmation liquidations are often touted as being particularly superior to Chapter 7 liquidations in the flexibility that they provide for the investment of funds. The United States Trustee provides extremely restrictive and cautious requirements for depositing and handling of cash by a Chapter 7 trustee (see appendix 4). Most creditors of bankrupt estates are willing to accept significantly greater risk in the management of the estate's funds in exchange for the higher expected returns. The liquidator may hold a substantial amount of funds for fairly long periods of time between distributions. Accordingly, the liquidator needs to obtain the highest "safe" interest rate available. Also, the liquidator should be required to invest money with an eye toward its availability to pay costs and make distributions. Investments involving substantial, early withdrawal penalties should only be undertaken, if other funds are clearly sufficient for anticipated cash needs.

Administration of Claims

The liquidator has the principal responsibility of processing and, where appropriate, objecting to claims filed by creditors. The liquidating plan of reorganization should be structured to encourage prompt resolution of claim disputes. Eliminating improper claims improves the payout to those creditors who are entitled to payment, and resolution of a claim objection helps speed payment to all creditors. Maintaining substantial reserves against frivolous and disputed claims for a long period of time can be frustrating to creditors and may create other problems.

The liquidating plan of reorganization often provides a deadline by which claim objections must be filed in order to resolve these disputes expeditiously. Similarly, the liquidator may be required to follow certain expediting procedures, such as the utilization of an alternative dispute resolution program. A delicate balance must be struck—such mechanisms should not cripple the ability of the liquidator to object effectively to claims or to amend objections at a later date. Frequently, the liquidator does not know enough about a claim to have formulated all possible objections by the objection deadline established under the plan. Accordingly, the plan should preserve the ability to amend claim objections, including the right to assert new theories, even after the deadline (see chapter 9).

Reporting to Stakeholders

A liquidator must report to the creditors on both the financial condition of the estate and the progress of the liquidation. The plan of reorganization and other instruments governing the liquidating trustee should provide appropriately customized reporting requirements. These requirements should take into account the legitimate need of an oversight committee or creditors generally, the court, or other parties in interest, to know what progress is being made in the estate's liquidation program. However, reporting requirements need not be so burdensome that they become a significant or debilitating expense to the estate (see chapter 6).

Powers of the Liquidator under a Liquidating Plan

Litigation

The ability to file lawsuits is one of the key powers of the liquidator. He or she is likely to take or threaten to take legal action against many parties. Businesses that owe money to bankrupt companies often withhold payment until taken to court. That task frequently falls to the liquidator (see chapter 8).

The power of the liquidator to bring all causes of action should be clearly stated in the plan of reorganization. The plan should also expressly provide for substitution of the liquidator as the party in any pending litigation. The plan should make clear which causes of action are preserved for the liquidator. The plan of reorganization may provide that some causes of action are released or otherwise compromised. The liquidator's authority with respect to such causes of action should be limited accordingly.

If the debtor or any of its assets have already been sold to a third party under the plan of reorganization, the purchase and sales agreement should make clear which causes of action are retained by the estate and which pass to the new owner. The liquidating plan of reorganization must preserve the liquidator's right to assert counterclaims. If a cause of action against a claimant were to be passed to a third party while the claimant retains his or her claims against the estate, the repercussions could be disastrous. Conversely, a third party acquiring the debtor or its operations may be justifiably concerned about exposure to liability for such claims and the resulting loss of revenues. Hence, joint control over counterclaims may be appropriately provided in the plan. Similar attention should be paid to potential cross claims.

The plan of reorganization should also provide the liquidator with authority to compromise controversies. Another advantage that liquidating trustees have over Chapter 7 trustees is their ability to compromise certain levels of claims without having to obtain court approval. In the event that court approval is required for a settlement, the plan can contain standards for compromises and procedures for their approval.

Care and Disposition of Assets

The liquidator must have the power to care for and dispose of assets. The plan should provide the liquidator with adequate latitude to perform his or her duties concerning preservation of the estate. To avoid excessive expenditures of funds in maintaining assets of no value, like a bankruptcy trustee, the liquidating trustee should be empowered to abandon assets or dispose of them through appropriate procedures. The liquidating trustee should also be given authority to sell property of the estate with or without approval of the bankruptcy court. While the ability to submit a sale to the Bankruptcy Court for approval may be appropriate, and perhaps even necessary under certain circumstances, the liquidation process should not be hindered by the requirement of frequent recourse to the court. The ability to involve the court in postconfirmation asset dispositions should be largely discretionary on the part of the liquidator or the supervisory creditor group, rather than mandatory (see chapter 8).

The liquidator should also be expressly empowered under the plan of reorganization to carry out the operations of subsidiary businesses controlled by the estate. At a minimum, he or she should have the power to vote any equity securities the estate may hold. The liquidator should also have the power, perhaps subject to certain limitations, to select and put in place management for operating assets of the estate. In this capacity, the liquidator may wish to select and employ deputies to assist in the performance of specified tasks or activities, as deemed appropriate by the liquidator. The committee should have limited control or oversight authority to ensure that the liquidator does not incur excessive costs in this endeavor.

General Administrative Powers

Other powers that may be necessary for a liquidator to operate are generally consistent with powers afforded a trustee under applicable state trust law. He or she may require authority to make purchases, to lease space, or even to engage in construction or similar activities (see chapter 7). Again, the test of what powers the liquidator must be given is determined on a case-by-case basis. The objective, however, remains the same: minimize the amount of time it takes to maximize the present value of the creditor's recovery.

Continued Bankruptcy Court Supervision of Liquidation

Even though a Chapter 11 plan is confirmed by the bankruptcy court and consummated by the transfer of assets into the liquidation vehicle, the bankruptcy court may retain jurisdiction over certain matters involving the debtor. However, the involvement of the bankruptcy court in the liquidation process under a Chapter 11 plan should not to be so pervasive that the court controls the process. To that end, the plan should provide that utilization of the bankruptcy court is largely discretionary. If court involvement is unnecessary, the continuing jurisdiction of the bankruptcy court probably should not be invoked.

To protect the interests of creditors and supervision of the persons conducting the liquidation, the bankruptcy court's involvement should only be triggered by a party in interest or several parties in interest. In other words, "We'll call you, judge, if we need you." The liquidator should exercise powers in accordance with governing instruments and not at the direction of the bankruptcy court.

This limitation is of particular importance and value in the operation of a business during the liquidation process—the bankruptcy statutes restricting business operations to ordinary course transactions should not apply. The liquidator should be allowed to purchase and sell property, subject to approval of the oversight committee, without first obtaining court authority. He or she should be able to retain and compensate managers as he or she deems appropriate. In short, postconfirmation operations under a liquidating plan of reorganization, absent special circumstances, should be as free of court control as would be the case of a debtor operating postconfirmation pursuant to a nonliquidating plan. Nonetheless, certain areas should be and typically are addressed in the plan of reorganization. As with any Chapter 11 plan of reorganization, a liquidating plan provides for retained jurisdiction in the bankruptcy court after confirmation.

Resolution of Disputes Involving Liquidator

Jurisdiction may be retained in the court in order to allow for removal or replacement of the liquidator. The court may also retain jurisdiction in order to mediate differences between an oversight committee of creditors and the liquidator. Although subject to the control of an oversight committee, the liquidator needs recourse to the court in the event that he or she believes that the oversight committee's instructions are improper. The plan of reorganization is likely to provide that the liquidator has fiduciary responsibilities to his or her constituency independent of those of any oversight committee. Under such circumstances, with two fiduciaries answerable to the same constituency, a dispute may arise regarding how the case should proceed. When a dispute is not clearly resolvable, the bankruptcy court is the proper forum for adjudication.

Composition and Conduct of Oversight Committee

The bankruptcy court may retain jurisdiction over the composition of the oversight committee (if one exists). If a committee member must be replaced, such replacement may also be subject to court approval, if desired. Similarly, if the conduct of a member of the committee is questioned, that dispute should, because of the court's familiarity with the case, be handled before the bankruptcy court.

Dispute Regarding the Plan and Confirmation

Disputes arising from interpretations of the language in the plan of reorganization should also be heard by the bankruptcy court. While many such disputes are peculiar to the liquidating plan and fall in that category of retained jurisdiction relating to protection of the liquidation process, other disputes are typical with any plan. For example, valuation of collateral issues and disputes over classification should remain in the bankruptcy forum.

Sale of Assets

Facilitation of the exercise of bankruptcy powers by the liquidator requires retention of jurisdiction by the bankruptcy court to review proposed sales. The continued jurisdiction of the bankruptcy court serves as a necessary mechanism for "cleansing" property prior to sale; that is, property that might be otherwise impossible to sell because of confusion regarding title or conflicting claims or liens may be cleansed and sold through the bankruptcy court. That said, the retention of jurisdiction should not be such that the liquidator and the oversight committee are forced into bankruptcy court at each step of the liquidation process. Not every sale requires bankruptcy court approval. The size of the transaction, the property involved, and the circumstances surrounding the sale (including the identity of the purchaser) dictate whether the liquidator needs the protection of the bankruptcy court.

Conducting a sale of property pursuant to order of the bankruptcy court also provides an opportunity for other parties in interest to have their say with respect to the sale. By providing notice of the proposed sale to the entire constituency, the liquidator affords all members of that constituency an opportunity to appear and be heard in the bankruptcy court with respect to the desirability of the sale. This opportunity not only provides the individual creditor with a role in significant aspects of the liquidation process, but also provides some added protection to the liquidator.

Resolution of Claims

The bankruptcy court retains jurisdiction to consider objections to claims. The bankruptcy court also retains jurisdiction in order to estimate claims for purposes of distribution or for purposes of establishing reserves against distributions.

Litigation

Bankruptcy court jurisdiction needs to be maintained over all the estate's litigation. It is a convenient and central forum for the preservation and pursuit of bankruptcy causes of action.

The Automatic Stay

The bankruptcy court should retain jurisdiction involving stay litigation. The plan should provide that the automatic stay survives confirmation of a liquidating plan of reorganization. The liquidating plan should contain clear provisions staying actions against the liquidator or the estate itself. Additionally, the Bankruptcy Code severely limits the party's (at least one with notice of the plan process) ability to pursue a claim against the estate or liquidator. In any event, whatever protection is provided to the liquidator and the estate under the plan should be enforceable by the bankruptcy court. Hence, the bankruptcy court should retain jurisdiction in order to ensure that such protection is given.

Taxes

The benefit derived from the powers of the bankruptcy court to hear and determine taxes should be retained. Since the liquidator may not be free of personal liability in connection with the payment of the estate's taxes, quick determination of tax liability in the bankruptcy court is critical in order to avoid maintaining substantial reserves, thus reducing distributions.

Reserves

The liquidator is required to maintain reserves at such times as distributions are to be made. The amount of these reserves should be subject to review by the bankruptcy court.

Investments

The bankruptcy court should have the ability to review the handling of funds by the liquidator, especially if the liquidator is given wide latitude in how funds are invested.

Reports

The bankruptcy court should have an opportunity to review and approve the report formats to be made by the liquidating trustee as well as the form of any security evidencing an interest in the estate being liquidated.

Deadlines

The bankruptcy court retains jurisdiction to modify deadlines set under the plan of reorganization, which might include the dates by which claim objections must be filed, certain assets must be disposed of, and distributions must be made.

Conclusion

While Chapter 7 is specifically structured for liquidations and Chapter 11 provides a vehicle for reorganizations, many liquidations are nonetheless carried out in Chapter 11. Sometimes what starts out as an attempt to reorganize evolves into a liquidating plan. On other occasions, a Chapter 11 filing may, at the outset, have been undertaken to facilitate an orderly liquidation.

Liquidating in the context of Chapter 11 plan offers a number of advantages compared to Chapter 7. Specifically, Chapter 11 plans provide greater creditor control, less pressure to sell assets prematurely, more investment options for the estate's cash, reduced cost compared to staying in Chapter 11 (costs associated with creditors' committees, lawyers, accountants, etc.), and overall flexibility in, among other matters, sorting out and dealing with the various classes of creditors. Flexibility and reduced cost have led to a huge upsurge in Chapter 11 liquidating plans implemented by a liquidating trustee. The liquidating plan must be drafted to insure proper supervision of the liquidation process and maximization of the benefits afforded by the Bankruptcy Code.

4

A Tale of Two Liquidations
Case Studies in Chapter 7 and Chapter 11

While the authors have been involved in numerous liquidations, two cases best illustrate the number and complexity of issues that a liquidator faces. These two cases—one a Chapter 7 and one a Chapter 11—provide a good framework within which to discuss the liquidation process. A Tale of Two Liquidations: Bank of New England Corporation (Chapter 7) and Friede Goldman Halter Inc. (Chapter 11) show how two companies came to liquidation down very different paths. Throughout the remaining chapters, Tales from the Bankruptcy Trenches draw primarily from these cases.

Friede Goldman Halter Inc.

Friede's Operations

Friede Goldman Halter, Inc. (FGH) and its various subsidiaries (collectively, Friede) comprised a multinational business engaged in the design, manufacture, conversion and modification of equipment for the offshore energy and maritime industries. FGH resulted from the merger of Friede International, Inc. and Halter Marine Group, Inc. in November 1999. Friede was based in Gulfport, Mississippi, with operations around the world, including significant operations on the Mississippi River and the Louisiana and Texas gulf coasts, and in Newfoundland, Canada. It was one of the largest shipbuilders in the United States. At its peak, Friede employed more than 4,500 people and operated in four primary divisions: an offshore segment, a vessel segment, a design and engineering segment, and an engineered products segment.

The vessels segment operated several shipyards principally dedicated to the new construction of marine vessels. Primary customers were offshore energy service companies, domestic and foreign governments, and other commercial enterprises. The offshore segment operated shipyards in Mississippi, Texas, and Newfoundland, where it constructed new offshore drilling rigs and performed conversion, repair, and modification services of existing offshore drilling rigs. Customers were primarily offshore drilling contractors.

The engineered products segment provided services that included the design and manufacture of heavy-lift marine cranes, mooring systems, marine deck equipment, jacking systems, and specialty mechanical systems, and a comprehensive aftermarket repair and retrofitting operation. Primary customers, in addition to the customers of the offshore segment, included offshore construction contractors, shipyards, commercial cruise-ship owners, general merchant marine operators, the fishing industry, on-land general construction contractors, and the U.S. government.

Friede's smallest operating division, the design and engineering segment based in Houston, Texas, was a well-established domestic naval architecture firm that specialized in offshore energy markets.

Friede's Cash Flow

Friede's revenue was primarily generated from large new-build construction, modification, and repair projects associated with marine vessels and offshore drilling platforms. Each of these projects typically involved numerous third-party vendors and subcontractors. Friede's projects typically involved progress billing to customers, whereby certain payments would be made by customers as contractually established milestones were reached in the construction process. The timing of payments to Friede varied greatly under these progress payment contracts; however, most of Friede's milestone payment contracts provided for back-ended payments. In other words, incurred construction costs typically exceeded the amount of customer payments received until completion of the project and final payment. Thus, sources of cash and liquidity were vital to Friede's' operations. The ability to borrow under Friede's revolving credit facility was essential to its survival.

As with any other commercial enterprise, obtaining new business was also crucial to the continuation of operations. Considerable customer deliberation went into each and every customer's project because of their size and nature. Additionally, potential customers could choose from a substantial number of builders offering competitive pricing. A number of relevant and important factors affect such customers' choice. One such factor that was typically at the forefront of any customer's decision was the confidence that the project would be completed on time and properly delivered. For example, a vessel operator that was looking to place a two-year $50 million vessel-construction project required a high level of confidence that the builder would complete the project. A number of factors created and sustained customer confidence in Friede, including Friede's access to the financial resources necessary to complete projects on time, access to its credit facility, and the ability to obtain payment and performance surety bonds. Additionally, Friede's customer revenues were essential to confirming operations, and continuing viability depended on new projects coming regularly into the pipeline. Without new customer contracts, operations would eventually grind to a halt.

Friede's Balance Sheet

Just prior to filing Chapter 11 in April, 2001, Friede reported real estate assets with a book value of $135.7 million and fixtures and equipment with a book value of $148.2 million. Friede's real estate consisted primarily of shipyards that were located across the Texas, Louisiana, and Mississippi gulf coasts. The personal property consisted of the equipment related to these yards, the inventory held at the yards, miscellaneous intellectual property, work in progress and accounts receivable from current jobs, and other items (e.g., software and computers).

Typical for a company of its size and industry, Friede had several layers and types of debt. Outstanding secured debt included a revolving credit facility and a term loan, secured by a senior lien on substantially all of its assets, owed to a group of lenders including the agent lender, Foothill Capital Corporation (Foothill). Foothill is known as a high-cost, asset-based lender. As of the bankruptcy filing, Friede owed approximately $70 million on the revolving facility and $40 million on the term facility. Friede also had additional secured debt, generally in the form of bonds issued or backed by governmental entities, that aggregated to approximately $38 million. Finally, Friede owed other miscellaneous secured obligations, including mortgages on its Texas shipyards, secured tax obligations, and other amounts due to subcontractors for work performed on construction projects that were generally entitled to statutory lien protections.

Friede's unsecured debt included approximately $185 million in principal amount in public bond debt. This debt, which called for semiannual payments, matured in 2004. In addition, Friede had obtained various surety bonds as required by certain of its construction contracts. Finally, at the commencement of the bankruptcy cases, Friede owed approximately $85 million in accounts payable, roughly evenly divided between the vessels and offshore segments.

Friede's Stock Price

FGH had a single class of publicly traded voting stock. In mid-2000, the stock traded at a high of approximately $15 per share on the New York Stock Exchange. The share price tumbled from that point to a share price of 94 cents just prior to the bankruptcy filing. FGH was de-listed from the New York Stock Exchange after the bankruptcy filing, although the equity continued to trade on the pink sheets.

The Friede Crisis

Operational issues caused a financial crisis from which it could not be saved, and Friede fell into bankruptcy. The primary crushing blows were delivered by unprofitable contracts with two companies, Ocean Rig and Petrodrill. Pursuant to these contracts, Friede was obligated to construct and deliver offshore drilling rigs at fixed prices and on time. For a variety of reasons, Friede almost immediately began to experience construction delays and increased costs. At the time of the Chapter 11 filing, Friede was still constructing the Petrodrill rigs and suffering enormous economic losses as a result.

Continuing losses led to significant, ongoing financial distress, which led to problems with Foothill, Friede's primary funding and liquidity source. Throughout 2000 and early 2001, Foothill was exceptionally tight with advances, and the possibility of an event of default and termination of the facility loomed. The borrowing difficulties exacerbated Friede's operational problems. Specifically, Friede was significantly behind in its vendor and subcontractor payments. This caused considerable friction between Friede and its vendors and even within the Friede organization, where ongoing projects and managers essentially competed for dwindling cash resources. Also, Friede found it difficult, if not impossible, to provide financial security in the form of letters of credit or otherwise to potential project customers, thus preventing Friede from pursuing and obtaining any significant new customer projects. In a sense, a perverse run on the bank had begun as Friede's financial difficulties became well known throughout the industry. Unless borrowing availability under the Foothill facility greatly expanded, Friede was doomed.

In February of 2001, the FGH board agreed to retain a crisis management firm in a last-ditch effort to negotiate borrowing relief from Foothill. At about this same time, the debtor and Andrews Kurth LLP (AK), its bankruptcy counsel, began to prepare a Chapter 11 filing. Business managers ultimately went to Atlanta to meet with Foothill. Although a brief reprieve was negotiated, Friede's commitments to Foothill, its ongoing operational problems, and the semiannual interest payment due on the publicly traded bonds on March 15, 2001, loomed.

In addition, Friede negotiated an agreement with Fireman's Fund Insurance Company, the bonding company for the Petrodrill projects, pursuant to which Fireman's would advance funds for the payment of wages to workers on the Petrodrill projects. Although bankruptcy was averted for the moment, friction over hard choices and the lack of a long-term resolution with Foothill and the viability of the Ocean Rig and Petrodrill projects led to the termination of the crisis management firm. During this period, Friede and its professionals were actively pursuing alternative financing sources with the goal of refinancing the Foothill debt and obtaining additional borrowing availability. These efforts were wholly unsuccessful.

The Friede Bankruptcy Filing

The inevitable occurred on April 13, 2001, when Foothill declared a default under the credit facility, based on alleged covenant defaults. Friede had five days to cure the default or face foreclosure by Foothill. With no other available options, on April 16, 2001 one of FGH's subsidiaries filed a Chapter 11. This subsidiary was a no-asset, nonoperating entity. It was filed to protect Friede's venue of choice—Biloxi, Mississippi—and to ward off an involuntary bankruptcy filing by the creditors against Friede in any other jurisdiction. On April 19, FGH and substantially all of the other Friede entities filed Chapter 11.

Like any large corporate Chapter 11 filing, the Friede petitions were accompanied by a number of first-day motions that sought a variety of operational and case administration relief for the debtors. These pleadings included applications to employ various professionals and motions relating to employee wages and benefits, the continuation of bank accounts and the cash management system, utility services, and cash collateral usage.

Frustration and Financial Forecasts

The cash-collateral issue dogged Friede throughout the case. While bankruptcy courts may permit a debtor's use of a secured creditor's cash collateral during a Chapter 11 case, a typical requirement for the granting of such authority is that the debtor provide credible cash forecasts for the period during which it will be used. Due to the emergency nature of the bankruptcy filing and the shortage of staff in Friede's financial and accounting groups, the debtors were not able fully to analyze their long-range cash receipts and needs at the petition date. Moreover, because of the recent merger, Friede's various units had separate and different accounting systems. The professionals quickly discovered that intercompany claims could not be reconciled and that no separate general ledger had been created for FGH, the parent. Its transactions were intermingled with those for Halter and the other operating subsidiaries. There was also no single list of real-property assets across the company, no reliable list of leases or contracts, and no single list of pending litigation. The situation was exacerbated as employees left to pursue other jobs or were shifted to help with the bankruptcy efforts. Meanwhile, the debtors' staff grew increasingly frustrated as the various professionals and management made similar and/or increasing demands for data. The demands, deadline pressure, and day-to-day uncertainty took their toll, not the least of which was the cost of the efforts, all borne by the company as administrative expenses to be paid before creditors saw any recovery. In addition to these challenges, the very nature of the business and the operational issues that immediately confronted Friede made the cash forecasting process exceedingly complex and lengthy for the duration of the Chapter 11 cases.

As expected, Foothill opposed Friede's use of cash collateral. Initially, the debtors attained interim, short-term authority to use cash collateral over Foothill's opposition. Subsequently, Friede and Foothill reached agreements by which the debtors could use Foothill's cash collateral to operate; however, there were a number of conditions (including substantial weekly cash payments to Foothill), and the agreements were fairly short-term due to cash-forecasting difficulties. While Friede could survive solely on the use of cash collateral (i.e., cash flow from the operations), survival was clearly going to be painful and short without some other financing source. Unless the Foothill relationship could be rectified through alternative financing, Friede was destined for liquidation.

The First Sale: BLM

One saving grace for Friede came in the form of the sale of the stock in Friede's French subsidiary, Brissonneau & Lotz Marine S.A. (BLM), a subsidiary within the engineered products division, during the first month of the bankruptcy. Fortuitously, the BLM stock had not been pledged to Foothill or any other lender. The BLM sale proceeds provided considerable liquidity, which gave Friede a bit of breathing room. Unfortunately, both Foothill and the unsecured creditors committee demanded the imposition of certain restraints on Friede's use of the BLM proceeds. Ultimately, the court restricted Friede's use of these funds. Nonetheless, the BLM liquidation proceeds provided temporary liquidity.

The Creditors Move Friede toward Liquidation

From the outset, Friede's management and professionals endeavored to reorganize the company and emerge from Chapter 11 with the operations intact and a restructured balance sheet. Unfortunately, events beyond Friede's control, primarily its inability to obtain alternative financing, doomed any prospect of a successful reorganization.

Prior to the bankruptcy filing, Foothill declared a default under the credit facility and ceased advancing new funds to Friede. Throughout the bankruptcy case, Foothill unequivocally demanded that Friede liquidate in order to provide the earliest possible repayment of the Foothill debt. Friede's efforts to obtain debtor-in-possession financing, in order to remove Foothill and to provide postpetition liquidity, were unsuccessful. This, coupled with significant prepetition unpaid trade debt, caused Friede's trade vendors, for the most part, to refuse any postpetition credit terms to Friede. Virtually all of Friede's postpetition vendors demanded cash-on-delivery or cash-in-advance for any postpetition deliveries. This lack of trade-vendor credit support further exacerbated Friede's lack of liquidity. Without financing and vendor support, Friede's existing and potential customers had little confidence that Friede could complete any significant construction project. The lack of customer confidence doomed Friede's ability to obtain new project contracts and required an extraordinary effort to maintain and continue the pre-existing project contracts. Lacking any new financing alternatives, it became clear that Friede would have to begin a partial liquidation in its pending Chapter 11.

The Liquidation Continues

Despite increasing operational difficulties, during the first several months of the cases the debtors continued to believe that a reorganization was viable. To this end, the debtors sought from the court an extension of the period during which the debtors had the exclusive right to propose a reorganization plan. This exclusive period gave the debtors the ability to manage their affairs in the early stages of the cases without the threat that the committee, Foothill or another creditor or creditors would propose a plan of their own. Because initial extensions are typically granted in many large cases, the debtors felt they stood a good chance of obtaining additional time to formulate a plan and to remain in control of their own destiny.

However, the unsecured creditors committee and Foothill opposed the debtors' request, although on slightly different grounds. Foothill's opposition was a continuation of its refrain that Friede should cease operations and liquidate its assets. The committee's primary issue related to the debtors' upper management. Simply, the committee questioned whether upper management was acting in the best interests of creditors and wanted to use its opposition to an extension of exclusivity to gain greater control over the direction of the cases, more influence over the debtors' day-to-day management, and a commitment that it would receive regular and substantial information regarding the debtors' operations.

Facing opposition from both the unsecured creditors committee and Foothill, as well as various other creditors, the debtors, now between a rock and hard place, realized that obtaining an extension was unlikely in the face of such diverse opposition. The debtors thus struck a deal with the committee to extend their exclusive periods, memorialized in an order that kept Foothill at bay but resulted in a shared control of the cases with the committee. The debtors' exclusivity was extended but in exchange for the committee's support, (i) the debtors could not propose a Chapter 11 plan without the committee's approval, (ii) the committee would receive weekly financial reporting; (iii) the debtors would commence a marketing process; and (iv) the debtors would rehire the crisis manager to be their chief restructuring officer (CRO). The court entered an order based on the agreement with the committee and in the process denied any effective relief to Foothill. FGH had nominally retained its exclusivity, but the handwriting was on the wall—at least a partial liquidation of the debtors was now in progress. The committee used its leverage to make sure that it had a seat at the table when decisions were made about how best to liquidate the debtors' assets. On the other hand, the hiring of a CRO was not necessarily a concession on FGH's part. Over the course of the first six months of the cases, the FGH board realized that it needed outside expert assistance to conduct the debtors' bankruptcy cases especially to help negotiate with the many lawyers and financial advisors that were now involved in the matter.

Liquidation Specialists Are Hired

The compromise over the debtors' motion to extend exclusivity presaged the long promised hiring of an investment banker to evaluate and market one or more of FGH's operating divisions. By early November 2001, when Houlihan Lokey Howard & Zukin (Houlihan) was engaged, it was clear to everyone that Friede could not be reorganized without selling one or more of its business units.

Foothill Requests a Chapter 11 Trustee

Determined to keep the pressure on, Foothill filed a motion for the appointment of a Chapter 11 trustee or the conversion of the cases to Chapter 7 on the grounds that the management of the debtors could no longer be trusted to operate as debtors-in-possession. However, the hiring of a CRO and the retention of Houlihan effectively blunted these arguments. The original management was no longer completely in control of FGH's reorganization efforts and at least a partial liquidation was being planned. There was no need for a trustee, and the court seemed to reflect that view when it did not set the motion for a status conference until nearly three months after the motion was filed. Ultimately, Foothill's motion would never be set for a hearing. (Now, under the 2005 amendments to the Bankruptcy Code, hearings on such motions are required to be set within 30 days of their filing.)

The Marketing of Assets

Houlihan's marching orders were not to sell everything but to start marketing the debtors' business segments. This would allow the board, the unsecured creditors committee, and the other constituencies in the cases to make informed decisions about how to proceed with sales, if any.

Sales Commissions Are Negotiated

Because of the somewhat unknown nature of its assignment, and the varying (and unknown) amounts for which the different segments might be sold, the unsecured creditors committee, the debtors, and Foothill, as well as Houlihan, sought some certainty within the terms of its engagement. Ultimately, the parties agreed that Houlihan would receive a flat fee of $1 million, paid from the sale proceeds, for each of the segments sold, rather than keeping track of its time and earning an hourly rate. Because there were four segments—offshore, vessel, design, and engineered products—Houlihan had the potential to earn $4 million for its work, plus expenses. Unlike many investment banks that advise companies in bankruptcy proceedings, Houlihan would not receive a monthly retainer and it would not receive anything if one or more of the segments were not sold. Houlihan's contract was subject to the comment of the United States Trustee, the views of which the bankruptcy court gave significant deference in matters of professional employment. In Houlihan's case, the United States Trustee agreed to the basic terms of the retention, insisting, however, that separate motions be filed before Houlihan was paid out of the proceeds from each sale, so that the United States Trustee and other parties had an opportunity to question the reasonableness of the fees in light of the results achieved. Foothill objected that no amounts to Houlihan should be paid from the proceeds of its collateral until Foothill had been completely paid. Houlihan ultimately received fees of $3.75 million.

The Marketing Process

Houlihan created a data room for prospective purchasers and teaser letters were sent to identify prospective purchasers. Houlihan sent marketing books, to its proprietary list of potential asset purchasers who responded to the teaser letters. AK created an asset purchase agreement (APA; see appendix 10) form, which was given to each interested bidder. Any asset purchaser had to first complete the form and draft any requested changes. This minimized the estate professionals' work and allowed the court and creditors to more easily compare competing bids.

Houlihan's personnel worked in Gulfport at the debtors' offices and in Houston and New Orleans with other estate professionals, and they traveled to the locations of the debtors' operations across the Gulf coast and in Minneapolis, Minnesota, to meet with the executives of the various business units. The segments' executives anticipated these meetings with both dread and hope. After months of trying to operate their divisions as part of Chapter 11 proceedings, all of them wanted to free their operations as soon as possible, but they had no way of being certain what came next.

This sentiment prevailed at AmClyde, the engineered products division based in Minneapolis. Its robust and established operations were only loosely tied to Gulfport, and management clearly chafed at its guilt by association with FGH. The CRO and Houlihan each decided that AmClyde was the place to start in terms of a potential sale, although Houlihan would work simultaneously to prepare all four operating segments for a sale. The CRO and Houlihan also knew that Hydrolift, which had purchased the stock of BLM, AmClyde's former French operations, was a natural buyer for AmClyde. Houlihan's challenge was to keep Hydrolift from believing it was or becoming the only prospective buyer and thus negotiate the best possible price for AmClyde.

The Second Sale: AmClyde

In planning its approach to the marketing of AmClyde, Houlihan's weapons were (i) its guile; (ii) its marketing efforts, through which other potential purchasers might be identified and brought to AmClyde's offices and operations for marketing tours and other due diligence activities; and (iii) the commitment of the unsecured creditors committee, the debtors and, to a lesser extent, Foothill, not to settle for any price that was too low. For its part, Hydrolift knew that if it could become the "stalking horse bidder" at an acceptable purchase amount, it would have significant momentum going into an auction and a sale hearing. A "Stalking Horse Bidder" is a first bidder on an asset that agrees to purchase an asset subject to other higher bids. Such a bidder frequently receives a cash "break up fee" should it be outbid at a later date. As such, it has certain protections that allow it some control over the process.

In January, 2002, Houlihan commenced negotiations with Hydrolift using the form APA as a starting point. Each of the debtors, including their CRO and AK, the unsecured creditors committee and its legal and financial advisors, and Foothill and its respective advisors, would review drafts of the APA, commenting on the particular terms of the document and providing their view of the price that should be sought. Because FGH remained a debtor-in-possession, the board retained and exercised final authority over the conduct of negotiations. Ultimately, FGH agreed to sell its AmClyde operations, which included substantially all the assets of four of the debtors, to Hydrolift for $36 million plus the assumption of certain liabilities. The APA also gave Hydrolift a $1 million break-up fee, or the amount it would be paid if it were outbid at an auction.

On February 19, 2002, AK filed a motion for approval of the sale and bidding procedures in conjunction with the proposed sale, and although the procedures were approved on March 15, no competing bids emerged. The bankruptcy court approved the sale and the sale closed on April 25. The closing of the sale, however, did not mean that additional funds were available for operations. In due course—and not as a surprise to the debtors or the committee—Foothill filed a limited opposition to the sale motion, asserting that all the proceeds of the sale were its collateral and should be paid to Foothill in partial satisfaction of the debtors' outstanding obligations. To resolve Foothill's objection, it was agreed that the proceeds of the sale would be held in a segregated account pending resolution of Foothill's claims. Thus, at closing, after certain adjustments and excluding $1 million set aside to pay Houlihan's fee, the debtors received $21,864,477. Because the APA had a feature commonly known as a purchase-price-adjustment escrow (a device used to allow a value to be assigned to working capital as of closing, by retroactively looking at the value of such property), the debtors would later receive an additional $13,756,517.

With the complete disposition of the assets of its engineered products segment, FGH became a smaller enterprise overnight. Downsizing would continue with the closing of the sale of the assets of its design and engineering division, Friede & Goldman Ltd. (FGL), which followed closely on the heels of the AmClyde sale.

The Third Sale: FGL

On the same day that the bankruptcy court approved the bidding procedures for the AmClyde sale, Friede filed a second sale motion for approval of the sale of the assets of FGL. With two sales on separate tracks, the professionals in the case now had their hands full, and this was true of no one more than the CRO. The CRO worked with Houlihan and AK to keep FGH's board apprised of developments in the sale process and try to carry out the board's wishes (and those of the unsecured creditors committee and Foothill) to move forward as fast as possible. But the sales were not the only items requiring his attention at this time. The CRO worked with AK on exclusivity and cash-collateral issues, both of which required multiple hearings throughout the spring of 2002, and the completion of a proposed employment and retention plan for the debtors' employees. The FGH board also directed him to work with AK on the formulation of a proposed plan of reorganization to provide some options to the debtors, should it be impossible to sell Halter and Offshore for acceptable amounts.

Houlihan, AK, and the unsecured creditors committee negotiated an agreement with a group of investors who formed FGL Acquisitions to buy the assets of the FGL for $8 million. On April 19, 2002, the bankruptcy court approved procedures for an auction, including a break-up fee of $250,000 for FGL Acquisitions as stalking horse bidder. As the date of the auction approached, it became clear that there was additional interest in FGL's extensive library of jack-up and other rig designs, as well as its highly experienced personnel. United Heavy B.V., a Russian company, qualified as a bidder under the procedures by executing an APA substantially similar to the one submitted by FGL Acquisitions and by complying with the other conditions established in the bidding procedures, including depositing 10% of the bid amount and providing financial information. On April 30 and May 2, 2002, as set forth in the procedures, Houlihan, AK, and the committee's counsel conducted an auction that resulted in United Heavy B.V. as the winner with a high bid of $15 million. The bankruptcy court approved the sale. FGH received net proceeds of $13,498,411, after payment of the break-up fee to FGL Acquisitions, certain other costs, and the escrow of another $1 million to pay Houlihan's fee. Again, after an objection by Foothill, all the proceeds were placed in a segregated account, awaiting further order of the bankruptcy court.

Thus, in approximately seven months, Houlihan had earned $2 million and the estate had received proceeds of approximately $47 million. However, the sales of the debtors two largest segments, in terms of employees and property and equipment—vessel (Halter) and offshore—remained to be completed.

The Fourth Sale: Halter

In the midst of the approval and consummation of the AmClyde and FGL sales, on March 22, 2002, FGH filed a proposed plan of reorganization and a disclosure statement. From the unsecured creditor committee's and the debtors' points of view, the proposed plan, which called for a reorganization around Halter and the offshore segment, was necessary to preserve their option to reorganize what remained of FGH, because the marketing of the Halter assets was not going well. Foothill and other creditors were highly skeptical of the proposed plan, and those parties immediately attacked it as a step in the wrong direction. Adding to the air of uncertainty surrounding the direction of the cases, the president of FGH resigned in early April, and the board appointed the CRO to assume complete control of the debtors. Friede now had two liquidators, Houlihan and the CRO.

Most of these issues began to disappear when Bollinger Shipyards, Inc., Halter's direct competitor, decided to make an offer for the Halter assets, instead of allowing another strategic buyer or, perhaps worse, a reorganized FGH, to become a reenergized competitor. Bollinger was basically the only serious potential buyer for Halter that Houlihan could identify. Bollinger agreed to buy the assets for the vessels segment for $48 million by executing an APA. Three days later, AK filed a motion for approval of the sale and the now familiar auction procedures, including a $2.5 million break-up fee for Bollinger. The motion drew another limited opposition from Foothill, which was resolved in the same manner as before, and in July 2002, the bankruptcy court approved the bidding and sale procedures.

Like the FGL sale another bidder appeared, Vision Technologies Kinetics, Inc. (VTK) an affiliate of a large Singapore-based ship and rig builder. VTK signed an APA and complied with the other conditions established in the bidding procedures to qualify to bid at the auction in Biloxi, Mississippi. With more than 10 estate professionals gathered for the auction, executives from VTK calmly bid against Bollinger with increasing $1 million increments for six hours. In the end, VTK prevailed with a bid of $67 million to Bollinger's $66 million. At a hearing later that day and the next, the debtors prevailed over Bollinger's argument that as a subsidiary of a foreign entity, VTK could not buy a U.S. shipbuilder.

Because of Halter's relative complexity, and because VTK personnel had had much less time than Bollinger's to perform due diligence prior to the sale, closing the sale was difficult and time consuming. VTK attempted to claw back every dollar it could, based on the working capital and other adjustment provisions in the APA. Some felt that Halter's executives were too eager to help the firm they hoped would be their next employer, pointing out ways that VTK could lower the price. Ultimately, however, the sale closed in October 2002. After paying certain tax claims, Bollinger's $2.5 million break-up fee, and setting aside another $1 million for Houlihan, FGH received $67.8 million, all of which was again placed in a segregated account awaiting resolution of Foothill's claims.

The Final Sale: Friede–The Offshore Segment

After the Halter sale, the estate had enough cash from liquidation to pay Foothill in full and to ensure the bankruptcy estate's continued administration. With just the offshore segment remaining, the debtors were now substantially smaller in size and easier to manage. Yet, marketing offshore presented additional complexities because of several municipal and government-backed financings that had been done to improve its shipyards. In addition, the relatively low entry cost into the rig-repair business—neither the equipment nor the shipyard is particularly specialized—suppressed the sales price. Thus, although the board wanted to sell the segment in order to move the bankruptcy cases toward a conclusion, the unsecured creditors committee wanted to reorganize the segment as a way of generating a better return for creditors. Part of the committee's motivation came from rumors that Friede's former chief executive officer/chairman of the board/largest individual stockholder intended to buy the assets at a discount and reconstitute the business. Given the antipathy that develops between creditors and former management, this was the last thing they would allow, perhaps despite the possible negative financial consequences.

Against this backdrop, a group of current and former executives put together a bid for the offshore segment. Ultimately, a sale to an entity formed by these executives, ACON Offshore Partners, L.P., was agreed for the price of $18 million plus the assumption of $61 million in debt—a significant savings for the debtors and a way of ridding the estate of several complicated financing arrangements. Although in the end, no other serious bidders appeared, committee's counsel insisted that no sale would proceed below $18 million. Ultimately, ACON agreed to pay that amount in cash. FGH received net proceeds of $13,675,000 after the payment of taxes, administrative claims, and a slightly reduced fee of $750,000 to Houlihan. Houlihan agreed to the discount in light of the fact that its marketing efforts had more or less run their course by the time ACON made its offer.

The Liquidating Plan

While the marketing and sale process continued, people began to focus on the Chapter 11 plan. The nature of the plan dramatically changed during the cases as the asset sale process evolved. The initial plan provided for a restructuring around the vessels and offshore segments, with the obligations owed to Foothill partially paid at confirmation and the remainder paid over time. Under this plan, equity in the reorganized entities would be owned by the unsecured creditors. This was fiercely opposed by Foothill. Additionally, the success of this initial plan depended upon postconfirmation working capital financing, which did not materialize. Despite the best efforts of the debtors and the committee, it soon became clear that the hurdles facing this plan were likely insurmountable, and in any event, the Halter marketing process was generating better-than-expected results. Given the results of the vessels-segment marketing, the decision was made to proceed toward the liquidation of all of the operating units.

The debtors and the committee began to modify the initial plan and the liquidating Chapter 11 plan came into being. The plan was structured in accordance with Bankruptcy Code's priority scheme, in that the plan provided for the satisfaction of secured claims and the payment in full of all administrative and priority claims. The plan was a "pot plan" for unsecured creditors, meaning that unsecured creditors were not assured any specific recovery. Rather, all assets remaining after satisfaction of senior priority claims would be available to partially satisfy unsecured claims. To implement this approach, the parties chose a liquidating trust.

Substantive Consolidation

The most difficult issue that faced the debtors and the committee in preparing the plan was the consolidation issue. The Friede enterprise consisted of 33 separate legal entities, each presumably with its own distinct assets and liabilities. Typically, the separate legal nature of entities must be observed so that each entity's creditors are satisfied by that entity's assets. Immediately, the debtors and the committee realized the virtually impossible task that faced them should they attempt to create a plan that recognized and gave effect to the separate legal entities. For years, Friede had blurred the lines between its various entities in such a way that it would have required a monumental forensic accounting process to even begin to apportion the assets and liabilities among the various entities. Quite simply, Friede had essentially operated and accounted for its business as if it were a single legal entity, not 33 separate entities. A number of financial and accounting tests were performed to determine the feasibility of separating the entities. The debtors and the committee ultimately realized that "substantive consolidation" was the only credible and appropriate course to pursue, even though such a plan could generate significant and costly litigation from various aggrieved or agenda-pursuing creditors. "Substantive consolidation" is appropriate where there is substantial identity between the bankruptcy estates to be consolidated and consolidation would be beneficial or avoid harm. Here it was clearly beneficial.

Releases

One issue that regularly caused disagreement in the plan-drafting process related to various releases that the debtors sought to incorporate in the plan. The committee opposed the debtors' proposed release of present and former officers, directors, and professionals. The committee had targeted certain of the debtors' prepetition officers, directors, and professionals as potential defendants in litigation over the merger between Friede International and Halter Marine. As a result, and in recognition of the committee's concern, the parties negotiated a full and complete release of any and all claims related to postpetition conduct and left alive claims related to prebankruptcy conduct.

Administrative Claims

Throughout the plan preparation process (and, in fact, all the way through confirmation), the debtors and committee were carefully tracking and assessing the administrative solvency of the debtors. A Chapter 11 plan cannot be confirmed unless the plan provides for the payment in full of all administrative and priority claims. Further, a confirmed plan may ultimately fail if the assets are not sufficient to satisfy such claims fully. At that point, conversion from Chapter 11 to Chapter 7 is the only option. As part of the anticipated confirmation fight, the proponents expected various parties to assert large administrative claims to prevent confirmation on feasibility grounds by showing that the aggregate of administrative claims exceeded the pool of assets available to satisfy such claims. This posed a considerable risk to confirmation that necessitated continuous analysis and management of the process to minimize, or prepare to litigate over, the magnitude of potentially allowable administrative claims. One potential administrative claim that hung over the process was a claim that had been threatened by the State of Louisiana Department of Environmental Quality (LDEQ). The LDEQ threatened, among other things, to assert a substantial administrative claim relating to allegedly contaminated property in Louisiana. A global resolution was ultimately reached with the LDEQ that led to the confirmation and consummation of the plan.

Postconfirmation Trust

The plan provided for a liquidating trust created under Delaware law and in accordance with Internal Revenue Service (IRS) regulations. As such, it could not engage in a trade or business except to the extent necessary to liquidate. All remaining assets of the debtors were transferred to the Liquidating Trust. At confirmation, the Liquidating Trustee was given authority to prosecute actions, abandon assets and do essentially all required to finish the Friede liquidation. A trust committee of committee members was formed to oversee the trust chairman, a/k/a the liquidator.

The Liquidating Plan Is Confirmed

The debtors and the committee finalized and filed with the court their Chapter 11 plan and a disclosure statement relating to the plan. The proponents also prepared and filed a related motion that sought court relief relating to plan vote solicitation, vote tabulation, and the confirmation process and deadlines. The court subsequently granted this motion and approved the disclosure statement. The debtors and the committee now focused their attention on the anticipated plan objections and the upcoming confirmation hearing.

A number of creditors filed objections to confirmation of the plan. Most of the objections, nonsubstantive in nature, required clarification and otherwise minor revisions to the plan. These were addressed relatively easily and did not, in the plan proponents' view, jeopardize the chances for confirmation. By the time the Friede plan was confirmed, the remaining assets consisted largely of causes of action that went into the litigation trust.

Bank of New England Corporation

Unlike Friede, Bank of New England Corporation (BNEC) in many respects began its liquidation long before it filed bankruptcy. By the time it did file Chapter 7, the vast majority of value to be derived for creditors came from litigation, not asset sales.

The BNEC Crisis

In the 1980s, BNEC was a bank holding company owning over 100 subsidiary corporations, including federally insured bank subsidiaries Bank of New England, NA (BNE), Connecticut Bank & Trust (CBT), and Maine National Bank (MNB). The ultimate cause of BNEC's demise is common—it grew too fast and paid too little attention to what it spent and got in return. From 1985 through 1987, its loan portfolio mushroomed more than threefold, from $8 billion to $27 billion. During an annual onsite review in 1986, the Office of the Comptroller of the Currency (OCC) discovered that BNE, BNEC's largest bank subsidiary, possessed a portfolio concentrated in risky real estate loans—a problem compounded by poor management and faulty loan assessments. During the next several years, and despite repeated warnings by the OCC, these problems caused BNE's financial condition to deteriorate.

As a result of the increasingly serious problems at BNE, the federal regulatory agencies—OCC, the Federal Reserve Bank (FRB), and the Federal Deposit Insurance Corporation (FDIC)—had a continuous presence at BNE commencing in the fall of 1989. In August 1989, the OCC entered into a formal agreement with BNE, which required BNE to address its problems. In response to the regulators' concerns over BNEC's capital, BNEC completed a bond offering in September 1989 and thereafter transferred most of the $250 million in proceeds to BNE, CBT and MNB.

During its 1989 onsite review of BNE, the OCC found that poor and rapidly deteriorating asset quality was threatening the viability of BNE. In December 1989, BNEC projected its 1989 loan losses to exceed $1 billion dollars, then the largest quarterly loss ever recorded by a domestic bank holding company. This prompted an investigation by the SEC, which determined that these losses had in fact occurred earlier. The SEC then required BNEC to restate its third quarter 1989 financials, and BNEC entered into a consent decree to that effect.

The Prebankruptcy Liquidation

At a BNEC board of directors meeting in December 1989, the regulators recommended that BNEC begin selling assets to raise cash to recapitalize its subsidiary banks. This program was internally known as the Asset Disposition Program. The regulators facilitated the program by causing BNEC to replace its existing senior management with management approved by the regulators. The Asset Disposition Program included the following, and more:

A substantial part of the proceeds of BNEC's September, 1989 bond issue were transferred to the subsidiary banks, including $171,000,000 to BNE, $2,520,000 to CBT and $300,000 to MNB.

BNEC forgave a $25 million debt obligation of CBT to BNEC.

The assets of BNE Mortgage Corporation were transferred to a subsidiary subsequently merged into BNE.

The assets of BNE Mortgage Services Corporation were transferred directly to BNE.

The stock of two vehicle-leasing subsidiaries was sold to General Electric Capital Corporation and the proceeds transferred to BNE.

BNEC's directly owned loan production subsidiary, New England Commercial Finance Corp., sold certain assets and the proceeds were transferred to BNE.

Assets of BNE-Old Colony valued at $76 million were sold and the proceeds transferred to BNE.

The stock of BNE Information Services, Inc., and BNE Data Services Corporation was transferred to the subsidiary banks.

Most of BNEC's $85 million federal tax refund was transferred to BNE and CBT.

The Asset Disposition Program was completed on December 31, 1990. All tolled, BNEC transferred over $500 million in cash and assets from BNEC to its insolvent subsidiary banks, including proceeds from public debt offerings and asset dispositions, mergers of directly owned subsidiaries into BNE, and miscellaneous transfers such as tax refunds, prepaid expenses, and trademarks.

As the Asset Disposition Program continued throughout the spring and summer of 1990, the institutional holders of BNEC's long-term public debt actively negotiated with bank officials in the hopes of restructuring over $700 million in BNEC bonds. In December 1990, after some eight months of negotiation, BNEC and its public-debt bondholders agreed to a tentative debt-for-equity swap. The bondholders withheld final approval for this plan, however, until assurances could be obtained from the regulators that the subsidiary banks would not be seized for a specified period of time.

On January 3, 1991, BNEC and BNE reported fourth quarter 1990 operating losses of approximately $450 million to the regulators. This information appeared in news reports the next day, which precipitated deposit runs on both BNE and CBT. For the first time since the Great Depression and the creation of the FDIC, depositors literally lined up outside the offices of a major federally insured bank to withdraw their funds. On Sunday, January 6, 1991, the regulators seized the banks.

The Chapter 7 Filing

BNEC filed its Chapter 7 bankruptcy petition the next day, January 7, 1991. On that same day, entities called bridge banks were created by the FDIC upon closure of BNE, CBT, and MNB. The bridge banks hired substantially all of the employees of BNEC and its bank subsidiaries. Soon thereafter, the bridge banks refused to turn over BNEC's deposit accounts, thereby leaving BNEC with no employees and no immediately available operating funds. Immediately upon the filing of a voluntary Chapter 7 case, an interim trustee was appointed. On March 21, 1991, a permanent trustee was elected at the first Section 341 meeting of creditors.

The Postbankruptcy Liquidation

As of the petition date, BNEC's books showed assets of over $941 million and liabilities of over $800 million, yet clearly BNEC was insolvent. Approximately 91% of the asset figure represented equity investments in subsidiaries and intercompany loans to subsidiaries, most of which were its bank subsidiaries seized by the FDIC. Any realization of value from those assets by the trustee was contingent upon the success of the trustee's litigation against the FDIC. In order to collect on receivables due from unseized subsidiaries, the trustee was required to sell and/or manage them on an interim basis, hoping that they would generate sufficient income to repay the obligations of the subsidiaries to BNEC. BNEC's investment portfolio, representing approximately 0.5% of these listed assets, was also illiquid, requiring significant effort on the part of the trustee to recover value for the estate. Of the remaining assets, 3.5% consisted of cash in accounts at BNE and MNB and furniture, equipment, and computers located at BNEC's former headquarters (all of which were seized by the FDIC), and 5% consisted of goodwill. The economic reality was that BNEC's remaining saleable assets were few: six operating subsidiaries with employees; over thirty inactive nonoperating subsidiaries; a portfolio of illiquid leveraged leases (see chapter 7) and a portfolio of illiquid private investments. Through careful analysis and shrewd negotiation, the trustee used these assets to build a war chest for pursuing a meaningful recovery for creditors through litigation.

The Litigation

In the two years following the bankruptcy filing, the trustee filed over 50 lawsuits, including suits against the FDIC to recover various assets allegedly fraudulently transferred to BNEC's hopelessly insolvent bank subsidiaries and BNEC's funds in accounts at the seized banks frozen by the FDIC; a suit against its accounting firm for its alleged failure to audit the company properly (see chapter 8); and suits against the recipients of preferential payments and fraudulent transfers. At the time of the bankruptcy, class-action litigation brought by BNEC's stockholders and bondholders was pending against BNEC's officers and directors, who were covered by substantial D&O insurance policies issued by Aetna and Lloyd's of London. The trustee and the FDIC both intervened in this action and thereafter embarked on complex multiparty negotiations.

BNEC was the sponsor of a pension plan, qualified under ERISA. The plan was overfunded by approximately $50 million, and the trustee asserted a claim to this projected surplus. The FDIC and the plan's participants also asserted claims to the surplus.

Each of the four principal litigations was ultimately settled, one during trial and three prior to trial. A few of the preference actions were tried but most also settled. At the end of the day, the trustee's litigation recoveries allowed the BNEC's senior creditors to be paid in full and its general unsecured creditors to receive a dividend of approximately $0.34 from a Chapter 7 estate many initially believed would be administratively insolvent (see table 4.1).

Table 4.1

FDIC	$140,000,000
Accounting firm	84,000,000
D&O	5,202,793
Pension surplus	12,748,321
Preferences	6,153,426
Total litigation recoveries	$248,104,540

Note. FDIC = Federal Depository Insurance Corporation; D&O = directors and officers insurance.

Conclusion

Every liquidation involves a unique set of facts. The recovery to Friede's creditors came principally from asset sales, while the recovery to BNEC's creditors came from litigation. The quicker the trustee becomes familiar with the company, its operations, its reasons for failure, and those parties primarily responsible for that failure, the easier it is to determine where the value lies.

5

Employee Issues

While the bankruptcy laws of this country are social legislation, they are not by any means the only social legislation applicable to the affairs of a business. Labor laws also fall within this category. The U.S. Congress seeks to protect the rights of the failed businesses' past and present employees as well as its creditors. Labor issues arise and must be resolved in almost all liquidations. While the rights of employees are not as sacrosanct as they are in certain European countries where job rights predominate over any other economic consideration, they still must be strictly respected. The liquidation of a business obviously affects its employees. They will either be terminated or be given the opportunity to transfer to a new employer who purchases all or part of the business. This is the major distinction between a liquidation and a reorganization—in a liquidation, many employees lose their jobs. Claims against their employer, the debtor, may be reduced or eliminated, and their future benefits are likely to be affected adversely.

Entire legal treatises have been written on bankruptcy labor law. This chapter merely provides a framework for the liquidator's analysis of key issues regarding the debtor's employees. Where a debtor is a party to collective bargaining agreements and the like, the liquidator should look to labor counsel for guidance.

Finally, as a result of amendments to the Bankruptcy Code under the Bankruptcy Abuse Prevention and Consumer Protection Act of 2005 (2005 Amendments), companies face much stricter rules governing employee retention and severance plans. While loopholes in the new Bankruptcy Code do appear to exist, this area of bankruptcy law will likely be the subject of much debate over the next decade.

Retention of Employees

The Practical Side

A substantial part of the value of many businesses is reflected in the knowledge base of the business' employees and their relationships with its customers and suppliers. In a liquidation, the employees of the estates' operating businesses find themselves in a difficult situation. They are concerned about their jobs, pension benefits and health benefits. They may also be owed back pay and vacation time. From the employees' perspective, all of these are now at risk. The senior managers of these businesses have additional concerns about their futures. No one wants to be the captain of a sinking ship. It does not look very good on a resume. In short, the employees of a firm that is liquidating itself are very worried.

The liquidator is now their ultimate boss and certain to feel empathy for them. While the liquidator is not empowered to look to the employees' needs at the expense of the estate's creditors, he or she does need these employees to do their part, if the estate is to preserve what value is left in the operating businesses. The liquidator walks a fine line between obtaining and maintaining the employees' allegiance and proceeding toward the overall objective of liquidating the estate for the greatest recovery for the claimants. The task is not an easy one.

The liquidator must act quickly to stabilize the situation in the estate's portfolio of operating businesses, particularly if those businesses are to be sold. Such businesses will sell for the highest price only if they are operating successfully. They must produce positive cash flows and, ideally, positive earnings before interest, taxes, depreciation, and amortization (EBITDA). They also must maintain their customer base and the integrity of their plant and equipment. Achieving such results requires effective management and adequate experienced staff.

Retaining Management

Bringing in new management from outside tends to be difficult and disruptive as the job is likely to be very short run. Accordingly, the liquidator usually works with existing management, even though this is the same group that was in charge as the ship was sinking. But much of existing management personnel may well be looking to their own future and hoping for an opportunity to move on.

Retaining the services of key managers almost always requires special efforts. Stay bonuses and performance bonuses are often required, both of which may be tied to the successful completion of a sale of the business at or above a certain price. The Bankruptcy Code places restrictions on these bonuses. The promise of a strong letter of reference is also often attractive.

Retaining Staff

While providing incentives for the retention of key managers is critical, the allegiance of the nonmanagerial employees is important. In many liquidations a certain amount of downsizing is necessary. Some employees must be laid off. Money for raises is tight or nonexistent. Those employees that remain, however, need to be retained in a way that earns their allegiance and productivity. If they see upper level management awarded generous stay bonuses, while their friends are being laid off and they are asked to take on additional responsibilities for no increase in pay, their morale is likely to suffer. Openness, honesty, and transparency are important. Most employees will understand that hard decisions must be made if anything is to be preserved for the troubled business' employees. The liquidator must explain to the workers that he or she is doing the best that can be done in a difficult situation. If any jobs are to be preserved, the business must be made as efficient as possible. Everyone must sacrifice for the common good. For this reason, incentives provided for the services of senior managers need to be large enough to retain them but modest enough so that the line workers do not become resentful. A balanced approach is needed. The liquidator needs to be very sensitive to the workforces' sense of fairness.

The Legal Side

Until 2005, retention bonuses of many millions of dollars were paid to management personnel who stayed through a Chapter 11 case. The 2005 Amendments significantly restrict these payments.

Executive Retention Bonuses

Prior to 2005, a debtor's initial filings with the Bankruptcy Court often included a motion seeking approval of a key executive retention plan (KERP). The 2005 Amendments put an end to that practice. A company is now required to show that each key management employee for which a retention bonus is sought has another offer that they will take if there is no KERP. This standard is nearly impossible to satisfy. It requires that each employee come to court and testify under oath that they have another offer and will leave absent the KERP. In addition, the debtor is required to prove that the services of the key employee are essential to the survival of the business. For many Chapter 11 companies, the crucial issue is not survival but value preservation for their constituents. Even if the company cannot show it will fail due to the loss of the employee, a successful liquidating plan usually depends on maximizing the value of the enterprise, which depends on retention of key managers. In addition, the retention bonus may not be more than 10 times the mean bonus to nonmanagement employees or, if no bonus was paid, an amount that is not more than 25%

of any similar bonus during the calendar year preceding that bonus. Essentially, the only bonuses available are those in effect prior to a debtor filing for bankruptcy, assuming those contracts can be assumed. A few courts have approved completion bonuses for executives who remain with a debtor, but even those arrangements are under fire.

Severance Payments

Severance payments, unless part of a program that is available to all full-time employees, are prohibited. The amount of the severance payment cannot be greater than 10 times the amount of the mean severance pay given to non-management employees during the calendar year in which the payment is made. Transfers made to, or obligations incurred for the benefit of officers, managers, or consultants hired after the date of the filing of the petition that are outside of the ordinary course of business and not justified by the facts and circumstances of the case are also prohibited.

Success Bonuses

The Bankruptcy Code, as amended in 2005, does not address incentive or success bonuses, other than a general provision that compensation must be justified by the facts and circumstances. Management compensation that includes a bonus based on a revenue or earnings target being achieved or a threshold sale price for an asset obtained appears to be allowed under the 2005 Amendments. The efforts of the manager receiving the bonus must be necessary to achieving the result for which the bonus is paid.

Termination of Employees

When a business is liquidated its employees are either terminated or, if they are lucky, given the opportunity of employment with the purchaser of the business segment for which they work. The termination of an employee can trigger obligations to comply with the federal Worker Adjustment and Retraining Notification Act (WARN Act), individual state WARN Acts, and even local labor laws. Termination of employment agreements give rise to claims against the debtor—some priority, some general unsecured. In this turmoil, the liquidator must do everything possible to preserve information held by such employees and seek their cooperation in future litigation brought by the liquidator.

The WARN Act

The WARN Act of 1988 was enacted to protect workers, their families, and communities from plant closings and mass layoffs by requiring companies to give advance notice of termination, so that affected workers have time to seek other jobs or retraining. Usually, 60 days' notice is required.

Application of WARN Act

Determinations under the WARN Act are extremely fact sensitive. Whether or not the company is required to give notice and if so, to which employees, requires fact-gathering by the liquidator. The exact number of employees and their status as full-time or part-time must be determined before applying the law to the facts to make the relevant determination. Assuming WARN Act notice is required, even for a limited number of employees, the company may be able to take advantage of the faltering company exception in order to provide less than the normal 60 days' notice of contemplated terminations.

WARN applies to a business or enterprise that employs (i) 100 or more full-time employees or (ii) 100 or more employees who work in the aggregate at least 4,000 hours per week, exclusive of overtime. A part-time employee, for purposes of WARN, is an employee who (i) works fewer than 20 hours per week on average or (ii) who has been employed for fewer than 6 of the 12 months preceding the date on which WARN notice is required. Two events are covered by the WARN Act—plant closings and mass layoffs, both of which frequently occur when a business is being liquidated.

Plant Closings A plant closing is defined as the temporary or permanent shutdown of a single site of employment, if such shutdown results in an employment loss for 50 or more full-time employees (excluding part-time employees, as defined by WARN) during any 30-day period. The term "single site" has been litigated in several contexts. When the duties for the workers in question require point-to-point travel or where the workers are stationed or work primarily outside of the employer's regular employment sites (e.g., airline workers, railroad workers bus drivers, salespersons), the single site to which such employees are assigned, work out of, or report to is generally accepted as the single site they are covered under for WARN Act purposes. Foreign sites of employment are not subject to or covered by WARN.

As far as a debtor is concerned, each regional location would be considered a single site of employment and WARN notice would only be required to the extent that the debtor terminates 50 or more full-time employees at each such site. Put another way, if fewer than 50 full-time employees are terminated at each regional location which the debtor plans to close, WARN Act notice is not required.

Mass Layoffs The second event covered by the WARN Act is a mass layoff. A mass layoff occurs when, in the absence of a plant closing, an employment loss at a single site of employment for any 30-day period is (i) at least one-third of the employees at the site and (ii) at least 50 full-time employees, or (iii) at least 500 full-time employees. In other words, a mass layoff occurs when a very substantial downsizing of the workforce occurs at a particular location.

WARN Act Notice

The WARN Act requires 60 days prior written notice of the plant closing or mass layoff. Notice of the decision to engage in a plant closing or mass layoff must be provided to (i) each representative of the affected employees as of the time of the notice (i.e., their respective unions) or, if the affected employees have no such representative, to each affected employee, and (ii) (a) the state in which the dislocated worker unit is located and (b) the chief elected official of the unit of local government within which the plant closing or mass layoff is to occur. If multiple local government units exist, the unit to be noticed is the one to which the debtor paid the highest amount of taxes for the year preceding the year for which the decision to terminate is made.

WARN Act Liability

An employer who violates the WARN Act by ordering a plant closing or mass layoff without providing the requisite notice is liable to each aggrieved employee for back pay for each day of violation and benefits under an employee benefit plan (as defined in Section 3 of ERISA). This amount is then reduced by the sum of (i) wages paid for the period of the violation, (ii) voluntary and unconditional payments which are not required by any legal obligation, and (iii) payments to a trustee or third party on behalf of the employee for the period of the violation (e.g., health benefits, payments to a contribution pension plan).

A liquidator who is required to provide notice under the WARN Act and terminates the requisite number of employees without doing so, would be liable for 60 days of back pay to each aggrieved employee, with reductions as set forth above. Any such liability has been held to constitute wages and is entitled to both an administrative expense (for postpetition terminations) and a priority (for prepetition terminations) in bankruptcy. However, any priority for prepetition wages (i) is limited to $10,000 and (ii) would be reduced by amounts employees receive on account of prepetition wages paid pursuant to the first-day employee-wage motions. An employer is only liable for each day of a violation. So, if the company gives no notice and terminates everyone immediately, the potential liability would be for a full 60 days of back pay to each aggrieved employee. However, if the company gave notice, but, for example 30 days later decided that enough was enough and let everyone go, the potential liability would only be for 30 days of back pay.

A strategy of firing the employees immediately prior to bankruptcy and rehiring them immediately thereafter has been considered. No WARN Act liability would be incurred by the debtor for this action, because the employment loss has not continued for the requisite 30-day period. Once the employees are rehired, however, the WARN Act notice period runs anew for any subsequent plant closings or mass layoffs, requiring a 60-day notice period. One might argue that, upon rehiring, all the employees would constitute part-time employees (as defined above) and not be covered by WARN. A bankruptcy court would, however, likely see through this thinly veiled attempt to skirt the WARN Act requirements and would be unsympathetic to the part-time argument; prior to the mass termination these were (presumably) full-time employees covered by WARN, and, even if hired back on a part-time basis, they *would have been* employed by the company for more than 6 of the preceding 12 months. Accordingly, little, if anything, is likely to be gained by a prepetition mass termination followed immediately by a mass rehiring!

Bankruptcy-Related Exceptions

The so-called faltering company exception provides that the 60-day notice period may be reduced if certain conditions are met. Specifically, if as of the time notice would have been required the employer (i) was actively seeking capital or business which, if obtained, would have avoided or postponed the shutdown and (ii) had a reasonable good faith belief that had notice been provided, it would have precluded the employer from obtaining the required capital or business, the notice period may be reduced. In this situation, the employer may provide less than 60 days' notice but must provide as much notice as is practicable and must give a brief statement of the basis for the shortened period. This exception applies only to plant closings, not mass layoffs, is narrowly construed by courts, and a causal connection between the shutdown and the failure to obtain the business or capital must be shown. A four-part test determines whether or not an employer may take advantage of the exception.

1. The employer must have been actively seeking the capital or business at the time 60-day notice was required, such as financing or refinancing through mechanisms such as loans, issuing stock, bonds, and so on, or additional money, credit, or business through any other commercially reasonable method. Specific actions taken must be identified.
2. The opportunity to obtain the business or financing must have been realistic.
3. If obtained, the business or capital sought must have been sufficient to avoid or postpone the shutdown, and this must be objectively demonstrated.
4. The debtor must show a reasonable good faith belief that giving the notice required by WARN would have precluded obtaining the necessary capital or business. Meeting this standard requires showing that the financing or business source would have chosen not to do business with a troubled company or with a company whose employees would be looking for other employment.

A court has discretion to reduce the amount of the liability or penalty provided for in WARN, if the employer can prove that the act or omission giving rise to the WARN Act violation was in good faith and that the employer had reasonable grounds for believing that the act or omission was not a violation.

Rejection of Employment and Severance Agreements

Employment agreements, including severance obligations thereunder, are executory contracts. Under the Bankruptcy Code the damages or claim against the debtor for rejection of these agreements are limited to one year's compensation under the agreement plus any unpaid compensation.

Cooperation and Preservation of Information

Access to personnel can be a particularly difficult problem. The liquidator is usually unable to pay a significant number of the debtor's former employees. Such persons have frequently had dealings with the debtor that give rise either to a claim by the former employee or a potential claim against the former employee. In resolving these claims, the liquidator should obtain from each such employee an agreement to cooperate in any further investigations. Similarly, if the liquidating plan of reorganization provides any sort of release of causes of action the liquidator might have against former employees, officers or directors, the release should be conditioned upon the cooperation of those individuals with the liquidator. To the extent that leverage exists in the plan to cause people to cooperate, that leverage should also be utilized. In drafting the cooperation language, the liquidator and his or her counsel should be cognizant of the fact that if the person released testifies on behalf of the liquidator in estate litigation the opposing party may seek to impeach the witness, alleging the release was given in exchange for favorable testimony.

Dealing with Unions and Collective-Bargaining Agreements

A troubled business may be burdened with a collective-bargaining agreement. Such an agreement may substantially affect the value of the enterprise. Under the Bankruptcy Code, a Chapter 11 debtor may seek court approval to reject a collective bargaining agreement. The debtor-in-possession has the burden of proving nine prerequisites.

1. The debtor-in-possession must make a proposal to the union to modify the collective bargaining agreement.
2. The proposal must be based on the most complete and reliable information available at the time of the proposal.
3. The proposed modifications must be necessary to permit the reorganization of the debtor.

4. The proposed modifications must assure that all creditors, the debtor, and all of the affected parties are treated fairly and equitably.
5. The debtor must provide to the union the necessary relevant information for evaluation of the proposal.
6. Between the time of the making of the proposal and the time of the hearing on approval of the rejection of the existing collective bargaining agreement, the debtor must meet at reasonable times with the union.
7. At the meetings, the debtor must confer in good faith and attempt to reach mutually satisfactory modifications of the collective bargaining agreement.
8. The union must have refused to accept the proposal without good cause.
9. The balance of the equities must clearly favor rejection of the collective bargaining agreement.

Determining what would constitute a successful rehabilitation involves balancing the interests of the debtor, creditors, and employees. A bankruptcy court must consider the likelihood and consequences of liquidation for the debtor absent rejection, the reduced value of the creditors' claims that would follow from affirmance and the hardship that would impose on them, and the impact of rejection on the employees. In striking the balance, the court considers not only the degree of hardship faced by each party, but also any qualitative differences between the types of hardship each may face.

If rejection is authorized, the debtor remains obligated to comply with National Labor Relations Act requirements to bargain in good faith, and the union is free to strike, even if a strike would put the financially troubled debtor out of business.

A union is allowed to file a general unsecured bankruptcy claim for its members' lost wages stemming from rejection of the collective bargaining agreement. Lost wages are recoverable as damages stemming from rejection of an executory contract and are not limited to the one-year period following the petition date. The union is allowed to deduct compulsory dues from the damages payable to individual employee claimants.

If the estate assets include a subsidiary that is a party to a collective bargaining agreement, the liquidator may be forced to file a Chapter 11 bankruptcy petition for the subsidiary in order to modify the agreement, thereby facilitating the sale. However, the union's claim may substantially affect the parent companies residual equity value in the subsidiary.

Benefit Plans

Defined Benefit Plans

Large firms going through liquidations frequently must deal with defined benefit pension plans that, when times were better, were set up to provide predetermined and calculable retirement benefits to employees. As the debtor firm proceeds toward liquidation, it must continue to manage its pension plan, but with a new objective—to dispose of the plan through termination or sale.

Typically, a debtor that establishes a defined benefit plan also serves as the plan's sponsor. Members of its management team often serve as the committee that decides ongoing plan matters, such as investing and benefit changes. In addition, the plan administrator, who serves the primary fiduciary role for the plan and manages its day-to-day activities, also is typically a member of the sponsor's management team. Within this incestuous set-up, huge problems arise when a firm must be liquidated.

Defined benefit pension plans maintain investment assets separate from an employer's assets in order to fund the benefit payments to current and future retirees. Accordingly, an employer has several responsibilities as a fiduciary. In particular, an employer must ensure that its actions and those of the pension plan comply with various federal laws that govern retirement plans, especially the Employee Retirement Income and Security Act of 1974 (ERISA).

Responsibility for administering a plan is likely to be thrust upon the liquidator after a company files bankruptcy. In dealing with a liquidating company's defined benefit pension plan, the plan administrator needs to achieve each of the following objectives:

- Manage and dispose of the plan in a way that minimizes the cost or maximizes the recovery to the debtor.
- Reach closure in a timely fashion while avoiding any subsequent exposure for the debtor and its manager.
- Ensure that the interests of the plan's participants are addressed appropriately.

Although these objectives are not mutually exclusive, conflicts sometimes arise among them. For example, looking after the interests of the participants by enhancing their benefits could reduce a plan's monetary surplus or increase its deficit to the detriment of the debtor. Accordingly, a plan administrator must take care to ensure that the interests of both the participants and the debtor are addressed properly.

Interim Management

The administrator of a debtor's pension plan is responsible for managing the plan as long as the debtor remains the plan sponsor. This typically involves determining eligibility for benefits; paying benefits to current retirees; advising participants or beneficiaries of their rights under the plan; directing investment policies; paying plan expenses; preparing necessary reports for participants; and maintaining plan compliance with ERISA, the Internal Revenue Code, and other relevant laws. For a liquidator serving as a newly designated plan administrator, the first order of business is to review the plan document or agreement in order to become familiar with benefit structures, eligibility, vesting, and provisions relating to plan termination.

Updating Participant Records Often when a company files for bankruptcy, and particularly when it proceeds towards liquidation, its corporate records, including those dealing with its employees, are in poor shape. Accordingly, an administrator initially must assess both the state of the participant records and the systems for determining participant eligibility and benefits. Disposing of a pension plan is likely to go most smoothly when its records are in good shape and its systems are effective. Files and data on participants, particularly their work histories, must be accurate and complete, and the systems for determining benefits must be in sync with benefit payment provisions of the plan document. A benefits consultant can assist with these tasks.

Outdated address information, particularly for former employees, is the primary deficiency typically found in participant records. An administrator must undertake a good faith effort to locate as many plan participants as possible before disposing of the plan. An intensive search should be undertaken to locate lost participants. Professional search firms specializing in plan participant searches are not particularly costly and often succeed in locating difficult-to-find participants.

While a plan's records are being "scrubbed," several other tasks should also be performed. Under current law, a retirement plan may provide for an involuntary distribution to a terminated employee, if the present value of the benefit is $5,000 or less. A plan document that does not include such a provision should be amended accordingly, and the plan administrator should direct payments of lump sum distributions to eligible participants. This procedure can reduce the number of participants substantially, which may make the plan more attractive to a buyer and thus make its sale ultimately easier to accomplish.

Portfolio Management A second task for the plan administrator is to restructure a plan's investment portfolio to reflect its new circumstances. The asset portfolio of an ongoing pension plan is managed for the long term, with an emphasis on growth. Benefit liabilities for such plans extend over many years and, for active employees, do not commence until some future date. The ups and downs of the stock market are a manageable problem for a plan that expects to continue well into the future, so its asset mix might be 50% stocks, 40% bonds, and 10% cash.

However, a plan that is to be terminated or sold should emphasize liquidity and capital preservation. It should not be left vulnerable to a precipitous drop in the stock market. Accordingly, such a plan's asset allocation should be shifted away from stocks and their inherent risk and toward bonds, which generally are less risky. Perhaps, an allocation of 15% stocks, 70% bonds, and 15% cash would be appropriate as a plan moves toward termination. If a lump sum distribution option is to be offered, the administrator should direct the fund managers to reallocate further in order to provide sufficient liquidity both to make that distribution and to make current payments to the plan's retirees.

Bonds, particularly long-term bonds, can also be a risky asset class to hold in a pension plan that is about to be terminated. Changes in interest rates could have a substantially adverse impact on a pension fund's assets and liabilities. Accordingly, a manager should carefully match the term structure (i.e., maturities) of interest-bearing assets to that of the plan's benefit liabilities. Investment reallocation toward bonds and away from stocks can be implemented in a manner that also effectively immunizes the plan; that is, by setting the duration of the assets equal to that of its projected liabilities, a plan's exposure to interest rate risks can be reduced to very modest levels.

Professionals and Administrative Staff Another important responsibility of a plan administrator involves hiring professionals with expertise in pension law, actuarial science, tax law, and other topics, to help manage and dispose of a plan. Although the fees of pension plan professionals tend to be high, their expertise is essential. All defined benefit pension plans should retain qualified, experienced benefits counsel, sometimes referred to as an ERISA attorney. The fees of senior actuaries are frequently higher than those of senior lawyers. Actuarial firms, however, can handle all plan management and termination functions using lower level benefits consultants, although their fees still amount to several hundred dollars an hour.

To help defray costs, a plan sponsor also should retain employees on the pension plan's payroll who helped administer the plan before the liquidation process began and should use them as much as possible to limit the need for outside professionals. Trying to limit the use of professionals in an effort to reduce costs can be tricky, however. What may seem like a simple matter could involve beneath-the-surface complexities. For example, pension plans are required to make annual filings with government agencies and to submit annual reports to plan participants. Often the instructions and rules governing the preparation of these filings and reports require expert interpretation. Whenever possible, a plan sponsor should avoid relying on outside professionals to administer the plan, but they should look to them for advice.

Finally, a profitable ongoing company often pays directly many of the plan's operating costs. The sponsor is ultimately responsible for the obligations of the plan. Accordingly, it makes little difference whether the plan or the company pays a particular expense, as long as ERISA regulations are met. However, when a company is to be liquidated and its plan sold or terminated, the sponsor should reevaluate expense payment policies. The debtor should make sure that every legitimate pension fund expense is paid by the plan rather than by the company. An ERISA lawyer can provide guidance on legitimate plan expenses.

Overfunded Plans

Sale of Plan The sale of a pension plan is a potentially precarious transaction for a plan sponsor. As mentioned earlier, a plan administrator is charged with managing a plan in the interest of its participants. If a new owner subsequently places the interests of plan participants at risk, the participants might bring a lawsuit against the debtor's manager who served as administrator of the plan, alleging that their interests were not protected in the transaction. By then, the debtor's estate may have closed after distributing all of its assets, and the trustee and former plan administrator could be found personally liable for damages.

Despite the risks inherent in the sales of pension plans of failed companies, a market for them exists. A seller transfers a plan's assets to a buyer who agrees to maintain the plan and pay its obligations. Buyers typically are attracted by a fund's surplus and will pay a price equal to a substantial percentage of that surplus. A buyer may intend to merge the plan with another it owns that has a deficit. If a plan is terminated rather than sold, any surplus is subject to a substantial federal excise tax, which can be as high as 50%. Therefore, selling a plan at a price in excess of 50% of its calculated surplus yields a value greater than the surplus, net of the excise tax that would be left.

If the surplus of a liquidating firm's pension plan is large enough to attract a potential buyer, the debtor firm manager should consider whether the plan can be sold without significant deal-killer issues. First, bankruptcy court approval of the sale most likely is required. A company's prior experience with the court concerning employee matters may provide an indication of how difficult obtaining court approval is likely to be. Also, depending on a deal's structure and possibly on previous transactions involving the sponsor, such as sales of businesses and substantial employee layoffs, a court may determine that plan document provisions increasing participant benefits have been triggered on the execution of the sale transaction. Change-in-control provisions are particularly thorny in this regard.

In short, a number of issues must be weighed in deciding whether the sale of a plan is worth the associated risks. A decision whether to proceed with negotiations with a buyer most likely hinges on the opinions of a firm's bankruptcy and ERISA attorneys.

Termination of Plan If sale of the plan proves to be unattractive, termination is the most viable method of exit. The ultimate objective of termination is to discharge the plan (and thereby the estate) of its liabilities to its participants; that is, all participants must be paid their benefits in some manner.

Two primary methods are used to pay such benefits: lump sum distributions and annuities. When a plan terminates, the benefits owed to a participant are usually paid as an annuity, unless the participant elects another option under terms of the plan. An ongoing plan's payment of a lump sum distribution of more than $5,000 to a terminated participant who has not reached retirement age generally is not allowed. However, a terminated plan generally can offer lump sum distributions in excess of $5,000 to participants who voluntarily choose this form of benefit. If the plan does not contemplate such distributions in the event of plan termination, it should be amended accordingly.

Once a company submits its initial filings to terminate a pension plan with the IRS and the Pension Benefit Guaranty Corporation (PBGC), the termination process is underway and a timetable of deadlines and expectations is established. Termination of a defined benefit pension plan requires a substantial amount of planning, however, so much work must be completed before the initial filings are submitted.

The administrator and other managers of a debtor firm should meet with its actuaries and ERISA attorneys to discuss plan termination. Becoming familiar with all of the tasks involved in a termination is important. The sponsor may be able to rely on lower cost alternatives to handle the substantial amount of administrative tasks that consume plan terminations. For example, after the termination commences, various notices regarding the termination and participants' benefits must be mailed and tracked. This process is time consuming and can be very costly, if handled by outside professionals.

A sponsor typically relies on actuaries to analyze a plan's surplus or deficit and ERISA lawyers to ensure that the plan is in compliance with all relevant regulations. Before the plan termination process is initiated, a debtor firm and its actuaries should assess the participant records to be sure that benefit calculations can be performed accurately and efficiently. Information that is consistently incomplete or inaccurate can preclude benefit calculations in accordance with the plan document and stop the termination process in its tracks.

Determination of Benefit The sponsor and the plan's actuaries should review the assumptions used to calculate benefits, particularly the discount-rate assumption. Although the law prescribes benchmarks for discount-rate determination, the timing of the plan's termination can impact a plan's benefit liabilities. For instance, interest-rate assumptions typically are determined as of the beginning of a plan's fiscal year. If interest rates are expected to rise by the beginning of the next fiscal year, delaying the start of the plan's termination until then would allow the factoring in of a higher discount rate, resulting in a reduction in the calculated benefit liabilities. On the other hand, if a plan termination is already underway and the interest rate is expected to fall by the beginning of the next fiscal year, the sponsor should contemplate expediting benefit payment, so that they occur before the end of the current fiscal year. If that is not done, such benefits are determined using the new lower interest rate thereby resulting in a higher calculated liability.

The determination of a participant's retiree benefit is typically a routine matter for an ongoing plan. It requires little actuarial or legal expertise. In the case of a plan termination, however, determining the current value of future retirees' benefits can be extraordinarily complex and involve a significant amount of judgment. Relying on actuaries and ERISA attorneys is critical to ensure that the calculation provides at least the minimum amounts due to participants.

When a plan terminates, all of its participants become fully vested, whether or not they were vested before the termination. A partial termination also can bestow full vesting on employees who were not fully vested. A partial termination occurs when a significant number of employees who are covered by the plan are excluded from coverage, either because the plan was amended or because their employment was terminated.

Additional vesting can substantially increase a plan's total benefit liability. A plan need not be terminated formally for full vesting to apply. During bankruptcies or liquidations, debtor companies frequently lay off most or all of their employees or sell all or a portion of their primary businesses. In these circumstances, a plan's partial termination could result in full vesting for all affected employees' benefits before any formal termination process commenced or before a sale of a plan was consummated.

Annuitizing the Participants When a plan is to be terminated, a third set of professionals typically are retained to help find an insurance company to provide annuities. The plan's actuary investigates each potential bidder in order to provide an opinion of its financial soundness. Only those deemed to provide the safest available annuity, in accordance with guidelines set forth by the U.S. Department of Labor, should be considered.

The next step is to contact each acceptable insurer and gauge its interest. Those who express an interest are provided with a packet of information detailing characteristics of the plan participants. Interested bidders are given a deadline for submitting a preliminary bid. Those who comply are placed in the initial pool. A second round of bidding is held, and the field is narrowed, possibly to three to five bidders. A final round of bidding is held, with submitted bids open for only a matter of hours. Once the final bids are reviewed, the winning company is quickly notified so it can put its hedge in place. Because interest rates fluctuate continuously, the winning insurance company will lock in a payment stream at current market interest rate levels.

The easiest task of the termination process is directing the pension trust to pay the winning insurance company the final bid amount, which, in turn, transfers the obligation to make payments to retired plan participants who did not elect to receive other forms of payment. Making lump sum distribution payments, on the other hand, is a labor-intensive process. It requires the plan administrator to institute various checks and balances in order to ensure proper benefit determinations and check preparations. After lump sum payments are made, a period of continuous follow-up is required in order to verify that checks were received and deposited.

Participants Who Cannot Be Located When a large pension plan is terminated, the current locations of at least a few participants are likely to be missing. Throughout the plan termination process, procedures should be put in place in order to identify those participants. These procedures can include using return receipt requests for all mailings to participants and documenting whether mailings are delivered successfully. A professional search firm should be hired to perform a diligent search to satisfy requirements that best efforts have been made to find all participants. As participants are located, they are paid, and the plan continues toward its ultimate objective of discharging its obligation to its participants.

The final acts of a plan's liquidation are final filings with the PBGC, which also involve turning over to the agency payment for benefit liabilities owed to the missing participants. At that point, the plan is discharged of all obligations to the participants.

Regulatory Oversight The IRS and PBGC typically monitor each step of the termination process. In its initial termination filing, a plan requests a determination letter from the IRS on the plan's compliance with appropriate laws. Several discussions may be required with the agency regarding a plan's operating compliance and its stated compliance, as represented by the plan document. The objective is to obtain a favorable determination letter from the IRS.

As long as a plan remains solvent, the PBGC focuses on when the termination will be completed and monitoring whether the estimates of the assets and liabilities, as reported in the initial filing, continue to be reasonable as the case progresses. However, the PBGC takes an active role in the termination of a plan whose liabilities exceed its assets.

The final tasks associated with the termination of a solvent plan involve filing documents certifying the plan's liabilities and related payments with the PBGC, directing the plan to remit any remaining surplus to the sponsor, and filing the employer's excise tax return with the IRS. Although the excise tax on the remaining surplus is generally 50%, a 20% rate applies to an employer who, as of the date of plan termination, is involved in a Chapter 7 bankruptcy or in similar proceedings under state law. For guidance on this rule as it relates to liquidations that are not carried out in Chapter 7, a skilled tax professional should be consulted.

Regardless of which rate applies in a particular case, to reduce the employer's tax burden, the plan should attempt to pay as many plan expenses as possible before the surplus reverts to the sponsor. Because of the way applicable taxes are calculated, paying these expenses out of the pension trust effectively costs a sponsor only 50% or 80% of the billed amount.

Claims on Surpluses

Typically, plan documents set forth who owns the surplus upon termination of a plan. However, the terms may be ambiguous. For example, where a plan provides that upon a change in control any surplus belongs to the participants, there may be litigation over whether a change in control occurred. Where one or more subsidiaries contributed to a plan on behalf of its employees, the creditors of a subsidiary may assert claims seeking a portion of the surplus. Such disputes must be resolved either by negotiation or litigation before the surplus can be distributed. Thus, among those who might file claims to a surplus are former employees of the debtor or its subsidiaries and creditors of subsidiaries. In the case of a large plan termination, the PBGC often files a contingent claim against the debtor which will not be withdrawn until it is satisfied that the termination was handled appropriately.

Underfunded Plans

In many bankruptcy cases, the plan is not in surplus. Nonetheless, the plan needs to be terminated in order to reduce the estate's exposures. Various parties including, the debtor's control group, its affiliate corporations, and its directors and officers may be exposed to liabilities that result from a distressed termination.

Typically, an insolvent plan that is sponsored by a firm in bankruptcy undergoes a distress termination, which requires it to submit detailed filings with the PBGC. The agency determines the degree to which a plan's assets are sufficient and notifies the plan administrator of its findings. If the PBGC determines that a plan's assets are insufficient to provide at least the guaranteed benefits to its participants, the agency proceeds to become successor trustee of the plan.

As an insurer of plan benefits, the PBGC guarantees payment of some basic benefits under a defined benefit plan, subject to limitations. If the plan's assets are deemed sufficient to provide at least the guaranteed benefits, the PBGC issues a notice to the plan administrator to close the plan and make its final filing with the agency. The plan administrator must then direct distributions covering the amount of guaranteed benefits to participants and allocations of any remaining plan assets in a manner specified by ERISA.

Generally, in the distressed termination of a plan that lacks sufficient assets to pay all benefit liabilities, the sponsor remains liable to the PBGC for the total amount of the plan's unfunded benefit liabilities. As a result, the agency files for and typically receives priority claim status in the debtor's bankruptcy case for the shortfall.

A defined benefit plan sponsor must seek authority from the court to conduct distressed termination while the company is in bankruptcy. To qualify, the

Tale from the Bankruptcy Trenches

At the commencement of the Friede case, the debtors had an underfunded defined-benefit pension plan. Because of the importance of retirement funds to the existing employees, issues related to the plan were highly sensitive and often threatened to crowd out more pressing operational issues. The debtors' management and its professionals spent a great deal of time making sure the plan was properly handled.

The pension plan covered approximately 1,613 people on the petition date and had assets of approximately $8.4 million. Future benefit accruals had been frozen in 1998. Although the debtors had made all required payments to the plan as of the petition date, it was underfunded on a plan termination basis in an unknown amount, but believed to be at least $4 million. The benefit levels in the plan were just below the maximum guaranteed by the PBGC. Thus, if the PBGC took over the plan, ultimately there would be no loss in terms of retirement benefits.

It became clear that the pension plan could never be afforded by a reorganized entity, because there would be no reorganized Friede. After additional discussions with the PBGC, and an audit of the pension plan's records by a PBGC team, the debtors filed a motion with the bankruptcy court asking it to authorize them to enter into a trusteeship agreement with the PBGC and to establish a termination date of the plan.

In contrast, when BNEC filed for bankruptcy protection, its pension plan was overfunded. Eventually, three groups asserted an interest in that surplus. First, BNEC as plan sponsor claimed ownership. Then the FDIC, as receiver of the failed banks (where the vast majority of the employees resided), claimed ownership. Finally, a group of employees and retirees of BNEC claimed ownership on behalf of plan participants. After a protracted set of negotiations, the three parties agreed to divide the funds. During that time, the surplus had grown from about $50 million to over $100 million. BNEC managed the termination with a combination of lump-sum distributions and the purchase of annuities.

company must (i) have filed a bankruptcy petition; (ii) not have had the petition dismissed; (iii) seek bankruptcy court approval to terminate; and (iv) the court must find that the debtor is unable to reorganize and remain in business unless it is allowed to terminate its pension plan.

When the plan is terminated, its obligations to the plan participants are turned over to the PBGC, who takes the plan's assets and makes the payments to plan participants. The PBGC has established maximum payout amounts, which are below the benefits promised to the higher paid executives of many pension plans. Accordingly, the PBGC's payments to some participants will be less than under the formula of the terminated plan.

The PBGC can assert two types of claims against the sponsor. First, the PBGC can make a claim for the difference between the liabilities of the plan that it assumed and the plan assets that it acquired. Second, it can make a claim for unpaid minimum funding under ERISA. These claims can be made against both the sponsor and the control group who are jointly and severally liable. A control group is comprised of those who own directly or indirectly at least 80% of the controlled business. The PBGC may also assert claims against related businesses, if they have a common ownership of 80% or more. The PBGC can also go back in time to a former parent in the case of spin-offs. Under ERISA pension plans must have named fiduciaries. These fiduciaries, and others who may have exercised substantial influence on the plan's management, may also be targets of claims.

Additionally, the officers and directors of the sponsor may be the target of lawsuits for failure properly to monitor a plan that undergoes distress termination. The courts seem to be expanding the obligation to an affirmative duty to warn plan participants of risks.

Role of Liquidator

A debtor firm's manager (e.g., trustee) who is also the plan administrator of the company's pension plan has potentially conflicting duties. A trustee is charged with marshaling the debtor's assets for the benefit of its claimants, yet in its role as plan administrator, the debtor firm's manager is charged with administering the pension plan in the interests of its participants. A plan administrator must do what is required to ensure that a plan meets its obligations to the participants. This obligation does not, however, mean that a sponsor or administrator must sacrifice the interests of a debtor in order to provide more value for participants than is called for under a plan.

One approach to its potential conflict is for the liquidator to retain two law firms, one to handle pension plan administration and termination issues and another to provide advice regarding the debtor company's bankruptcy, claims, and liquidation. When a plan's termination is scrutinized by various groups of participants and their attorneys, the trustee-plan administrator's decisions are viewed in a better light if they are backed by the opinions or advice of counsel specializing in pension-plan administration rather than bankruptcy law.

A large defined-benefit pension plan with a sizable surplus can provide substantial value to a debtor. Extracting as much of this value as possible via a sale or termination can be worth the significant effort. However, a plan that has a deficit can create headaches for the estate administrator. Whether dealing with a surplus or a deficit, a liquidator must recognize early that the disposition of the company's defined benefit pension plan is a major undertaking that requires thoughtful planning in order to minimize costs and risks to the firm and its manager.

Defined Contribution Plans

Defined-contribution pension plans are typically much easier for a liquidator to terminate than defined-benefit plans. First, the plan document is reviewed to see if it needs to be amended to comply with current law or to correct any obvious disqualifying defects. If necessary, amendments or corrective action should be taken. The bankruptcy trustee then files a motion for authority to (i) amend, if necessary, and terminate the plan; (ii) fully vest all plan participants in any unvested account balances; (iii) take any necessary action to maintain tax qualification of the plan upon termination; and (iv) distribute the assets. If the termination occurs outside of bankruptcy, the governing body (i.e., board of directors, managers, receiver, etc.) passes a resolution authorizing the same. The liquidator should (but is not required to) submit the plan to the IRS for a determination that the plan is qualified upon termination.

Employees who have left the company are entitled to immediate distribution prior to plan termination and prior to receipt of any determination letter from the IRS. They are provided with a distribution notice and may elect a direct rollover, taxable distribution, or deferral of distribution. Until the plan is terminated (and IRS letter received in most cases), the liquidator cannot require them to take a distribution, but they may elect to take a distribution. The liquidator should attempt to distribute as many voluntary distributions as possible prior to termination.

Any employees who remain employed through the liquidation and any former employees who do not elect to take a distribution prior to termination must wait until the plan is terminated before they receive a distribution. If a participant does not return a distribution form, the plan administrator is required to set up an individual retirement account (IRA) for the participant and roll the benefits into the IRA. Other than the distribution tax notice, no notice to participants or anyone else is required.

Sometime down the road, the IRS will issue a determination letter on the plan. The liquidator may, but is not required, to wait for the determination letter before distributing the assets. The reasonable administrative expenses of plan termination and winding up can be charged to the plan accounts before distribution, if necessary. The preferred method is to obtain the creditors' approval to allow the company to pay the expenses.

Problems occur when the plan trustee or plan administrator has abandoned the plan. The custodian of the assets usually will not release the funds without direction from the plan trustee. In that situation, typically the bankruptcy trustee assumes the responsibilities of trustee of the plan. Once all assets are distributed to participants or rolled into IRAs, the plan trustee can resign, assuming he or she hasn't already disappeared from the scene.

When the debtor has not made the requisite contributions, the PBGC normally asserts a claim to recover these amounts. This claim has priority status. Members of the board of directors and other key executives may have personal liability.

401(K) Plans

In the course of business operations, a company frequently establishes and maintains a 401(k) plan, a retirement plan qualified under Section 401(a) of ERISA, for the benefit of its employees. The debtors' employees who satisfied certain age and service requirements are given the opportunity to participate in the plan. As a result, at the time of bankruptcy, current and former employees of the debtor are entitled to their plan account balances.

In a liquidation, the 401(k) plan is typically no longer a necessary or meaningful component of the debtors' operations or bankruptcy estate. As long as the plan remains in effect, the debtor will continue to incur expenses for ongoing administration and will incur legal expenses as the plan is amended to comply with changes in the law. Under ERISA, these expenses can only be paid by the debtor or from the assets of the Plan. These expenses become completely unnecessary and of no benefit to anyone, since the participants are able to continue to receive the tax benefits provided under the 401(k) plan by transferring their assets to an IRA or to a plan maintained by a new employer. Accordingly, as part of the ongoing resolution of the debtors' affairs, the liquidator should file a motion with the court for authority to terminate the 401(k) plan and make appropriate distributions to the participants.

After the plan's termination, each remaining participant receives a distribution equal to the amount held in his or her account after the payment of allocable costs and expenses incurred by the termination. Individual participants may elect either to have their amounts taxed currently or defer taxation by transferring the amount distributed to an IRA or a plan maintained by a new employer. The sooner the liquidator takes the necessary action to terminate the 401(K) plan, the better.

Deferred Compensation Plans

A deferred compensation plan (deferred comp plan) typically allows a highly paid executive to defer a portion of his or her annual compensation until retirement. In order to avoid income tax on this compensation in the current year, the obligation must be an unsecured contractual obligation of the employer/company. These are not Keogh, 401(k), or other qualified plans. Upon bankruptcy, these executives become unsecured creditors of the estate with respect to their deferred compensation claims, and any plan assets become property of the estate. These plans are often called "rabbi trusts," because the first such plan was created as part of financial planning for a rabbi.

Split-Dollar Life Insurance Policies

Split-dollar life insurance policies are yet another executive fringe benefit that often must be dealt with by a liquidator. These plans split the premiums and

Tales from the Bankruptcy Trenches

Friede

On the Friede petition date, its deferred comp plan had approximately 72 participants, of which approximately 50 were still employed by the debtors. A rabbi-trust account held approximately $2.5 million, against approximately $3.7 million in obligations under the terms of the plan and $3 million of actual, total employee deferred compensation and contributions into the plan. Thus, the plan had a shortfall of more than $500,000 even with employee contributions that had been set aside. Although the funds in the deferred comp plan were segregated, the deferred comp plan was not an ERISA-qualified plan. It was extremely likely that the bankruptcy judge would rule that the funds were general property of the estate and available to all creditors. Almost all of the senior managers of the debtors had accrued substantial benefits in the deferred comp plan, so the shortfall and the fate of the remaining funds were very hot topics of conversation as the bankruptcy case commenced. A compromise was reached among the debtors and their creditors. In exchange for working toward the completion of the bankruptcy cases and giving up any claims they had to the unfunded amounts owed under the deferred comp plan, the managers would receive the funds owed to them in increments tied to progress in the cases.

BNEC

The BNEC deferred comp plan held approximately $8 million with obligations far in excess of that amount. The participants, principally board members and executives, filed proofs of claim in the millions of dollars. As part of the settlement of the trustee's lawsuit against the officers and directors, the directors and officers gave up their deferred comp claims, and the trustee received a portion of the D&O insurance proceeds.

benefits of a life insurance policy between the employer and employee. Typically, the employer pays all the premiums and is entitled to a portion of the death benefit equal to its cumulative premiums paid or the cash value. The employee's beneficiary receives the balance of the death benefit. The employee has current taxable income equal to the economic benefit rather than the full premium.

PBGC approval is not required for this type of nonqualified plan. Policy cash values show as an asset on the balance sheet of the debtor. Unlike the expense of other fringe benefits, a split-dollar plan can be structured so that the business eventually recovers the cost of the policy, while offering the employee an exceptional fringe benefit of permanent life insurance protection. Plus, income tax-free proceeds are received by the employee's beneficiaries. Putting together a split-dollar plan can be a complicated process but not nearly as complicated as taking one apart. In the liquidation of a company, the policy typically cannot be surrendered for its cash value. The liquidator must either wait for the employee

Tale from the Bankruptcy Trenches

On Friede's petition date (April 13, 2000), the debtors faced a significant workers' compensation issue. They had approximately 2,000 employees in over four states. Because they were engaged in heavy marine construction, accidents and even deaths were not unknown in recent memory. In addition, Friede had just settled a Racketeer Influenced and Corrupt Organizations (Act) [RICO] action brought by Liberty Mutual, its insurer, that alleged that Friede had intentionally manipulated the experience rating of its workforce to garner lower workers' compensation rates.

To meet these challenges prior to the petition date, Friede had procured a policy with Zurich Insurance Company that had a $250,000 per incident self-insured retention—meaning that, although legally Zurich was responsible for all the claims, under its contract with Friede, the debtors were responsible for the first $250,000 of all medical and legal bills associated with injured employees. On the petition date, hundreds of workers' compensation claims were outstanding—most not covered by the new Zurich Policy but by a group of other companies—and the debtors were spending hundreds of thousands of dollars every month to pay for them. Shortly after the petition date, the debtors stopped paying its current retention obligations, forcing Zurich to do so. The contract came up for renewal in September 2001. The debtors' vice president of risk management was in London on September 11, 2001, and resigned from Friede in absentia, without negotiating a renewal of the Zurich policy.

Workers' compensation insurance was critical, and Friede would have been required to shut down all operations if no policy was in effect. For its part, Zurich wanted no part of the bankruptcy and quoted a $17 million premium for a replacement policy. Ultimately, Zurich was convinced that forcing a shutdown of operations would create an avalanche of claims against its policy, precisely the result it feared. Two successive two-week extensions were negotiated. During the second extension, a new member of the management team rapidly negotiated a new, cheaper policy that allowed the debtors to continue to operate. Litigation with Zurich would continue well beyond confirmation, with Zurich claiming it was owed over $3 million in actual and future loss amounts.

The debtors also stopped paying their older claims, which collectively had loss reserves of more than $7 million. The insurer backing these claims, Reliance National Indemnity Company, was placed in an insurance liquidation by the State of Pennsylvania effective October 31, 2001. Without Reliance, employees sought the protection of the state workers' compensation guaranty funds. Still, the information for the defense of the claims had to come from someplace. An employee was found who would ultimately serve as the coordinator of all these actions. At the time of the confirmation of the plan, approximately 175 workers' compensation cases were open in five states, and the coordinator spent much of his time on the road attending hearings. Because Friede was in the maritime construction industry, most if not all of the claims were covered by the Longshore and Harbor Workers Compensation Act, and adjudicated by administrative law judges at the Department of Labor (DOL). When some of these judges refused to allow the cases to proceed because of concern over the automatic stay, the DOL filed a global request for relief from stay. The debtors and the DOL reached a stipulated order allowing the proceedings to go forward as long as defense was being provided to the debtors by an insurance company or a guaranty fund.

to die or sell the residual interest in the policy. The logical purchaser is the insured employee. When the employee has affirmative claims against the company, the company's right to recover premiums paid or cash surrender value can be used as currency to settle the claim.

Postretirement Health Benefits

A Chapter 11 trustee or debtor-in-possession must pay retiree benefits as an administrative expense of the bankruptcy estate. Retiree benefits are limited to health care, accident, disability, and death benefits, and do not apply to give priority to claims by trust funds that administer only pension benefits for retired workers. Likewise, premium payments for retiree health benefits are entitled to priority status as an administrative expense. Premiums are due annually, and the employer is required to pay a full year of premiums, even though it has plans to cease doing business shortly after the premium due date.

A bankruptcy procedure, separate but similar to the rejection of collective bargaining agreements, is used in evaluating whether the requirements for termination or modification of retiree health benefits have been met. Unless the benefit plan is modified, the employer must continue retiree benefits. These procedures require that prior to seeking modification of retiree benefits, the employer must bargain with a representative of the retirees, either the union or a separate retiree committee. If bargaining is not successful, the employer can then seek modification of retiree benefits.

Workers' Compensation Insurance

All states require that a company either have workers' compensation for its employees or have a bond on file with the state to satisfy any obligations that may arise under the policies. Premiums are typically based on the experience rating of a company's workforce. The lower the incident of injury, the lower the workers' compensation rates. Operating without workers' compensation insurance is illegal.

Conclusion

Employee issues frequently arise in large liquidations. In some cases, the liquidator needs to retain existing employees in order to maintain its subsidiaries' viability long enough to sell the operating businesses for the best prices. In other cases, the need may be to downsize by laying off employees and closing plants. Special incentives may be needed to entice key employees to stay. Incentives should not, however, be so large that they create problems with other employees who are asked to stay and make financial sacrifices. Particular care is required in implementing plant closings and mass layoffs. The WARN Act may impose substantial penalties on a firm that terminates large numbers of employees without adequate notice. The liquidator should proceed with due care and caution.

Terminating pension and other employee benefit plans is complex. If the plan is solvent, the surplus (after paying required taxes) represents a potential recovery for the estate and its creditors. If the plan is insolvent, the deficit represents another source of claims. In either case, the sale or termination of the debtor's various qualified and nonqualified benefit plans requires a number of carefully executed steps to satisfy the requirements of the IRS, PBGC, and other interested parties and to maximize residual values for the estate.

6

Day-to-Day Management

The liquidator must not only dispose of assets, resolve claims, and pursue litigation, he or she must also effectively manage the estate on a day-to-day basis. This typically requires the liquidator to secure office space, hire staff, take custody of the company's records and establish internal controls for the day-to-day handling of funds (see appendix 4). The liquidator must also maintain records for the liquidation and ensure ongoing compliance with applicable federal, state, and local laws. This process includes the filing of tax returns and other financial reports. Finally, the liquidator must quickly become familiar with the executory contracts on which the company remains obligated in order to determine whether they should be rejected (resulting in claims against the estate) or assumed (because they are advantageous to the estate) and assigned to third parties.

Office Space and Staff

To manage the liquidation, the trustee usually needs office space and staff. Typically, a Chapter 7 panel trustee handling numerous cases has office and staff in place. The liquidator handling a large case may need to maintain separate offices and staff. If the company no longer has suitable space, the liquidator leases space. Furniture and office equipment should be kept to a minimum and leased where economically efficient. No one needs to be impressed. Sub par, subleased space as a gypsy tenant can suffice.

Suitable candidates for the liquidator's staff may be found in the company. These employees can be particularly valuable due to their institutional knowledge of the company and its operations. When employees are not available, outsourcing and temp agencies may be used. In the rare instances where more senior managerial positions must be filled, restructuring firms often hire out professionals for that purpose. Premium prices may have to be paid to staff these positions due to the limited timeframe of the engagement.

The Debtor's Records

The liquidator must contend with numerous issues involving the debtor's records or the lack of them. The first step is to arrange for the records' secure storage and maintenance. The liquidator, litigants, and creditors are all likely to require access to the debtor's records. The files may need to be reorganized—or even organized for the first time—in order to render them usable. The liquidator governs access to those records and should make sure that he or she does not incur any liability by reason of turning over records to a third party. Notice and, if appropriate, a hearing in the bankruptcy court may be necessary to protect the liquidator. The liquidator succeeds to the debtor's attorney-client privilege. Thus, no documents of the debtor may be withheld from the liquidator on the basis of privilege. The liquidator can require the debtor's law firms to surrender files.

One of the most burdensome problems for the liquidator involves disposing of the debtor's records. Many records may have to be maintained long after the liquidation is concluded in order to satisfy legal requirements as well as the needs of others (see chapter 11).

The Liquidator's Records

In addition to dealing with the debtor's records, the liquidator must properly maintain the records of the liquidation process. This is just like the paper end of running most businesses. Savings certificates, savings account books, evidence of investments (e.g., stock certificates and bonds), cash, blank checks, estate checks, deeds, and other items of value should be kept in a safe or locked cabinet. All estate files, including paper and electronic accounting records, should be stored in secure facilities. For a sizeable estate, the liquidator should develop and maintain a written business-interruption or disaster recovery plan for the estate's financial and administrative records, as well as for its computer systems and data. A printed copy of the plan should be stored in the estate's office and at an offsite location known to the staff. Generally, estate records may be kept in paper form, electronic form, or some combination of both. Except for the items listed below, original documents may be scanned and discarded after the scanned image has been verified against the original. A bankruptcy trustee is legally required to retain the following items:

- Bank reconciliations, bank statements, canceled checks and returned items, if any
- Blank deposit slips and check stock; voided checks (if in the trustee's possession)
- Investment certificates and other evidence of estate investments
- Promissory notes for installment sales and other original documents evidencing estate assets
- Business interruption or disaster recovery plan
- Any original documents the trustee is required to retain pursuant to local bankruptcy rules.

Estate files should be logically organized and readily accessible. Filing should be up-to-date. Financial records should be segregated from the other case administration records (e.g., pleadings). Records available electronically from the court do not need to be kept in the estate's files.

Accounting Issues

The maintenance of the estate by the liquidator includes numerous accounting functions. These are burial expenses for the business. Regardless of how successful the liquidator is in liquidating property or pursuing litigation, a failure in the accounting area can taint an entire case. In a liquidation, the liquidator almost always hires an independent accounting firm to undertake a variety of tasks. In a large case, the liquidator is also likely to retain a small staff in order to assist in day-to-day accounting. The independent accountant should help set up accounting mechanisms or modify existing ones to suit the needs of the case. The accountants assist the liquidator with compliance obligations in numerous ways: (i) financial reporting to the United States Trustee, bankruptcy court and creditors; (ii) filing federal, state; and local tax returns; (iii) annual state organizational filings; and (iv) SEC reporting. Additionally, accountants often work with the estate as seller in connection with the disposition of estate assets and with the estate as plaintiff with the forensic accounting often required in estate litigation. To perform duties properly and effectively administer a case, the liquidator must establish an appropriate accounting system and maintain financial records on a contemporaneous basis. Computer software programs help make this task manageable.

Financial Reporting by Chapter 7 Trustee

A Chapter 7 trustee is required to employ a uniform record keeping and reporting system for financial reporting to the United States Trustee. This system consists of Uniform Transaction Codes (UTCs), akin to a uniform chart of accounts, and three primary records: the Individual Estate Property Record and Report (Form 1), the Cash Receipts and Disbursements Record (Form 2), and the Summary Interim Asset Report (Form 3). This system is used throughout the country. Utilizing these records, the trustee provides an interim report (or trustee interim report, TIR) to the United States Trustee at least annually and upon request. The TIR must be submitted to the United States Trustee no later than 30 days after the end of the reporting period. If the report cannot be submitted by the due date, the trustee must obtain a written date-specific extension from the United States Trustee prior to the deadline. The United States Trustee reviews the report within 60 days of receipt and provides the trustee with written notice of any deficiencies.

Individual Estate Property Record and Report

The Individual Estate Property Record and Report provides a blueprint for the liquidation. All assets of the debtor, as shown on the debtor's original petition, schedules, and statement of financial affairs, are listed. These are referred to as scheduled assets. In addition, all assets added by the debtor on amended schedules and statements and all other assets identified by the trustee must be recorded. These are referred to as unscheduled assets. The report details all estate assets, both scheduled and unscheduled, and reflects the status of their disposition. It compares the debtor's assessment of each scheduled asset's fair market value, the trustee's estimated net value to the estate for each estate asset, and the actual value realized by the trustee. It also supports the decision regarding administration of each asset. For assets not administered, the report reflects abandonments, whether past or future, formal or informal. For assets administered or to be administered, it reflects the amounts realized and the anticipated remaining value of assets not completely liquidated.

The report also includes a statement of the estimated dollar value of each asset. This value is assigned either (i) by the debtor in the petition, schedules, and statement of financial affairs or (ii) by the trustee, if the asset was not originally scheduled by the debtor. It also shows the estimated net recoverable value determined by the trustee. Estimated recoverable value is the dollar amount of the property less any security interest and any other appropriate adjustment, such as costs to maintain and preserve the asset, costs to sell, realtor commission, property taxes, or capital gains tax.

The disposition of assets is recorded by indicating the abandonment of any asset, or the gross amount received from its sale or other liquidation. The status of the liquidation process should be reflected as either (i) the value determined by the trustee prior to liquidation, (ii) the remaining value of an asset that has been partially liquidated, or (iii) that an asset has been fully administered by the trustee.

The report contains other information such as the status of assets not fully administered or abandoned, pending litigation, dates of hearings or sales, projected date of closure of the estate, and other relevant actions. A Summary Interim Asset Report (Form 3) is prepared and submitted at least annually to the United States Trustee as part of the interim report.

Cash Receipts and Disbursements Record

The trustee must prepare a Cash Receipts and Disbursements Record (Form 2) that shows all receipts, disbursements, and bank account transfers in the case. All receipts are identified by the reference number assigned on Form 1. Each entry also includes the check number, name of the payer or payee, the date of the transaction, a description of the transaction, and the applicable UTC. The trustee must maintain a separate Form 2 for each estate bank account, including certificates of deposit.

All transactions must be entered on Form 2 in chronological order, as they occur. Transactions may not be backdated, except for interest, which is posted within 30 days of the period to which it applies.

Reporting in Chapter 11 Cases

A Chapter 11 debtor is obligated to file monthly operating reports with the United States Trustee, which include the following items:

- Balance sheets comparing assets and liabilities at the petition date to the last four months
- Schedule of postpetition liabilities
- Aging of postpetition liabilities and accounts receivable
- Postpetition statement of income (loss)
- Schedule of postpetition cash receipts and disbursements
- Postpetition cash account reconciliation
- A schedule of postpetition payments to insiders and professionals

In a Chapter 11 case, the committee and debtor often agree that additional information will be provided by the debtor to the committee during the plan negotiation and formulation process. This agreement could, for example, commit the debtor to provide items such as weekly cash flow reports and operating budgets. The members of the committee are frequently asked to sign confidentiality agreements that prohibit them from disclosing any material nonpublic information provided to them for this purposes and prohibit them from trading the debtor's securities. The court may ask that this information also be provided to it under seal. The debtor is also obligated to pay quarterly fees to the United States Trustee, determined by a statutory formula. The maximum fee per quarter is $10,000.

Reporting by a Liquidating Trustee

The reporting requirements of a liquidating trustee under a Chapter 11 plan are set forth in the plan or the related plan documents. Typically, the liquidating trustee must provide the oversight committee and the court with an accounting of monies collected and disbursed during the reporting period. These reports are frequently kept simple to avoid unnecessary costs.

Tax Returns

Tax returns must be prepared and filed when due. A company can be out of business and still owe taxes. The Bankruptcy Code provides a mechanism by which a liquidator quickly tests the estate's tax return. Eliminating or at least minimizing the estate's tax liability enhances the funds available for payment to the other creditors. Accordingly, a liquidator is likely to take fairly aggressive positions on the estate's tax return. Thus, large reserves may be maintained until the procedure contemplated by section 505 of the Bankruptcy Code is completed. Clearly, creditors benefit from the prompt completion, filing, and processing of tax returns.

Federal Tax Filings

Partnership and Corporate Debtors The filing of a bankruptcy petition by a partnership limited liability company (LLC), limited liability partnership (LLP), or corporation does not create a separate taxable entity. The accounting period of the entity is continuous and the return, filed under the debtor's tax identification number, must reflect the debtor's pre- and postpetition income and deductions.

Unless a corporation is exempt from income tax, corporate returns must be filed by the liquidator regardless of whether or not the corporation has income. The liquidator must file state income tax returns for a corporation, unless the corporate debtor lacks postpetition net taxable income for the entire period during which the case is pending. Upon application to the IRS district director, the IRS may waive the requirement to file federal returns if the corporate debtor has ceased business operations and has neither assets nor income. For partnership cases, the liquidator must file the federal and state tax returns regardless of the amount of gross income.

Employment Taxes and Other Tax Forms If the debtor was an employer, the liquidator must file the Employer's Quarterly Federal Tax Return for any withheld federal income and FICA taxes, and the Employer's Annual Federal Unemployment Tax Return for unemployment taxes, if the appropriate form was not filed by the debtor. Failure to file these returns on time may cause the liquidator or estate to be penalized.

In addition, the liquidator must withhold all applicable federal and state income taxes, social security taxes, and Medicare taxes from any wage claims paid by the estate. The withheld taxes must be properly and timely deposited with a financial institution or paid with the return. Further, depending upon the business that the debtor conducted, the liquidator may be required to file sales, excise, and other tax returns in order to establish the amount of the taxing authority's claim.

If the liquidator pays wages, including prepetition wage claims, the liquidator is responsible for preparing and filing W-2 forms and for sending copies to the employees. For those cases in which the debtor paid wages during the calendar year of the bankruptcy petition, the trustee will receive requests from the employees for withholding tax information in order to complete their personal income tax returns. In these circumstances, the liquidator may either complete W-2 forms and provide them to the employees based on the corporate records or may make those records available to the former employer or former employees to assist them in reconstructing the information. In any event, an employee who is unable to obtain Form W-2 for wages paid by the debtor prepetition should be instructed to obtain Form 4852 from the IRS and attach it to Form 1040 in order to be credited for the estimated amount of taxes withheld. (For further information, the liquidator should consult IRS Circular E [The Employer's Tax Guide].)

The liquidator may also be required to file information returns, 1099s, if certain types of payments have been made. For example, Form 1099-INT must be supplied to the payee and to the IRS when the liquidator makes a payment of interest aggregating $10 or more. Similarly, the liquidator is required to file Form 1099-MISC when $600 or more in fees are paid to attorneys, accountants, and other professionals. Payments made to an attorney whose fee cannot be determined (e.g., anticipated payment from a settlement) must be reported to the IRS and the attorney without application of the $600 limitation.

Reporting Gains and Losses The estate recognizes a taxable gain or loss on the sale of estate property. Any resulting tax liability is treated as an administrative expense. The estate succeeds to the holding period and character of the property, and the estate is treated as the debtor with respect to such asset. The estate is liable for any taxable gain upon the sale of property, even if the proceeds are abandoned. Therefore, the liquidator should abandon rather than sell assets that will not generate net proceeds sufficient to pay any tax liability generated by the sale. The abandonment of or failure to abandon property by the liquidator in a corporate or partnership case does not affect the tax consequences to the estate of a subsequent sale or foreclosure.

Failure to Pay Taxes The liquidator should be mindful of the obligation to file appropriate returns and to pay tax liabilities on behalf of the estate. A liquidator who fails to comply with the federal withholding provisions runs the risk of being held personally liable for trust-fund taxes not collected and paid to the government. Similarly, the liquidator may be held personally liable when an estate does not have sufficient funds to pay the taxes due from the sale of estate assets.

In some circumstances, the liquidator can seek relief from penalties for failure to pay certain taxes. Relief is conditioned upon showing that (i) the failure to pay taxes incurred by the estate resulted from a court order finding probable insufficiency of funds, or (ii) the tax was incurred by the debtor prepetition, and either the petition was filed prior to the tax return due date or the penalty was imposed after the petition was filed. Relief is not available for cases involving the failure to pay employment taxes.

Quick Audits The Bankruptcy Code allows a trustee to request determination of unpaid estate tax liabilities incurred during the administration of the case by filing the tax return and requesting determination from the appropriate tax agency. The procedure, known as a 505(b) request or quick audit, allows the liquidator to resolve the administration of the case expeditiously. It is an important and valuable tool that is often used.

To obtain a quick audit of the estate's federal tax returns, the liquidator must file a written application with the IRS district director for the district where the bankruptcy case is pending. The application must be (i) executed under penalty of perjury, (ii) accompanied with an exact copy of the return(s) filed by the trustee, and (iii) include a statement telling where the original return(s) were filed. Any tax shown owing on the return must have been paid.

The IRS must give notice within 60 days if the return has been selected for audit and has a total of 180 days to complete the examination, unless an extension is granted by the court. If the IRS does not give notice or complete its examination within the time limits, the trustee is discharged from liability, absent fraud or a material misrepresentation in the return. The trustee also is discharged upon paying the tax determined to be due by the agency or by the court upon completion of the quick audit.

State and Local Tax Returns

As part of the liquidator's investigation of the debtor, he or she determines in what state the debtor is incorporated or organized (corporations are incorporated, limited liability companies are organized). In what other states does the debtor do business or have assets? Does the debtor have any subsidiaries? If so, what are the states in which they are organized, do business, and own assets? Once this information has been compiled, the liquidator, in consultation with accountants and lawyers, must determine the debtor's state and local tax obligations.

Other Federal and State Agencies

The liquidator may also be responsible for filing other (non-tax-related) reports on behalf of the debtor and its subsidiaries. These can include, for example, annual corporate reports with the secretary of state, the State Workforce Commission, environmental, and industry-specific supervisory agencies.

SEC Filings

Contrary to popular belief, filing for bankruptcy does *not* exempt a company from making periodic filings with the SEC. As a result, unless relief is available, the debtor must make the disclosures and filings mandated by the SEC and file reports under the jurisdiction of the bankruptcy court.

Prior to bankruptcy, the company should have provided full and timely disclosure of its deteriorating financial situation and liquidity problems, including risks associated with defaults under credit agreements. In 2005, the SEC initiated enforcement proceedings against K-Mart for failing to disclose its financial and liquidity problems leading to its bankruptcy filing. Expanded disclosure requirements on Form 8-K require the company to file a current report within four days in the event of material financial changes and defaults. As a condition to requesting no-action relief from the SEC, the company should take steps to inform investors of its financial problems, beginning before the bankruptcy filing.

Prior to and during bankruptcy, a distressed company faces difficulties in making timely SEC filings, including (i) reduced accounting staff, (ii) the cost of quarterly reviews and the annual audit required for SEC filings (when cash is particularly tight), (iii) retaining auditors for a high-risk audit, (iv) management's inability or unwillingness to sign or certify filings, and (v) the duty of the company and trustee to preserve the estate and contain costs. Nevertheless, the SEC takes the position that investors are entitled to full disclosure from periodic filings unless the company is entitled to terminate its SEC filing obligations because specific conditions have been met—the number of investors is less than 300 or trading activity is minimal.

SEC filings provide business information and analysis beyond the financial information included in United States Trustee reports discussed above—for example, management's discussion and analysis of financial condition and results of operations, disclosure of known trends and uncertainties, and business disclosures. In addition, SEC filings entail reviews and certifications such as disclosure controls and procedures, an independent audit, and certifications by chief executive and chief financial officers.

Why Should the Debtor Be Required to Make SEC Filing?

Investors in a bankrupt company have varying degrees of interest in the disclosures provided by SEC filings, depending on their status as an investor and their access to information from the bankruptcy negotiations. For example, an equity investor that is not also a creditor may have an interest in continued SEC filings, which include management's assessment of the company's prospects and, by extension, the likelihood of any residual value for equity owners. Equity investors are more interested in upside potential, which is more fully disclosed in SEC filings than in bankruptcy court filings. An insider investor, meaning a large holder with board or creditor committee representation, has regular access to the kinds of financial information and analysis ordinarily included in SEC filings. An insider investor may support discontinuing SEC filings in order to reduce expenses or may want the company to continue to make full disclosures in SEC filings to permit continued insider trading in the company's distressed securities. A small investor without board or committee representation may want access to information in SEC filings in order to monitor the company's financial prospects and the status of negotiations with creditors. Following a bankruptcy filing, the company and trustee are legally responsible for complying with the securities laws. They could become subject to inquiries or enforcement proceedings by the SEC for failing to make required filings.

Should the Debtor Seek Relief from SEC Filing?

The company's ability to make timely SEC filings during bankruptcy generally requires resolution of a number of bankruptcy-related problems, such as disputes with the auditor, internal control deficiencies and weaknesses, and potential restatements of prior periods, as well as demands on accounting staff related to the bankruptcy. Often the debtor wants relief from its reporting obligations.

The liquidator should monitor trading and the number of security holders in order to determine whether the company may be entitled to terminate its SEC reporting obligations. He or she should also create a roadmap of options to obtain relief from SEC filings and consider SEC filing requirements when planning strategy and agreements with creditors. Depending on the circumstances of a particular company, time in bankruptcy, number and type of investors, trading volume, and engagement of auditors for other reasons, the company may be able to terminate its filings requirements or propose modified filing procedures by obtaining a no-action letter.

If the company is a voluntary filer, it may qualify to file Form 15 and cease reporting immediately, if it has fewer than 300 security holders. A company with low trading volume may be able to seek no-action relief from the SEC and propose modified reporting procedures, typically filing monthly operating reports with the SEC within four days after the reports are filed with the bankruptcy court. Requesting no-action relief often requires correspondence with the SEC over a period of time, with attendant costs. The company must provide information regarding low trading volume and should describe the reasons that modified reporting is consistent with the protection of investors.

A reorganized company or liquidating trust may be able to operate without the obligation to make SEC filings, if the number of security holders or beneficial owners is limited and transfers of securities of trust interests are restricted. Bankruptcy counsel should consult with securities counsel to facilitate compliance with securities laws as the company's bankruptcy plan is drafted and approved.

Compliance Timeline

During the period of financial distress that precedes a bankruptcy, the company must:

- Disclose financial problems and known trends and uncertainties that could affect the company's liquidity, financial position, and results of operations.
- Provide appropriate information to the independent auditors, without causing the company and its management to be perceived as withholding information or interfering with the audit in violation of the Sarbanes-Oxley Act.
- Disclose on Form 12b-25 the reasons for any delayed filings, carefully providing full and accurate reasons that do not understate the company's financial distress.

As the company makes its bankruptcy filing, it should remain current with its SEC filings by doing the following:

- Promptly file a current report on Form 8-K disclosing the bankruptcy filing, as well as bankruptcy-related disclosures, such as noncompliance with listing standards, disputes with the auditors, and defaults in debt covenants.
- File posteffective amendments to all share registration statements and registration statements for employee stock plans, removing such shares from registration. The company should terminate all of its registration statements before filing its annual report on Form 10-K in order to avoid renewing its SEC filing obligations for an additional year.

While under jurisdiction of the bankruptcy court, the company must:

- Continue to make SEC filings on a timely basis. Failure to make SEC filings as required could result in SEC enforcement proceedings against the company and could compromise the company's ability to seek relief from the SEC to modify its reporting requirements.
- Promptly after filing for bankruptcy, assess alternatives that would permit the company to terminate or modify its reporting obligations.

As the bankruptcy plan is being negotiated, the securities aspect should be considered, including the following:

- If the company's assets are transferred to a liquidating trust, the plan should include provisions to ensure that the trust does not become a reporting entity under the Securities and Exchange Act.

- If the company's old equity is canceled in the bankruptcy proceeding and new equity is privately held, the company should seek appropriate relief that may be available from the SEC to terminate its reporting obligations.
- If the company's business is winding down and trading volume is minimal, the company should again determine whether it may seek no-action relief in order to terminate its reporting obligations.

Reporting Takes Time and Money

The independent accountants and any personnel maintained by the liquidator play a significant role in compiling the numbers for these reports. This costs money. In addition, the liquidator may have to file reports regarding, or on behalf of, subsidiary debtors with the bankruptcy court and as otherwise required under state or federal law. The necessary reports should be identified early in the liquidator's administration and care should be taken to ensure that they are filed on time.

Intercompany Issues

Interentity or intercompany issues sometimes play a role in the liquidation process. Often the liquidation involves a number of entities, one or more of which is a debtor. The several entities may share personnel, office space, and equipment. To the extent that each entity has a distinct creditor group and the entities have not been substantively consolidated, the liquidator needs to account carefully and accurately for each corporation for its use of staff and facilities.

Employment and Supervision of Professionals

Day-to-day management of a liquidation often requires a host of professionals, all of whom must be monitored by the liquidator. Liquidators managing medium sized and large liquidations are almost certain to employ professionals, including attorneys, accountants, appraisers, and auctioneers to represent or assist in performing their duties. In a bankruptcy case, professional fees are subject to court approval. Those professionals may be awarded reasonable compensation for actual and necessary services and reimbursement for actual and necessary expenses.

In a Chapter 7 case and prior to the confirmation of a Chapter 11 liquidation plan, the employment of professionals must be approved by the court prior to the rendering of any services. Generally, courts do not authorize compensation for services rendered prior to court-ordered employment. However, some courts permit retroactive or *nunc pro tunc* orders of employment in special circumstances (see appendix 1).

Leases and Executory Contracts: Assets or Liabilities?

The Bankruptcy Code provides huge benefits for those liquidating under its protection, not the least of which is the debtor's ability to assume or reject executory contracts. As defined by the courts, an executory contract is a contract where substantial performance remains to be completed by both the debtor and nondebtor at the time bankruptcy is filed. Leases make up a separate and special category of executory transactions. The trustee of a liquidating estate has to decide whether to accept (assume) or reject these obligations. Usually, the debtor assumes executory contracts that are beneficial to the estate (e.g., below-market leases) and rejects those that are not beneficial (e.g., above-market leases). The assumed beneficial contracts can be sold or assigned to third parties for cash. When business units are being sold, potential purchasers are often required to specify in their bids which contracts relating to that unit they would agree to assume. A purchaser's assumption of contracts can add value to a transaction. The liquidator might otherwise be forced to reject a contract, which would result in an unsecured claim against the estate.

Rejection of the executory contract constitutes a breach of the contract. Typically, the third party whose contract was rejected has an unsecured claim against the estate for damages. It will simply receive its pro rata share of the liquidation proceeds.

A trustee who wishes to assume a contract in default must cure the default, pay past due amounts, and give adequate assurance for future performance of the debtor's ongoing obligations. Contract clauses that state that executory contracts cannot be assumed in bankruptcy are unenforceable. Court approval is necessary for assumption or rejection. The standard for approval, however, is the debtor's business judgment, an easy standard to meet. Most controversy deals with whether a contract is executory or substantially performed. Performance contracts cannot be assumed or rejected. Most important, if the trustee elects to assume the contract and then fails to perform, the third party is entitled to a postpetition administrative priority claim for any resulting damages. This claim can reduce the funds available to pay the trustee.

While the Bankruptcy Code permits the rejection of executory contracts, a secured transaction is not subject to simple rejection. Accordingly, analysis of claims against an estate based on an agreement that bears a title that it is a lease should include a careful assessment of whether or not the particular agreement contains a (nominal price) purchase option at the end of the lease term; whether or not the lessee obtains equity in the property over the life of the lease; whether the lessee assumes a risk of loss, and whether the lessee pays taxes, insurance, and other expenses related to the property. An adverse analysis of these questions can lead a court to find that the instrument is in fact a loan. These determinations vary under the laws of the various states.

Conclusion

The day-to-day management of a liquidating estate involves many of the same matters as running an on going business, except that the goal of the process is to reach the point where nothing is left to manage. Important day-to-day matters include: keeping and maintaining records; paying federal and state income taxes, excise taxes, and employment taxes during the administration of the estate; submitting required SEC filings (although certain exemptions are possible under certain circumstances); and finally, identifying and analyzing executory contracts.

7

Locating and Disposing of Assets

In order to convert assets into cash, the liquidator must first identify the assets. Occasionally, this task was completed prior to the liquidator's appointment. If not, locating assets is one of the liquidator's first jobs. The assets then must be evaluated in order to determine whether they should be sold or abandoned and, if they are to be sold, the appropriate disposition method and expected price.

Locating Assets

As discussed in chapter 2, in a normal liquidation, a company's balance sheet, general ledger, and bankruptcy schedules provide a roadmap for identifying the company's assets, but actually locating them is another matter. If the business was conducted from one location, the assets theoretically should be located there, but that is not always the case. Businesses conducted at multiple locations tend to generate more work for the liquidator in tracking down assets. In distressed situations, assets frequently walk out the door with the employees, especially employees who are laid off—everything from computers to coffee cups disappear. Assets also may have been fraudulently transferred to third parties prior to the filing.

Searching for Assets

In some instances, assets cannot be located simply because of the poor state of the company's records. The liquidator can undertake an investigation much like a judgment creditor would try to determine if a judgment debtor has assets. Title companies can be hired to search records for real estate held in the company's name. Asset-location companies can be hired to locate other types of assets.

Uncovering Fraud

The liquidator may uncover fraud or embezzlement in the course of the liquidation. The moment illegal activity is suspected, the liquidator has a duty to investigate. Certified fraud examiners can be hired for this purpose. The most common discovery is that assets were fraudulently transferred out of the company prior to bankruptcy.

Only one of the two kinds of fraudulent transfers involves true fraud. The classic fraudulent transfer occurs when a debtor transfers an asset to a third party with the actual intent to hinder, delay, or defraud its creditors. For example, the company's president might transfer to his spouse a piece of real estate owned by the company, or an employee could set up a bogus vendor number and make payments to the "vendor" on false invoices. This type of fraudulent transfer is recoverable in a civil action under both state and federal law. Such actions may also be a crime under the Bankruptcy Fraud Prevention Act and under the penal code in some states.

The second kind of fraudulent transfer is known as a constructive fraudulent transfer. It involves the transfer of assets by the debtor for which reasonably equivalent value was not received at a time when the debtor was insolvent, inadequately capitalized, or unable to pay its debts as they became due. No fraudulent intent need be present. (Fraudulent transfers are discussed in greater detail in chapter 8.)

A current fad among heavily leveraged individuals is to transfer their assets into offshore spendthrift trusts, such as Cook Island trusts. Certain states, such as Alaska and Delaware, have passed legislation enabling these trusts, which are intended to place assets beyond the reach of a debtor's creditors. Often a liquidator must pursue these assets, which have frequently been fraudulently transferred. This requires hiring special counsel and attaching the trust assets and/or pursuing criminal fraud charges against the transferor of the assets.

Evaluating the Assets

The true value that a particular liquidator brings to the situation is his or her ability to evaluate assets and maximize the recoveries from these assets. Assets may be classified as liquid assets, illiquid assets, disputed assets, and contingent assets.

Liquid Assets

Liquid assets have an easily determined market value, such as the price that the market establishes for publicly traded stocks, bonds, and other securities. This category also includes assets having an active secondary market, such as agricultural products, metals, and various other minerals. Realizing maximum value from such assets is primarily an issue of timing: Should the estate sell now or sell later? Realizing value quickly involves the least risk but is by no means always the most attractive course.

An estate cannot be closed until all of its outstanding business and legal issues are resolved. Often there are complicated issues (e.g., tax liabilities and claims for refunds, pension plans, claims disputes, causes of action) that take time to resolve. If such issues require leaving the estate open for a substantial time, the liquidator has the flexibility to choose the best time to liquidate individual assets. The liquidator for an estate whose outstanding issues can be quickly resolved does not have the flexibility to wait for the best price on its liquid assets.

Funds held by a bankruptcy trustee must be invested in very secure and therefore very low return securities (see appendix 2). Accordingly, it may be better for the estate to retain liquid assets that can reasonably be expected to generate a significantly higher return than treasury bills. They can always be sold when the estate needs the funds to pay expenses or is ready to make a distribution to claimants. For instance, the higher return on a portfolio of mortgages may more than offset the slightly higher risk. Moreover, the sale of the mortgages involves transactions costs, which are avoided or reduced if the estate simply keeps the portfolio and collects the scheduled principal and interest payments. The longer one holds the mortgages, the more interest and principal will be received and the less will need to be sold.

To varying degrees, the liquidator has an affirmative obligation not to speculate and should not hold onto particularly risky assets that could be sold. On the other hand, holding moderate to low-risk liquid assets (e.g., diversified portfolios of mortgaged-backed securities, investment grade corporate bonds) might be reasonable. A (poorly diversified) position concentrated in junk bonds, however, probably would not be a reasonable investment, even if the indicated yield seemed attractive.

Illiquid Assets

Illiquid assets are salable with significant effort or over time. Moreover, certain illiquid assets can be risky to hold due to the uncertainty of their market values. The only available sale may be at a significant discount from the intrinsic value to an investor in a position to hold on for the long term. Realizing value from such assets involves prudent timing, maintenance, and pricing. Illiquid assets include real estate, investments in nonpublic companies, and wholly and partially owned subsidiaries.

Wasting Assets

Wasting assets are those destined to lose value as time passes. Such assets include businesses whose customer and supplier relationships tend to be adversely affected by the financial distress of their parent corporation, equipment that becomes increasingly obsolete as technologies change (e.g., computers), and assets that provide a tax shelter that is lost when their owner does not generate income to shelter. Clearly, the estate needs to ascertain the values of wasting assets, do what it can to protect these values, and then sell them as quickly as possible.

Nonwasting Assets

Nonwasting assets may or may not appreciate through time but at least they are not subject to an automatic downdraft. Many assets in this category either automatically liquidate (e.g., private debt instruments) or are designed to evolve into liquid assets in the future (e.g., venture capital investments of businesses that plan to go public). If the estate can avoid making a premature sale, these types of investments generally reward the wait. Potential buyers for such assets (prior to their reaching a natural exit point) usually seek and indeed demand a very substantial discount from the illiquid assets' intrinsic values. Unless potential buyers are offered the asset at such a discount, they will not buy it. Put another way, if the would-be buyer expects the asset to be worth some value x when the company goes public a year from now, their offer may be 50% of x. Thus the buyer would demand and expect to receive a 50% one-year return on the investment in order to purchase it. If the liquidator can wait a year for the asset to mature, he or she is likely to obtain a much better recovery for the estate.

Some illiquid assets will not self-liquidate within a reasonable time. Examples run the gamut from real estate (developed and undeveloped) to wildcat oil wells to works of art. Such assets may or may not produce income, but they are not likely to turn into cash on their own no matter how long one holds them. The liquidator must sell them in order to realize their value. The first step in selling an asset is to understand it. What is it worth to someone who would have a good reason to own the asset? The liquidator may perform a substantial amount of research in unfamiliar businesses in order to understand some assets' values. The objective is to find a buyer who is willing to pay a fair price for putting the asset to its highest and best use.

Disputed Assets

Disputed assets are either liquid or illiquid assets (including wasting and nonwasting) with positive value whose ownership is in dispute. For example, the estate may have an asset that it either purchased or sold just prior to bankruptcy. Because of disagreements over fully satisfying the terms of the contract, the asset's ownership is now subject to competing claims. Such assets cannot generally be sold to a third party without clear title. Sometimes ownership can be resolved first, either by court decision or negotiation. At times, the prospect of a sale may give the impetus for a resolution of ownership issues. At still other times a sale can proceed without resolving ownership. Each claimant simply sells his or her respective interest (whatever it may be) with the sale funds held in escrow until ownership disputes are resolved.

Depending on the circumstances, a liquidator in bankruptcy may be able to utilize the law to obtain a larger percentage of the value of a disputed asset. The bankruptcy court may be asked to act as a shield in order to protect the bankrupt estate's interest in the disputed asset (e.g., apply the automatic stay, allow the rejection of executory contracts, etc.). The manager of a bankrupt estate should look to the Bankruptcy Code for the many weapons to use in a fight over a disputed asset.

Sometimes a disputed asset is held by a nonbankrupt subsidiary of the insolvent estate. Continuing to operate such a subsidiary outside of bankruptcy has both advantages and disadvantages. In dealing with parties raising a dispute, the protective powers of the bankruptcy court provide a useful tool. However, this protection tends to be quite expensive. At times, the mere prospect of putting the subsidiary into bankruptcy helps the estate successfully negotiate a resolution. At other times, putting the subsidiary into bankruptcy facilitates the resolution of competing claims and allows the sale of its assets to proceed with the protection of the bankruptcy court.

Contingent Assets

Assets that have the potential to generate value but ultimately may have no value are viewed as contingent assets. The principal group of contingent assets are the causes of action that have to be pursued in a court of law for any realization, although contingent assets also include things such as potential federal, state, and local tax refunds and purchase options.

Causes of Action

With contingent assets such as potential lawsuits, one must put at risk the cost of funding the lawsuit. In exchange, the litigant receives the prospect of succeeding sufficiently to collect enough money to justify the undertaking. Clearly, the liquidator needs to evaluate carefully the costs and benefits of pursuing each contingent asset (see chapter 8). Essentially, one treats each cause of action as a potential investment and computes its net present value (NPV). Only if the NPV is positive does one proceed.

Miscellaneous Found Money

Rarely do third parties come forward voluntarily to turn over funds to a liquidator, but a good liquidator finds assets that do not appear on the balance sheet. He or she identifies and derives value from many unlikely sources. The liquidator can cancel unnecessary insurance coverage and demand premium refunds. For example, historically, BNEC acted as a self-insured with Travelers Insurance Company, acting as the third-party administrator of worker's compensation casualty and other such umbrella insurance coverage for BNEC and its subsidiaries. When the financial condition of BNEC and its subsidiaries deteriorated, Travelers suggested that the preexisting format be changed so as to have BNEC obtain full coverage and pay monthly premiums of approximately $1 million to Travelers. Travelers then estimated each month the number and amount of claims filed or estimated to be filed for the preceding period in order to calculate whether the premiums were overpaid or underpaid. The program was terminated on the petition date but the trustee pursued recovery of a sum of money from Travelers asserting that the terms of the policy provided for a refund when actual experience with insured losses under the policy were below estimated losses. The trustee recovered a refund from Travelers.

The liquidator also can determine if deposits or bonds were made with foreign, state or local government entities and request return of the deposits. For example, at its formation, a BNEC subsidiary filed a $100,000 bond with the Arizona Insurance Board in order to conduct a re-insurance business in Arizona. The trustee dissolved the subsidiary and received $100,000 from the state. Other ways to find funds include

- applying for federal, state, and local tax refunds for the debtor and all its subsidiaries;
- analyzing purchase options and stock options to determine whether they are in or out of the money; and
- analyzing leases to determine if any are below market, so they can be assumed and assigned in exchange for cash.

Sale of Assets

Valuation of Assets

In evaluating whether an asset has value to the estate, the liquidator must determine whether the asset is encumbered and whether the value of the asset exceeds the amount of the secured creditors' liens. The liquidator must also consider whether the cost of preserving the asset or tax consequences of any sale would significantly erode or exhaust the value from the asset, which can be realized for general unsecured creditors. If the sale of an asset would result in little or no benefit for unsecured creditors, the trustee should abandon the asset if the cost of preserving it would be greater than the revenue from a sale.

Most of the debtor's assets are classified and valued somewhere on its balance sheet. Unless the asset is traded in an established liquid market and the debtor has "marked to market" the asset on its balance sheet, the accounting, or book, value that appears on the balance sheet for assets is unlikely to be a very reliable estimate of its intrinsic value. An asset's accounting value is a constructed number. That number is arrived at by starting with the asset's original cost and then is mechanically adjusted for the impact of the passage of time as it relates to the expected life of the asset (depreciation, etc.). The process rarely corresponds to what is actually happening to the asset's underlying market value to a potential buyer. Thus preparing fair market value estimates for most of the debtor's assets requires some work on the part of the liquidator. The Chapter 7 trustee is required, for reporting purposes, to place a realizable value on the individual components of the debtor's portfolio of assets. It is equally important for other liquidators, because having such a set of valuations is crucial to the process of deriving value for the estate. To determine if the price being offered is in line with the asset's intrinsic value, one needs an accurate understanding of that intrinsic value. How do you perform a valuation analyses? Simply put, the three basic approaches to estimating asset values are market method, replacement cost method, and income method (discounted cash flow).

Market Method

To obtain a valuation based on market comparables (also called market transactions), one observes the prices at which similar assets are being bought and sold in the marketplace. Valuation means include the NADA or Kelley Blue book for automobiles; information acquired from real estate agents, as well as county records regarding recent sales of comparable real property; and advertisements for the sale of like goods This approach also works well for highly marketable assets such as actively traded stocks and bonds. The market comparables approach can also be reliable for one-of-a-kind assets, when the more generic asset is part of an active market. For example, the value of a downtown office building could be estimated by observing sales of similar buildings. One would make appropriate adjustments for differences in size, condition, and location. Similarly, equipment such as airplanes, railroad rolling stock, oil rigs, and construction equipment have relatively active markets. A derivative of the market comparables method is the market multiple method. Transactions involving entire businesses are frequently negotiated based on a multiple of earnings or revenue. For example, businesses in one industry may typically sell for ten times earnings while businesses in another industry may typically sell for three times earnings. Many assets are so unique that the comparables approach is largely useless.

Replacement Cost Method

The replacement cost method seeks to establish a value based on the cost of replicating the asset. Clearly, most buyers are not likely to pay more for an existing asset than it would cost to produce something equivalent. Having the asset immediately available may add premium to the value when producing another one takes time, but the impact of this consideration is likely to be small. So, the replacement value approach may provide a relatively useful number for the upper limit to how much a buyer might pay. Thus a replacement cost valuation is at best only an estimate of a ceiling to the true valuation. The actual value may be significantly below its ceiling, particularly if the market is well supplied with such assets. The replacement cost method is most often used for a unique asset such as, say, a church building.

Income Method (Discounted Cash Flow)

While the market method and replacement value method have their uses, the income approach is often the preferred method for valuing assets, especially for inactively traded, one-of-a-kind assets. The income approach is based on the propositions that an asset is worth the current value of the income that it is expected to produce. The income method is the most sophisticated and difficult to apply, yet it is the most flexible and reliable, as long as the information needed is or can be made available (see appendix 5).

When an asset in the estate involves scheduled future payments, a liquidator must attempt to discount the future income stream to an appropriate present value and liquidate the asset as expeditiously as possible. If the discounted payments cannot be liquidated, or the asset cannot otherwise be assigned for the benefit of creditors, the trustee must consider interim distributions to creditors as funds become available, provided that claims are resolved and sufficient funds are reserved to administer the estate.

Which Valuation Approach Is Best?

No one approach to valuation is best. The liquidator must evaluate each situation individually. If a ready market exists for the asset in question, the market method should be explored. If a meaningful market comparable price can be constructed, it should provide a relatively reliable index of the asset's value. Even when comparables are available, some effort to assess the asset's replacement value provides a check on the underlying value estimate. Recall, however, that assets will not necessarily sell for their replacement values if a large quantity of such assets is available on the market relative to the demand. Often neither the market comparable nor the replacement value approach can provide a useful or reliable estimate of value. One is therefore forced to use the income approach with many types of assets. If the business's income is highly predictable and dependable (e.g., a mortgage or other well-defined payment stream), the pure income approach is appropriate. Otherwise, the market multiple approach is indicated. If the liquidator hires an investment banker to assist with the sale, you can be rather sure that one or more of the techniques outlined above will be used. The liquidator, however, must understand these methodologies in order to work effectively with investment bankers.

Appraisers and Investment Bankers

Local appraisers typically have access to local and regional data that will assist them in the valuation. Investment bankers not only bring industry-specific data to the valuation process, they are of great assistance in identifying strategic and financial buyers for business units.

The role of the investment banker can be very broad. As seen in the Friede case study, they assist the liquidator in (i) making a preliminary valuation of the asset, (ii) preparing marketing materials and a data room for potential buyers to use for due diligence, (iii) targeting identified buyers, and (iv) negotiating the terms of the sale. Often their fee is success based. While Houlihan worked for a flat fee in the Friede case, monthly retainers and percentage-of-proceeds fees are also common.

The role of the appraiser is more limited. An appraiser essentially provides the liquidator with an opinion of value on an asset, based on specialized knowledge of an industry. For example, BNEC owned an art collection. The trustee identified and obtained court approval to hire an art dealer to appraise the art. Thereafter, the dealer's assignment included the negotiation of private sales by the dealer of individual pieces, after the trustee concluded that private sales would bring the highest value. The dealer was not able to place all the pieces privately and ultimately he arranged for and oversaw the auction of the remaining pieces at a reputable art auction house.

Identifying Potential Purchasers

There are basically two types of business buyers, strategic and financial. Strategic buyers seek to acquire operating businesses that fit into their existing portfolio of business units. They hope to create synergies by combining the new business with their existing operations. Because the strategic buyers expect to earn an enhanced income from the acquired business and to derive savings from economies provided by the combination of the acquired operations and the existing portfolio of businesses, the acquisition is often worth more to the strategic buyer than it is to a financial buyer. The strategic buyers typically compete in and for the same business as the entity to be sold. As seen in the Friede case study, Bollinger Shipyards, Halter's direct competitor, decided it would be in its best interest to bid for Halter's assets instead of allowing another strategic buyer or, perhaps worse, a reorganized Friede to become a re-energized competitor.

Financial buyers are in the business of buying and selling operating companies. Their goal is to acquire such companies as cheaply as possible, using a lot of debt and relatively little of their own money. They then hope to operate the newly acquired businesses for a few years, squeeze out inefficiencies, pay off some of the debt, and put them in shape to resell. Such a sale could be either to another company or to the public through an initial public offering.

When looking to sell a business, it is important to identify and contact as many strategic and financial buyers as possible. With more interested buyers making bids, the liquidator is more likely to obtain a good price.

Terms of the Sale

Typically, the liquidator and the buyer initially agree on a price and the general terms of the sale, which will be documented in what is called a term sheet. The term sheet forms the basis for drawing up the terms of the sales contract, referred to as the asset sale agreement (ASA; see appendix 10). The key terms of the ASA are the purchase price and assets to be sold. It may also include representations, warranties, indemnities, and the like. Although lawyers draft these agreements, liquidators negotiating asset sales must know which issues to address in the term sheet. An ASA is not typically needed for the sale of individual assets. Title is transferred pursuant to a simple bill of sale. An ASA is more often used when a business unit is being sold.

Purchase Price

Generally, all sales should be paid for in cash equivalents, such as certified checks, cashier's checks, money orders, or wire transfers. The liquidator should not accept a promissory note or installment payments and should avoid sales that structure payments to extend beyond one year. Sometimes, however, a sale involving periodic payments, which do not delay case closing, may be in the best interest of the liquidation. When the purchase price is paid in installments, the liquidator also should obtain and perfect a security interest in the estate assets sold and take other suitable precautions to protect the estate against default.

Assets to Be Purchased

Purchasers are typically reluctant to buy the stock of a subsidiary of a bankrupt company. They prefer to purchase assets, particularly when the debtor and its subsidiaries file a consolidated tax return. The purchaser does not want to become liable for back taxes of another member of the consolidated group.

When a business unit is sold, the ASA covers all assets integral to the business, including inventory, accounts, and equipment as well as intangible assets such as trademarks, software, customer lists, and other intellectual property. Causes of action belonging to the unit are frequently carved out of the asset description and retained by the liquidator. The ASA should make clear which litigation remains with the estate and which is transferred with the assets to the purchaser. Employees and contracts should also be addressed. The ASA should specifically identify contracts to be assumed by the debtor and assigned to the purchaser and contracts to be rejected. If offers of employment will be made to some of the debtor's employees, a deadline should be set so that the liquidator can terminate those employees who will not receive an offer.

Representations and Warranties

Representations and warranties are assurances which the seller provides to the buyer that the asset to be sold has certain characteristics. For example, the seller may warrant that all tax returns have been filed and no outstanding tax claims exist; that all required business licenses are in place; that the buyer has good title to all real estate free and clear of liens; that all accounts receivables are collectable; that inventories are of a certain size, and so forth. These assurances are designed to give the buyer comfort that the seller is going to deliver the property in the condition that the buyer expects. For these assurances to have any value to the buyer, some means of redress must be available. Usually, the buyer wants the right to seek appropriate damages from the seller, if any of the warranties are breached (i.e., turn out to be false). This is not easy to do.

Frequently, a liquidation sale is "as is, where is," with no representations or warranties. The buyer must rely solely upon its inspections and investigations. This type of sale is the safest course for the liquidator but may not always result in the highest possible value. When the liquidator does provide a means of redress, he or she cannot be put in a position to keep the estate open because representations, warranties, and other postclosing obligations to the purchasers are still in force. Accordingly, the contract must provide for a termination date of all obligations made by the liquidator/seller. Usually, the termination is set to expire after a certain period of time has elapsed (e.g., 12 months after closing) or earlier, if the estate is ready for closure. Additionally, a cap should be placed on the amount of damages for which the estate could be liable. Typically, some portion of the purchase price is deposited into an escrow account, often called a basket. These funds are available to the buyer during the indemnification period. The purchase and sale agreement should provide a procedure for the buyer to assert its indemnification in writing to the seller during the indemnification period. The ASA resolution procedure provides for mediation or arbitration, if the parties are unable to agree upon the amount to be withdrawn from the account.

Postclosing Adjustments

Postclosing adjustments are the changes or adjustments made to the purchase price after the closing of the sale. When the purchase price of an operating business unit is based on a formula tied to the balance sheet as of a certain date (typically closing), the parties must wait until after closing for a final (often audited) balance sheet. Funds may also be escrowed to cover postclosing adjustments. This was done in the Friede sale of AmClyde, its engineered products segment (see chapter 4). Of the $36 million purchase price, only $21 million was received at closing. The remainder was received several months later, following a final calculation of working capital as of the closing date.

Overbid Protection

Sales of estate assets in a bankruptcy proceeding are subject to higher and better offers. Accordingly, one of the first terms the initial winning bidder (commonly referred to as the "stalking horse") negotiates into the term sheet is "overbid protection." An overbid, or topping amount, is a minimum amount that a competing buyer must offer above the initial buyer's bid. Bankruptcy courts approve reasonable overbid provisions in order to protect the initial winning bidder from a subsequent bidder who relies on the initial bidder's due diligence and offers a nominally higher bid. The term sheet also often requires the subsequent bidder to (i) deposit some portion of the purchase price in escrow, (ii) accept the transaction on the same terms as the initial winning bid, and (iii) demonstrate the financial ability to consummate the transaction. In Friede's sale of its design and engineer segment, the competing bidder, United Heavy BV, was required to deposit 10% of the bid and provide extensive financial information to the debtor and committee, including sources of financing.

Breakup Fees

A breakup fee is that amount paid to the initial winning bidder when that bidder is not the ultimate successful bidder because a third party has topped his bid. The fee can be either a fixed dollar amount or a percentage of the purchase price. Typically, the topping amount is more than the breakup fee and covers not only payment of the breakup fee but also the associated additional legal fees of the liquidator.

Breakup fees are used in transactions both inside and outside of bankruptcy. In bankruptcy these fees are intended to attract an initial bidder, establish a floor for other bidders and attract additional bidders. For breakup fees to be allowed in bankruptcy they must be approved by the bankruptcy court. To be approved the fee must (i) be reasonable in relation to the proposed purchase price, (ii) encourage rather than discourage bidding, and (iii) be negotiated at arm's length (i.e., not manipulated or marked by self-dealing). For example, in the

Friede case, a breakup fee of $250,000 was approved on FGL Acquisitions' $8 million bid on the design and engineering segment (3.125% of the bid), and a $2.5 million breakup fee was approved on Bollinger Shipyards' $48 million bid on the vessel segment (5.20% of the bid). Neither FGL Acquisitions nor Bollinger ended up as the successful bidder, and Friede paid those breakup fees. The $1 million breakup fee approved on Hydrolifts' $36 million bid for Am-Clyde (2.77% of the bid) was not paid because Hydrolift was ultimately the successful bidder. Each of these breakup fees was vigorously negotiated, ranging from 2.77% to 5.2% of the underlying bid.

Sale Procedures in Bankruptcy

The bankruptcy trustee is permitted to sell property of the estate only after notice to creditors and a court hearing. The only exception allowed to the notice requirement occurs when the contemplated transaction is in the ordinary course of the debtor's business. The liquidation of estate assets by a bankruptcy trustee rarely qualifies as an exception. A trustee, therefore, must comply with the notice and hearing requirements before proceeding to liquidate an estate asset. Exigent circumstances may require liquidation of assets immediately after the case is filed. In these instances, emergency motions should be filed.

A liquidating trustee under a confirmed plan may be authorized to sell assets without court approval. Often the plan provides that approval of the oversight committee or board is all that is needed.

Notice and Timing

For liquidations in active bankruptcy cases, creditors on the service list must receive 20 days notice of a proposed sale of estate property. The court, for cause shown, may order a shorter notice period. Frequently, this procedure becomes necessary for emergency situations. A hearing on the sale or an order authorizing or confirming the sale is not required unless an objection is filed. Objections to the sale must be filed within 15 days from the mailing of the notice or within the time fixed by the court. Unless the court orders otherwise, objections to a sale must be filed and served five days before the date set for the proposed action. An objection to a sale is deemed a request for a hearing and the matter proceeds as contested.

Notice of a proposed use, sale, or lease of property of the estate must be provided to the clerk of the bankruptcy court, debtor, United States Trustee, and all creditors. The following information should be included in the notice:

- Type of sale (private, auction, etc.)
- Location, date, and time of public sale
- Description of assets

- Terms and conditions of sale
- Factors used to establish value (appraisal, book value, etc.) in a private sale
- Procedure and time period for filing objections
- Amount of liens and identity of lien holders
- In a private sale, identity of purchaser and relationship, if any, to any creditor or party in interest

Sale Free and Clear

The ability to sell assets free and clear of existing liens often enhances their value. Property of the estate can be sold free and clear of a third-party interest, only if one or more of the following apply:

- Applicable nonbankruptcy law permits a sale of such property free of the interest.
- The third party interest holder consents.
- The interest is a lien and the sale price is greater than the aggregate value of all liens on the property.
- The validity of the interest is in bona fide dispute.
- The entity could be compelled in a legal or equitable proceeding to accept a money satisfaction of its interest whose amount is less than the net sale proceeds.

The bankruptcy court may approve a sale over objections of a lien holder or any entity with an interest in the property, with liens attaching to the proceeds.

A lien holder cannot be charged with general expenses of administration, the expenses of the case, or costs of preservation of the property, except as incurred for the lien holder's benefit. If the liquidator can establish that the sale was necessary to the preservation of the lien holder's interest in the collateral, the estate may be able to recover sale expenses from the sale proceeds.

Sale of Jointly Owned Property

The estate is allowed to sell both the estate's interest and the interest of any co-owner in property in which the debtor had an undivided interest, if specific conditions are met. An action to obtain approval to sell jointly owned property must be brought by the trustee as an adversary proceeding.

Sale of Secured Property

A secured creditor can protect its own interests in the collateral subject to the security interest. In certain limited circumstances, however, a bankruptcy trustee may properly sell secured property that would generate proceeds for the benefit of unsecured creditors. If the estate retains equity in the property, the trustee may seek to sell it. If the estate does not retain equity, the trustee may still sell the property. For example, a liquidator may be able to satisfy in full a blanket security interest on multiple units of property by selling only one unit. Similarly, a trustee may be able to obtain a higher price from an aggregate sale of assets than from selling the assets individually. Finally, the sale of a secured but wasting asset may be indicated in order to minimize the deficiency. Administering fully secured property should always be viewed as the exception taking into account the particular circumstances of each case.

When selling fully secured property, the liquidator must administer the sale in a manner designed to avoid a diminution of funds otherwise available for unsecured creditors. He or she should obtain an agreement in writing from the secured creditor to recover the costs of sale from the collateral. The liquidator must disclose the terms of any agreement between the liquidator and the secured creditor at the outset, for example, in the notice of proposed sale, and in the trustee's final report and request for compensation and reimbursement of expenses.

Sales to Insiders

A trustee or affiliated officer of the court may not legally purchase directly or indirectly or otherwise deal in property of the estate for which the trustee serves. A trustee is not specifically prohibited from purchasing assets from an estate administered by another trustee. Nonetheless, the practice should be avoided in order to minimize any appearance of impropriety. Similarly, sales to professionals regularly retained by a trustee should be avoided. A trustee or a professional regularly employed by the case trustee, including the auctioneer, a family member of the trustee or professional, or an employee of the trustee or professional, are not permitted to bid or to buy property at a private sale or at an estate sale conducted by the auctioneer. The United States Trustee will object to any proposed sale of estate property to either a trustee or a professional person regularly employed by the case trustee, a family member of the trustee, or an employee of the trustee. If the trustee becomes aware of any indications of sales to insiders or of collusive bidding, the sale should immediately be stopped, and the matter reported to the United States Trustee. People have, in fact, been sentenced to jail for violating this law.

Postsale Activity

Upon completion of the sale, an itemized statement of the property sold, the names of the purchasers, and the price received for each item must be transmitted to the United States Trustee and filed with the clerk of the bankruptcy court. When an auctioneer sells the property, the auctioneer must file the statement. If the property is not sold by an auctioneer, the trustee must file the statement.

Prohibition on Collusive Bidding

Collusive bidding occurs when bidders conspire to control the sale price of assets. Collusive bidding is prohibited under the Bankruptcy Code and subjects the violator to punitive damages. The bidders must control the sale price, not merely affect it. For example, if two buyers agree to bid together for a pool of assets and split the assets after closing, they affect the sales price but do not control it.

Rights of First Offer/Refusal

A right of first refusal gives the holder the legal right to purchase the debtor's asset (typically real estate) on the terms and conditions of sale contained in a bona fide offer by a third party to purchase the asset, if the debtor is otherwise willing to accept the offer. A long-term lease that gives the tenant a right of first refusal to purchase the property if the landlord decides to sell is common. Bankruptcy courts typically enforce prepetition rights of first refusal granted by a debtor, if the right is contained in a contract that is assumed, such as a lease. The holder of a right of first refusal is not bound by a sale procedure requirement of a topping bid or topping fee, if the holder is prepared to meet the final offer of a competing bidder. The sale of BNEC's leveraged lease portfolio (discussed at the end of this chapter) involved a right of first refusal granted in a lease by a nonbankrupt subsidiary. It was ultimately exercised by the holder.

The liquidator or his counsel must identify holders of rights of first refusal *prior* to the marketing process, so that these holders receive notice of the proposed sale *and* other potential buyers are aware of the right of first refusal. Even where the right of first refusal can be eliminated through contract rejection, the holder of the right should be notified of the sale. Since the right of first refusal is typically exercised at market value, if the holder is willing to pay the fair market value for the asset, the holder is not prejudiced.

An option contract is an agreement, which gives the optionee the power to purchase an asset from a debtor at an agreed price and within an agreed time period. Option contracts have been held by courts to be executory contracts, which may be rejected. For example, a stock option agreement giving the optionee the power to purchase a majority of the stock of a debtor's subsidiary for a dollar a share may be rejected if the fair market value of the stock greatly exceeds a dollar a share. An option to purchase at the market price, which is triggered by bankruptcy, is also unenforceable.

Auctions

363 Auctions

A sale in bankruptcy court is often referred to as a 363 auction. Rather than an auctioneer conducting the sale, the bankruptcy judge or designated counsel conducts the sale. Typically, bid packages have been distributed by the liquidator to potential purchasers. Those interested have had the opportunity for some type of due diligence, perhaps access to an electronic data room. A court date is set and the interested buyers come to court to bid for the assets. Often bids are submitted in writing. Ultimately, the judge calls for best and final offers and ultimately announces the winner.

Other Auctions

The liquidator commonly employs an auctioneer to sell different types of property, including furniture, equipment, artwork, and inventory. The auction is conducted at the debtor's place (or former place) of business or at an auction house, after appropriate advertisement of the sale and opportunity for viewing by prospective purchasers. The asset is sold to the highest bidder and title is transferred by a bill of sale.

Hiring an Auctioneer

A bankruptcy trustee must obtain court approval to hire the auctioneer as a professional person. The liquidator must actively supervise the auctioneer to ensure that the estate is properly protected against loss, that property is sold for reasonable prices to independent buyers, that auction proceeds are promptly and fully remitted, that auctioneers timely submit accurate sale reports, and that auctioneer expenses are actual and necessary and paid in accordance with legal requirements. Methods by which a trustee can supervise auctioneers include personally attending auction sales, thoroughly reviewing auctioneer reports, and independently verifying reported information. A bankruptcy trustee must advise the United States Trustee of concerns with respect to auctioneers and must promptly report any situations, which could result in a loss to the bankruptcy estate. Failure to supervise auctioneers appropriately may result in claims against the trustee.

Compensation The compensation of an auctioneer hired by a bankruptcy trustee must be approved by the bankruptcy court. Any buyer's premium must be fully disclosed in the employment application and considered in determining the reasonableness of the total compensation.

Auctioneers usually deduct their commissions and expenses from the sales proceeds and remit a net amount to the seller. This practice, however, is prohibited in the handling of bankruptcy estate funds, unless specifically authorized by the court. However, the order authorizing employment may specify the percentage charged by the auctioneer and authorize the deduction of the commission and the costs of sale from the sales proceeds, with the auctioneer remitting the net sales proceeds to the trustee. In those cases, the auctioneer must present with the report of sale an affidavit or declaration listing all incurred costs and expenses.

Bonding Insurance The liquidator must ensure that auctioneers are adequately bonded in an amount that is sufficient to cover all receipts from the sale, prior to allowing them to take possession of property. For a bankruptcy auctioneer, the bond should be in favor of the United States of America and is distinct from any other auctioneer's bond required under state law. The amount of the bond is established by local bankruptcy rule or the United States Trustee. The trustee should confirm that the auctioneer is bonded in an amount appropriate to cover all estates in which the particular auctioneer has been employed. All original bonds should be forwarded to the United States Trustee, who routinely monitors the adequacy of the bond.

When the auctioneer assumes control over estate property for a period of time prior to sale, the trustee should keep an inventory of the items stored and periodically verify that the assets are still under the auctioneer's control and are in good condition. The liquidator also should ascertain that the auctioneer maintains insurance for lost or stolen property. Insurance claims for lost, stolen, or destroyed property should be made promptly, and a bankruptcy trustee should inform the United States Trustee of such claims.

Turnover of Proceeds The auctioneer must not be allowed to commingle auction proceeds with the proceeds of business, personal, or other accounts. Whenever possible, the auctioneer should immediately turn over auction proceeds to the liquidator. In any event, all proceeds of a bankruptcy estate must be turned over within 30 days of the end of the auction. The United States Trustee may have additional requirements in this area.

If an auctioneer fails to account for or to turn over auction proceeds within 30 days, the bankruptcy trustee should promptly notify the United States Trustee. A liquidator should take immediate action to recover the funds, including initiating a proceeding against the auctioneer's bond.

Auctioneer's Report The auctioneer should provide to the liquidator an itemized statement of the property sold, the name of each purchaser, and the price received for each item, lot, or for the entire property, if sold in bulk. A bankruptcy trustee must ensure that the auctioneer's report is promptly submitted to the court upon completion of the auction. If the report has not been provided within 30 days after the auction, the bankruptcy trustee should request a copy and ensure that it has been filed with the court and United States Trustee and as otherwise provided by local rules and practices.

The liquidator should compare the auctioneer's report to the original inventory and obtain an explanation for any discrepancies. The liquidator also should scrutinize items marked stolen or missing. As noted earlier, the liquidator should attempt to recover the value of lost, stolen, or destroyed items by filing a claim with the auctioneer's insurer or by initiating a proceeding against the auctioneer's bond, as appropriate.

Internet Auctions

If the liquidator considers that it would be advantageous to sell assets through an Internet auction Web site, he or she should examine its suitability to sell each particular asset, review the fees charged by Internet auction providers, and carefully review the terms and conditions for use of a particular Internet auction Web site.

An Internet auction provider usually does not take possession of assets, call auctions, collect proceeds of sale, or in any way act as a liquidator's agent. Instead, most sites merely provide an automated venue for the liquidator to conduct an auction. Because of their limited role in a sale, Internet auction Web site providers should not be considered auctioneers or other professionals requiring an order of employment, unless they specifically contract to perform substantial additional services beyond providing a Web site to market the estate's assets.

The liquidator should consider obtaining guidance from the court regarding the need for court approval of Internet auctioneer employment in doubtful cases. For example, if an Internet auction provider collects deposits or sale proceeds, or takes physical possession of the property to be sold, the provider is rendering substantial additional services and an order should be obtained. Whether or not there is a need for authority to retain the auctioneer as a professional, the liquidator should always fully disclose the terms and conditions of the proposed sale and the respective duties and responsibilities of the Internet auction provider in an appropriate sale motion filed with the court and properly noticed to creditors.

Statutory Foreclosures

Foreclosure of real estate "on the courthouse steps" is a type of auction that is strictly governed by state statute. The automatic stay under the Bankruptcy Code stays or stops any foreclosure of a lien on the debtor's assets. However, in some instances the debtor *is* the lienholder. The liquidator may, in the pursuit of assets, be required to foreclose liens on and take possession of commercial or residential real estate. The liquidator as the creditor normally is the buyer at the foreclosure sale because he or she can credit bid (i.e., bid the amount of the debt rather than pay cash). Thereafter, the liquidator must sell the real estate. This is typically allowed in a private sale in order to maximize value. For example, the authors represented a debtor that owned a mortgage company with a portfolio of other real estate owned (OREO), which was obtained through foreclosure on defaulted mortgages. Liquidating the portfolio of real estate for the best price requires maintenance of the properties prior to sale—landscaping must be maintained; gas, water, and electricity must be functioning, and insurance must be in effect.

Environmental Issues

When appropriate, the liquidator should take the necessary steps to abate or prevent environmental contamination by or to estate property. If property of the estate has no value and may be hazardous to the health or safety of the general public, the trustee should give careful consideration to abandoning that property expeditiously. Before abandoning the property, however, the trustee should take appropriate precautions possible in light of the available assets of the estate and consult with appropriate federal, state, and local authorities. Common sense plays a role here. If the debtor was involved in an environmentally sensitive business, the trustee should make an inquiry as to the extent of the estate's exposure. Consultation is advised to ensure adequate notice and appropriate consideration of public policy issues. A notation of the consultation in the estate file is recommended.

Abandonment of Assets

A trustee should abandon any property that is burdensome or of inconsequential value to the estate, when the total amount to be realized from its sale would not result in a meaningful distribution to creditors or would redound primarily to the benefit of the trustee and professionals. In determining whether property has consequential value to the estate, the trustee should consider a number of issues, such as

- amount, validity, and perfection of purported security interests against such property;
- estimated market value of the property;
- tax considerations; and
- administrative expenses and litigation costs to be borne by the estate, resulting from the recovery and sale of the property.

The trustee should be able to justify the decision to abandon estate property. Any documentation in support of this decision should be kept in the estate file.

Scheduled property that is not administered before the case is closed is deemed abandoned upon entry of the order closing the estate. However, the trustee should not rely on the deemed abandonment provisions when property

Tale from the Bankruptcy Trenches

The Chapter 7 debtor Bank of New England Corporation had a subsidiary, BNE Capital Corporation, which owned subsidiaries. This group of subsidiaries, which we will call the BNE Lease Group, owned real estate leases. A Bank of Tokyo affiliate (BOT) managed and administered the portfolio. While no new leases were being booked, the existing portfolio required management and, in some cases, periodic additional equity payments. The nine leveraged leases that comprised the portfolio included (i) BASF Inmont, a paint facility in Linden, New Jersey; (ii) Fleming Foods, a refrigerated warehouse in Geneva, Alabama; (iii) Garrett Airline Repair, a maintenance facility in Anniston, Alabama; (iv) GECC Park Plaza, an apartment building in St. Louis, Missouri; (v) Hechinger, consisting of thirteen home improvement stores scattered among several states; (vi) Florida National, an office building in Jacksonville, Florida, leased to First Union Bank; (vii) Bank of Baltimore-Bethesda, an office building in Bethesda, Maryland; (viii) Bank of Baltimore-Flagship, an office building in Baltimore, Maryland; and (ix) Federal Mogul, an office building in Southfield, Michigan. Three of these leases presented special issues.

Preserving the Value of the Assets

BNE Realty Leasing Corporation (BNE-RL), a subsidiary of BNE Capital, leased the Park Plaza Apartment Building in St. Louis, Missouri to General Electric Credit Corporation (GECC). When BNEC filed bankruptcy, BNE-RL was in default on a $1,802,631 payment. Once the payment was made, BNE-RL became entitled to a $943,758 rebate. The cure period was scheduled to expire June 30, 1991. The trustee obtained an agreement with GECC that gave BNE-RL a 90-day extension until September 30, 1991, in exchange for an immediate payment of approximately $20,000 (representing interest for the 90-day period).

Cushman and Wakefield was retained to analyze the property and BNE-RL's lease position. The trustee also worked with Winthrop Financial Associates to evaluate BNE-RL's options. The trustee concluded that the value of the lease justified making the payment. Failure to make the payment would result in the forfeiture of BNE-RL's interest in the lease. The trustee applied to the court for permission to make that payment from the proceeds of another asset sale. The court allowed the trustee to make the payment resulting in a net outflow of $858,873 to protect the investment.

As year-end 1991 approached, BOT notified the trustee that staged equity payments of approximately $500,000 on the Hechinger and Florida National leases were due to GECC on March 31, 1992. Similar payments were due every six months thereafter for seven periods. An initial analysis by the trustee supported making the payments totaling $2,323,915.56 to protect the investment.

"Cleaning Up" the Assets for Sale

In connection with prepetition sales of some of the former BNEC Group's Leverage Lease Portfolio, the BNE Lease Group was encumbered by a servicing and remarketing agreement with BOT. This agreement provided for monthly servicing fees of .1125% of the average net book value of each

(continued)

Leverage Lease and, upon the disposition of each Leverage Lease, at the end of the lease term, a payment of 80% of the net disposition proceeds in excess of the book residual value.

After considerable internal discussion and research, the trustee concluded that attempting to sell the leveraged leases with the BOT agreement in place was inadvisable and unworkable. Prospective buyers would be reluctant to bid knowing that they were locked into a partnership with BOT. And yet because the current market values of the properties were well below the level at which the residual sharing with BOT would occur, the trustee doubted that prospective buyers would be willing to pay enough to buy out the remarketing rights. Most potential buyers also wanted to do their own servicing. Accordingly, the trustee concluded that the best course of action was to propose to BOT that the trustee buy them out of the agreement. The trustee also analyzed the alternative of putting the BNE lease entities into bankruptcy and rejecting the leases and BOT Agreement but concluded that the risks of that strategy outweighed the potential gain.

After extensive negotiations, an agreement with BOT was reached. The principal elements were as follows: (i) BOT released the BNE Lease Group from the original BOT agreement; (ii) the trustee paid BOT $1 million at closing and agreed to pay BOT $800,000 out of the first dollars received from the leveraged leases sales; (iii) BOT continued to service the leveraged leases at a reduced fee until the leases were sold or the original expiration date for servicing was reached; and (iv) limited releases for acts under the original BOT agreement were exchanged.

Sales Efforts

The trustee conducted due diligence and gave consideration to packaging the leveraged leases into a vehicle (e.g., a REIT, RELP, or grantor trust) for sale or distribution to creditors. Ultimately, the trustee concluded that the portfolio was too small to justify creating such a vehicle. An outright sale of the leveraged lease portfolio was pursued. The trustee contracted with First Winthrop to market the leveraged leases for a brokerage fee of 5% of net proceeds plus out-of-pocket expenses. Immediately following the approval of First Winthrop's retention, First Winthrop began to market the portfolio, and prepared a sales brochure. The trustee also contacted certain lessees who might have had an interest in purchasing their respective properties. None of these initial efforts resulted in a transaction.

The trustee received several bids for parts of the portfolio and two parties indicated an interest in the entire portfolio, Dana Corporation (Dana) and XXVII Corporation (XXVII Corp.). The trustee received competing bids until both were above $17,000,000. The trustee then asked each bidder to present its highest and final figure. Dana bid $18,050,000 for the *assets,* while XXVII Corp. bid $17,950,000 for the *stock* of BNE Capital. After careful consideration, the trustee selected the Dana bid. Both XXVII Corp. and First Union entered objections to the estate's proposed sale to Dana. XXVII Corp. asserted that its bid was higher (taking into account the different structure and transaction costs). First Union complained that the trustee had not complied with First Union's right of first offer on the Florida National Property. The trustee contended that the tax risk of the XXVII Corp. proposed structure made their offer unattractive. The trustee responded to First Union's objection that he had complied with the first offer provisions and that, alternatively,

(*continued*)

First Union's right applied only to the underlying asset, not to the proposed sale of the partnership that owned the property.

Prior to the hearing, XXVII Corp.'s attorney deposed the trustee and his accountants and finally sought to make a competing bid. XXVII Corp. made an offer to the estate that exceeded the value of Dana's bid. The upset bid, however, did not comply with the court's sale procedure order in three respects. It did not exceed the Dana bid by 5%, it was not proffered within the required time period, and it did not have the required deposit. At the hearing, the trustee advised the court of the XXVII Corp. bid and its deficiencies. The court refused to accept jurisdiction regarding First Union's right of first offer issue but otherwise overruled both objections. In December 1993, the Court entered an order approving the estate's proposed sale but held that it did not have jurisdiction to rule on First Union's right of first offer. Both XXVII Corp. and First Union entered appeals of the bankruptcy court's order. First Union withdrew its objection based upon the trustee's agreement to give First Union 10 days prior notification of the estate's intention to close the Dana sale. Subsequently, XXVII Corp. also withdrew its appeal.

After lengthy negotiations with Dana, the parties ultimately signed an asset purchase agreement. The APA included all the properties in the leveraged lease portfolio, including the Florida property, but provided that the Florida property could be kicked out in the event that First Union offered to match the purchase price that DCCC allocated to the Florida property. Several months later, the trustee closed the sale with DCCC absent the Florida property. The estate received approximately $5,578,997.00 net of

Table 7.1

Purchase price	$18,652,881.30
Less: GECC payoff	3,420,027.71
Closing fees	32,340.04
Title charges	106,757.15
Escrow holdback	911,573.05
Alabama transfer tax	18,950.25
Legal fee	90,955.63
Florida transfer tax	266,242.20
NY tax stamps	13,575.00
NY transfer tax	52,895.94
Relco payoff	75,000.00
BOT fees	824,897.50
Winthrop commission	925,360.54
Net purchase price	$11,914,306.29
Less: Taxes	1,845,117.00
Initial BOT fee	1,000,000.00
Staged equity payments to preserve asset	3,202,788.50
Estimated legal fees	100,000.00
Total proceeds at closing	$5,766,400.79
Plus: Escrow holdback released	911,573.05
Ultimate recovery	$6,677,973.84

Note. GECC = General Electric Credit Corp., BOT = Bank of Tokyo.

(*continued*)

expenses and outstanding indebtedness relating to the leveraged lease portfolio and was relieved of liability from the underlying lease documents. An additional $935,559.00 was placed in escrow pursuant to an escrow agreement. No claims were made by DCCC against the escrowed amount, and the amount was released to the estate in 1996.

In June 1994, the trustee, in accordance with a right of first offer contained in the lease agreement with First Union, offered the Florida property to First Union for the price that DCCC had allocated to the Florida property under the APA. First Union exercised its right of first offer. At the closing of this transaction, the estate received a cash payment to BNEC of $6.75 million and the assumption of all the seller's obligations and liabilities under the transaction documents. Table 7.1 provides a summary of the value ultimately derived from the leveraged lease portfolio.

may expose the estate to some type of liability. Unlike normal circumstances, the trustee should immediately abandon fully secured property or uninsured property of no value to the estate. If, however, the asset's value is likely to appreciate faster than the claim against it, the asset may be retained. Immediate consideration should be given to abandoning property of no value to the estate that may be hazardous to the health or safety of the general public. Such property should be abandoned, if possible, after consultation with appropriate federal, state, and local authorities.

Creditors are entitled to notice of a proposed abandonment. A notice of abandonment should identify each asset to be abandoned by reference to the description provided in the debtor's schedules and any unlisted assets should be clearly described. The notice should also provide information that is needed to demonstrate the basis for the decision to abandon.

Tax Considerations

Deciding how to structure the sale of an asset or how to formulate a liquidating plan should begin with a careful analysis of the debtor's existing tax attributes. The laws concerning bankruptcy taxation are enormously complex and invariably require consultation with a bankruptcy tax expert. But a liquidator needs to have a general understanding of the overall parameters of bankruptcy taxation.

As noted in chapter 6, careful attention must be paid to the debtor's basis in the assets that are to be liquidated. If the debtor's basis in the assets is equal to or above the amount the asset is likely to bring in the liquidation, the estate may not realize any taxable gain from such disposition. By comparison, if the debtor's basis in the assets is extremely low, the estate could realize significant taxable income upon the disposition of the assets. The tax attributes of any operating subsidiaries must also be carefully considered. The operation of the subsidiaries by the liquidator may result in the estate being exposed to liability for taxable income generated by such operations. Moreover, the tax attributes of the subsidiaries may significantly impact the method chosen to dispose of the subsidiaries. A sale of the shares of the subsidiary may have a vastly different result from a sale of its assets.

A debtor whose tax attributes are extremely favorable—such as a debtor with substantial net operating losses, investment tax credit carryovers, capital losses, and/or a high tax basis in its assets—should be used as the liquidating entity in order to preserve the debtor's favorable preconfirmation tax attributes. Courts have held that if the debtor's assets are transferred into a liquidating trust (termed a "grantor trust") pursuant to a plan of reorganization, the debtor's preconfirmation tax attributes remain with the debtor and the resulting creditor's trust is not a taxable entity and therefore operates tax-free. However, this result may not be achieved if a Chapter 11 trustee is used under the plan.

Conclusion

The primary objective of the liquidation is to raise money and pay claimants. One way to obtain monies for distribution is by identifying and deriving value from the estate's assets. Locating the assets may or may not be straightforward. Deriving value from the assets is often a challenge. The estate's assets come in many different forms including liquid and illiquid, wasting and nonwasting, disputed and undisputed, contingent and noncontingent. One of the most important tasks in disposing of assets is to obtain an accurate understanding of their worth. Various approaches are helpful, including replacement cost, discounted cash flow, and comparables. Marketing the assets and negotiating the purchase and sales contract are other important tasks.The BNEC trustee's sale of a subsidiary's leveraged-lease portfolio is particularly illustrative of the complex situations that can arise in a sale. It involved steps to preserve the asset, enhance its value, market the asset, establish a sale procedure with a break-up fee, and deal with a disgruntled bidder and with a holder of a right of first refusal.

8

Pursuing Litigation

In addition to the dispositions of property that realize proceeds for the benefit of creditors, the liquidator's principal means of increasing the funds available to creditors is by bringing litigation as a plaintiff. What litigation opportunities exist and where to pursue them varies from case to case. In almost every liquidating bankruptcy case involving a sizeable debtor, the estate owns preference and fraudulent transfer actions by reason of Chapter 5 of the Bankruptcy Code. Other common types of litigation available to the liquidator include claims for misfeasance of officers and directors, professional malpractice and claims against third parties to collect accounts receivable or other amounts due by reason of contractual relationships with the debtor. Not all litigation disputes seek a monetary award, however. For example, the ownership of an asset may be in dispute as may be the terms of a contract or the validity of a patent or trademark. In such cases the principal relief sought may be a court order (e.g., cease and desist) designed to resolve the dispute. Thus, estimating the value of successful litigation involves estimating the value of the sought after relief.

The liquidator must analyze potential litigation from an economic prospective. A net present value analysis can be a useful tool in this process. If litigation is commenced, the liquidator must periodically reconsider the advisability of the litigation in light of the passage of time and the arrival of new information. Documented analysis should provide a strong safeguard against allegations that the liquidator did not make the decision wisely. Furthermore, although much litigation settles before trial, the liquidator must be prepared to fund litigation properly or earn the reputation of someone who does not have the funds to litigate and settles cheap.

Investigation

A bankruptcy trustee has a fiduciary duty under the Bankruptcy Code to investigate the financial affairs of the debtor, which includes an obligation to investigate potential causes of action and initiate lawsuits on behalf of the estate. In a complex liquidation, numerous matters warrant investigation. The liquidator should seek the fastest, most effective route for determining whether or not a cause of action has positive value. An early assessment of the prospective defendant's ability to pay a judgment is necessary. Careful review of legal theories also is necessary to determine whether or not any potential cause of action is worth pursuing. A preliminary factual investigation normally precedes these two steps. The liquidator should monitor the factual investigation carefully to ensure that the investigation continues only as long as a reasonable prospect of positive return to the estate exists. Litigation is often much like drilling for oil: for every well that comes in as a producer, there are several dry holes. One of the greatest burdens of the liquidator is to identify and, as soon as is possible, abandon a dry hole.

The trustee is given powers under the bankruptcy rules to conduct examinations and compel the production of documentary evidence in order, among other things, to investigate potential causes of action. The effective use of these powers can be critical to the trustee's requirement of avoiding frivolous lawsuits. However, factual investigation is not always done by formal discovery. The investigation typically requires interviews with employees, a review of records, and possibly some forensic accounting. A trustee should also be prepared to deal with the risk of spoliation of evidence by potential targets of litigation.

"Spoliation" is defined as the destruction or the significant and meaningful alteration of a document or instrument. When businesses fail, spoliation is common. When a party knows or reasonably should know that there is a substantial chance of litigation and that certain evidence will be material and relevant to the litigation, the party has a duty to preserve and produce that evidence. Even though intentional destruction of and reckless failure to preserve and produce relevant information can lead to sanctions by the court, officers and directors who view themselves as potential targets of litigation may not be motivated to preserve embarrassing and potentially damaging evidence. The trustee should immediately take all reasonable steps to preserve a debtor's data, particularly electronic data. This can involve maintaining licenses to software so that data can be retrieved.

Statutes of Limitations

As with the evaluation of any potential litigation, the liquidator must determine whether the statute of limitations (i.e., the time period within which he or she can bring the lawsuit) has run. For preferences, fraudulent transfers under federal law, strong-arm causes of action, set-off causes of action, actions to avoid statutory liens and to recover postpetition transfers, the limitations period runs until two years after the appointment of a trustee or such times the case is closed or dismissed, whichever is earlier.

For causes of action that arise outside the Bankruptcy Code, the state or federal statute of limitations relevant to that cause of action is applied with the following exception: The filing of bankruptcy generally tolls the statute of limitations for two years from the petition date. Consider this hypothetical: The debtor has a state law breach of contract claim against Acme, Inc., which arose May 1, 1998. The applicable statute of limitations is four years. The debtor filed bankruptcy on April 20, 2002. Since limitations would not run until May 1, 2002, the liquidator, on behalf of the debtor, had until April 2, 2004, to file suit against Acme, Inc. However, if the debtor filed bankruptcy on May 3, 2003, limitations would have run, and the bankruptcy filing could not revive the cause of action. For the trustee who believes he or she has a statute of limitations problem, all is not lost—in certain instances the discovery rule, the doctrine of adverse domination, and the like allow the trustee to maintain the cause of action notwithstanding the apparent limitations problem. A trustee coming up quickly on the statute of limitations should consider offering to enter into a tolling agreement with the potential defendants.

Discovery Rule

Many states' discovery rules provide that the statute of limitation does not begin to run on a cause of action, until the injured party discovers or by exercise of reasonable diligence and intelligence should have discovered, facts that form the basis of the cause of action. A trustee may rely on the discovery rule to move the expiration of the statute of limitations on a cause of action until after bankruptcy, thus gaining the advantage of the two-year tolling period. The discovery rule can be particularly important to a liquidator outside of bankruptcy who does not benefit from the Bankruptcy Code's tolling period.

Adverse Domination

The adverse domination doctrine may extend the statute of limitations period applicable to a debtor corporation's causes of action against the directors and officers who were in control of the corporation. The doctrine provides that the statute of limitations does not begin to run against a corporation's officers and directors until that corporation has a majority of its directors who are not culpable. Since breach of fiduciary duty claims belong to the corporation, this equitable doctrine can be of benefit to a liquidator.

Tolling Agreements

A tolling agreement is a written agreement between the liquidator and a potential defendant executed prior to the expiration of the applicable statute of limitation in which the defendant agrees to exclude the tolling period from the statute of limitations applicable to the claim. For example, suppose that the statue of limitations on an action expires on March 1, 2005. On February 20, 2005, the liquidator and the potential defendant execute a tolling agreement, whereby the statute of limitations is tolled from February 20, 2005, through September 30, 2005. The liquidator must settle or commence litigation on or before September 30, 2005. Tolling agreements benefit both the liquidator and the potential defendant. The liquidator is not forced to expend estate funds in filing suit before he or she is ready and the potential defendant avoids the negative publicity and costs associated with the lawsuit. When a potential defendant refuses to execute a tolling agreement, a bankruptcy judge often allows the trustee to file a short complaint and then immediately file a motion to stay the case, thus allowing the trustee time for further investigation and potential settlement discussions.

Forum Selection

Use of a centralized forum is one of the cost benefits gained through a liquidation in bankruptcy. Typically, a trustee files most, if not all, of the estate's litigation in the bankruptcy court where the case is pending. Nevertheless, any one of a number of factors may lead the liquidator to choose a forum other than the bankruptcy court for specific litigation. Bankruptcy courts are not set up to conduct jury trials. In cases involving professional malpractice and the like, the trustee, as plaintiff, may view a jury as more receptive to awarding large sums of money to the estate. While a creditor may waive its right to a jury trial by filing a proof of claim in the bankruptcy proceeding, a trustee is not prevented from seeking a jury trial. The trustee may obtain a jury trial by filing suit in state court or in a federal district court (in or out of the district where the bankruptcy is pending), if jurisdiction and venue are otherwise proper. A defendant may seek to have venue transferred, but the court typically defers to the trustee's choice of venue.

Where the debtor has commenced litigation in state court prior to the bankruptcy, procedural rules allow the debtor in many instances to remove the case to federal court, where it is then referred to the bankruptcy court. However, the federal court may choose to abstain and allow the case to proceed in state court where cases have been pending for a long period prior to bankruptcy.

On rare occasions, the liquidator may be forced to arbitrate a claim rather than file suit. When a liquidator is pursuing a claim arising out of a written contract that contains an arbitration provision, courts frequently enforce such provisions and require the trustee to arbitrate.

Avoidance Actions

The trustee has authority to recover for the benefit of the bankruptcy estate certain property transferred from the debtor to a third person before or after the filing of the petition. To accomplish this, the trustee may *avoid* unauthorized, unperfected, or preferential security interest in, or preferential transfers of, property of the estate. This enables the trustee to invalidate transfers that unfairly benefit particular creditors. These strong-arm provisions of the code, vitally important to all creditors, ensure the policy of equality of distribution among creditors of equal standing. Most of the litigation commenced by a bankruptcy or liquidating trustee is avoidance actions under Chapter 5 of the Bankruptcy Code—preferences and fraudulent transfers.

Preferences

The trustee is authorized to avoid certain transfers made within 90 days of bankruptcy that would otherwise benefit one or more creditors at the expense of other creditors. Such transfers are termed "preferences." All of the following elements must be present to avoid a transfer as a preference.

- A transfer,
- of property of the debtor,
- to or for the benefit of a creditor,
- on account of an antecedent debt
- made while the debtor was insolvent,
- occurs within 90 days prior to filing of the petition (or within one year, if the transferee was an insider), and
- prefers the creditor receiving the transfer, by allowing it to receive more than it would have in the bankruptcy proceeding.

A preference may occur if a creditor such as a bank shored up its loan by obtaining a security interest in additional collateral within 90 days of the bankruptcy filing. The bank may lose its security interest as to the additional collateral because the creation and perfection of a contractual lien (e.g., taking and recording a trust deed on real estate or a security interest in personal property) is a transfer. Judicial liens are transfers even though not consensual. A transfer is made for preference purposes on the date it takes effect between the transferor and transferee.

Certain transfers that would otherwise be preferential are not avoidable by a trustee. For example, a trustee may not avoid a transfer to the extent it was *intended* by the parties to be a substantially contemporaneous exchange for new value given by the debtor and was in fact, a substantially contemporaneous exchange. The most important exception to the preference rule shelters ordinary course transactions from preference attack. A trustee may not avoid a transfer that was made (i) in payment of a debt incurred by the debtor in the ordinary course of business or financial affairs of the debtor and transferee, (ii) in the ordinary course of business or financial affairs of the debtor and transferee, and (iii) according to ordinary business terms. Also shielded from preference attack are certain transfers that create a security interest similar to a purchase money security interest. The security interest must secure new value that was given to *enable the debtor to acquire* particular property and was in fact used to acquire such property. Finally, a transfer may be protected from preference attack to the extent the creditor gave *new value* to the debtor after the transfer. Some creditors have floating liens in the debtor's inventory and/or receivables. To the extent such creditors do not improve their net positions in the collateral during the avoidance period, perfected liens on new inventory and/or receivables (and their proceeds) are not avoidable as preferences. Preferences provide a key source of revenue for the liquidator (see appendix 6).

Fraudulent Conveyances

There are two types of fraudulent transfer actions. One requires showing actual intent to commit fraud. The other, referred to as a constructive fraudulent transfer, does not.

Actual Fraud

The trustee may avoid a transfer of the debtor's property (or avoid an obligation incurred by the debtor) made with actual intent to hinder, delay, or defraud an existing or future creditor. A classic example is the culpable corporate director who sells his $1 million Aspen home to his brother for $50,000 prior to his trial. But fraud is often more subtle. Thus courts allow intent to be shown by circumstantial evidence and typically look for what they call "badges" of fraud. These include the following activities and circumstances:

- The transfer or obligation was to an insider.
- The debtor retained possession or control of the property transferred after the transfer.
- The transfer or obligation was not disclosed or was concealed.
- Before the transfer was made or obligation was incurred, the debtor had been sued or threatened with suit.
- The transfer was of substantially all the debtor's assets.
- The debtor absconded.
- The debtor removed or concealed assets.
- The value of the consideration received by the debtor was not reasonably equivalent to the value of the asset transferred or the amount of the obligation incurred.

- The debtor was insolvent or became insolvent shortly after the transfer was made or obligation was incurred.
- The transfer occurred shortly before or shortly after a substantial debt was incurred.
- The debtor transferred the essential assets of the business to a lienor, who transferred the assets to an insider of the debtor.

This list of badges of fraud is not inclusive, and courts can find actual intent to defraud even in the absence of any of the enumerated badges. Likewise, even if traditional badges are present, actual intent may not necessarily be presumed if the debtor has legitimate and independent reasons for the transfer.

Constructive Fraud

The trustee may also avoid a transfer of the debtor's property or an obligation incurred by the debtor if the debtor received less than a reasonably equivalent value or fair consideration in exchange, *and* the debtor

- was or became *insolvent* as a result of the transfer;
- was engaged in business and was left with *unreasonably small capital* after the transfer;
- intended to incur debts after the transfer or believed he or she would incur debts after the transfer, that would be *beyond his or her ability to pay* as they matured.

Reasonably equivalent value is defined as property, or satisfaction or securing of a present or antecedent debt of the debtor. The consideration received from a noncollusive, real-estate mortgage foreclosure sale conducted in conformity with applicable state law conclusively satisfies the reasonably equivalent value requirement, rendering a transfer not voidable.

The Bankruptcy Code allows for the avoidance of a transfer within the one-year period prior to bankruptcy. State uniform fraudulent transfer laws provide for a longer "look back" period, typically four to six years.

The recipient of the transfer may have done nothing illegal or unethical and nevertheless be liable to a trustee for the difference between the value received and the value given to the debtor in exchange. For example, debtor has a piece of equipment with a fair market value of $10,000. The debtor sells the equipment for $5,000 in order to obtain cash to make an interest payment thereby delaying a bankruptcy filing for two months. The buyer thinks he just got a great deal. The trustee can challenge the exchange of a $10,000 asset for $5,000 as not constituting reasonably equivalent value.

Other Causes of Action

The debtor is generally the best source for identifying causes of action other than avoidance actions. Management is usually acutely aware of the wrongs done by third parties. While the debtor may therefore be the primary source for identifying such potential litigation, the liquidator must determine the viability of any such potential litigation through independent investigation.

Many of the same concerns previously discussed with respect to bankruptcy causes of action have equal application to nonbankruptcy causes of action. Statutes of limitations must be identified, evidentiary problems must be addressed, and proper attention must be paid to the economics of the situation. While economics generally govern what litigation should be pursued, occasionally the liquidator takes on the role of defender of the system. To the extent that fraud or other wrongdoing has been perpetrated on the debtor or its estate while the bankruptcy is pending, the liquidator may have no choice but to pursue the matter. Similarly, if any impropriety existed in the administration of the estate prior to confirmation, the liquidator may have to act.

As previously noted, the nonbankruptcy causes of action often relate to actions of the debtor's officers, directors, and prepetition professionals. But they may also include breach of contract actions, patent infringement, and other business torts.

Directors and Officers

Frequently a case is brought against the directors and officers of the defunct company for failure to perform certain of their fiduciary duties properly. The directors of a corporation owe fiduciary duties to the corporation. In addition, the directors of a corporation owe fiduciary duties to its creditors when the corporation enters the zone of insolvency. A trustee is legally entitled to and should enforce all claims on behalf of the estate.

The fiduciary duties owed by directors and officers include loyalty, due care, and good faith. The officers and directors are also expected to avoid corporate waste. In order to assert a cause of action for breach of fiduciary duty, a liquidator must assert facts sufficient to overcome the presumption of the business judgment rule. The business judgment rule is a presumption that, in making a business decision, the directors of a corporation acted on an informed basis, in good faith, and in honest belief that the action taken was in the best interests of the company. The business judgment rule is rebutted when the plaintiff shows facts that any of the following four elements were not present: (i) a business decision, (ii) disinterestedness and independence, (iii) due care, and (iv) good faith.

Breach of Duty of Loyalty

The duty of loyalty requires that the best interest of the corporation and its stakeholders take precedence over any interest of a director, officer, or controlling shareholder not shared by the stakeholders generally. A director is independent when his or her decision is based entirely on the corporate merits of the transaction and is not influenced by personal or extraneous considerations. A breach of the duty of loyalty occurs when an interested director controls or dominates the board as a whole or fails to disclose his interest in a transaction to the board, and reasonable board members would have considered the existence of the material interest a significant fact in deciding whether to approve the transaction. Another situation that gives rise to a breach of the duty of loyalty is the abdication of directorial duty. However, even if a trustee is successful in establishing that one director engaged in self-dealing with respect to a transaction considered by the board, the business judgment rule presumption does not vanish with respect to the other unconflicted directors on the board. Where the liquidator's goal is to invoke director and officer insurance coverage—one culpable director is enough.

Breach of Duty of Due Care

A board is held to have breached the duty of due care when the directors individually and the board collectively failed to inform themselves fully and in a deliberate manner before voting. A director violates the duty of due care when he or she renders a negligent decision or exhibits an unconsidered failure to act in situations in which due attention would arguably have prevented the loss to the corporation. A breach of the duty of due care occurs when the directors fail to exercise appropriate attention to potentially illegal corporate activities. Director liability for such a breach may arise from a board decision that resulted in a loss because the decision was ill advised or from an unconsidered failure of the board to act in circumstances in which due attention would arguably have prevented the loss.

Breach of Duty of Good Faith

Good faith is demonstrated when the board acts in a manner that can be attributed to a rational business purpose. Accordingly, in order to hold directors liable for a breach of duty of good faith there must be no rational business purpose for actions taken by the directors that lead to the loss.

Corporate Waste

A claim for waste arises when the directors authorize a transfer of property of the corporation that is so one-sided that no businessperson of ordinary, sound judgment could conclude that the corporation had received adequate consideration. The transfer must either serve no corporate purpose or be so completely devoid of consideration that such transfer is in effect a gift. The business judgment rule does not apply to the waste cause of action. A board that authorizes a fraudulent transfer may thus become personally liable for the corporation's losses.

Claims against Professionals

The former accountants and lawyers for the liquidating company also have their activities examined for negligence. Causes of action asserted against professionals typically include professional negligence, malpractice, breach of contract, negligent misrepresentation, and breach of fiduciary duty.

Professional Negligence

In order to prevail on a claim for ordinary or professional negligence, a liquidator must prove (i) the professional had a legal duty to conform to a standard of conduct; (ii) a breach of this duty; (iii) a causal connection between the conduct and the resulting injury; and (iv) damage suffered by the debtor. The duty owed by professionals is to use skill, prudence, and diligence such as professionals of ordinary skill and capacity commonly possess and exercise in the performance of the tasks that they undertake. The presumption is that professional services are undertaken in an ordinarily skillful manner must be overcome through the use of expert testimony. Expert testimony typically demonstrates that the professional's conduct was so unreasonable that it constitutes a significant deviation from the profession's standards of care.

Professional Malpractice

A professional malpractice action is essentially a professional negligence action. Malpractice is a dereliction of professional duty, whether intentional, criminal, or merely negligent, by one rendering professional services that result in injury, loss, or damage to the recipient of those services or those entitled to rely on them. Again, the liquidator through expert testimony must prove the failure of one rendering professional services to exercise that degree of skill and learning commonly applied under all the circumstances in the community by the average prudent reputable member of the profession.

Breach of Contract

The elements of a breach of contract claim are the breach (i.e., failure properly to perform services) of a contract (i.e., the underlying engagement letter) and the resultant damages to the debtor. Minimum damages would be the fees paid by the debtor for the professional services. Consequential damages may also be available.

Negligent Misrepresentation

The elements of a negligent misrepresentation claim are (i) the defendant's negligent supply of false information to the debtor, (ii) the debtor's reasonable reliance upon that false information, and (iii) economic injury resulting from such reliance. A lawyer or accountant who negligently supplies inaccurate information to the debtor can be held liable for damage to the debtor resulting from the debtor's use of such information.

Breach of Fiduciary Duty

The elements of a breach of fiduciary duty claim are (i) the existence of a fiduciary duty (ii) breach of that duty and (iii) damages proximately caused by the breach. The existence of a fiduciary relationship includes a confidential relationship, such as that with a company's attorneys and auditors. A relationship is confidential when one party is so situated as to exercise a controlling influence over another or when, from a similar relationship of mutual confidence, the law requires the utmost good faith.

Deepening Insolvency

The deepening insolvency damage model is viable in some states. It requires allegations that the defendants caused an injury to the corporation's property from the fraudulent expansion of the corporation's debt and prolongation of the corporation's life. Even if a corporation is insolvent, its corporate property may have value. The fraudulent and concealed incurrence of debt can damage that value in several ways. For example, to the extent that bankruptcy is not already a certainty, the incurrence of new debt can force an insolvent corporation into bankruptcy, thus inflicting legal and administrative costs on the corporation. When brought on by unwieldy debt, bankruptcy also creates operational limitations, which can hurt a corporation's ability to run its business in a profitable manner. Aside from causing actual bankruptcy, deepening insolvency can undermine a corporation's relationships with its customers, suppliers, and employees. The threat of bankruptcy, brought about through fraudulent debt, can shake the confidence of parties dealing with the corporation, calling into question its ability to perform and consequently damaging the corporation's assets, the value of which often depends on the performance of other parties. In addition, prolonging an insolvent corporation's life by incurring debt that cannot be repaid may cause the dissipation of corporate assets. These harms can be averted and the value within an insolvent corporation salvaged, if the corporation is dissolved in a timely manner. The allegation that a person deepened the insolvency of a company must be coupled with a negligent act that caused it. It is not an independent cause of action. For example, an accounting firm negligently audited a debtor. As a result of the bad audit, the debtor was unaware of its true financial condition and borrowed additional money (i.e., deepened its insolvency), which put the debtor in default of its loan agreement.

Insurance Coverage

The existence or nonexistence of insurance coverage can be a significant factor in the decision to pursue litigation, particularly against former officers, directors, and professionals of the debtor. Such policies, if they exist, must be reviewed to determine the coverage period, notice requirements, and any relevant exclusions.

Coverage Period

For a claim to be covered under a policy, the claim must first be asserted during the period of coverage of that particular policy. Any later claims that are related to a claim already made under a particular policy are deemed part of the earlier claim. A liquidator must ensure that claims are filed on a carrier in a timely manner. This consideration is in addition to the statute of limitations.

Exclusions

One of the most important parts of an insurance policy is the exclusion section (i.e., what it does *not* cover). A common exclusion in a D&O policy is the insured-versus-insured (IVI) clause. IVI clauses are exclusions that preclude directors' and officers' insurance coverage when the dispute is between the corporation and its directors or officers. These exclusionary clauses became prominent after a wave of litigation in the 1980s in which corporations attempted to recoup operational losses by filing claims against D&O policies. Thus, IVI exclusions are commonly thought to serve the purpose of preventing collusive litigation that results in insurance companies being tapped to cover a company's operational losses.

For a reasonably healthy company that is operational, the IVI exclusion makes sense. But what happens when the company runs into financial trouble (or the company is doomed by the misdeeds of its insiders) and enters into some form of formal insolvency proceeding? Is the person responsible for conducting the liquidation of that business an insured under the exclusion, or is that person sufficiently distinct so that any harm done to the company by its directors or officers is covered by the insurance policy? The law is not completely settled, but the emerging rule is that the IVI exclusion applies only when the debtor brings the claim. It does not apply to statutorily appointed bankruptcy trustees, a litigation entity or trust that has been assigned the debtor's claims pursuant to a plan of reorganization, a state or federal receiver, or an assignee for the benefit of creditors.

Another relevant exclusion precludes recovery when the officers and directors received a direct monetary benefit as a result of their alleged wrongful conduct. The fraud exclusion eliminates coverage for embezzlement as well as for preferences or fraudulent transfers received by an officer or director. Skillful attorneys draft a complaint to avoid invoking the fraud exclusion and thereby losing insurance coverage.

Fee Arrangements

Litigation is costly. A liquidator must determine the most economically efficient method of funding the litigation. Negotiations with counsel over fee arrangements can be as important to ultimate creditor recoveries as asset sales. A liquidator can use one of the following four basic legal fee arrangements:

1. *contingency fee*—percentage of what the liquidator recovers
2. *hourly fee*—services rendered by the attorneys and often by their support staff at fixed rates
3. *flat fee*—predetermind amount for services, regardless of the outcome
4. *blended fee*—combines two or more of the above

Liquidators often use contingency fee agreements when the claims are relatively small (under $10,000), because hourly fees could well exceed the amount of an individual claim. A liquidator also may reason that an attorney will work harder if the fee is linked to the amount recovered. These arrangements work well for preference actions. A liquidator with substantial claims may find paying legal fees on a straight hourly basis to be less costly, if the estate has sufficient cash to do so. Sometimes the estate cannot afford to fund the litigation upfront. At other times the estate, while technically capable of paying the litigation costs as they are incurred, may wish to avoid the risk of spending a lot of money on a lawsuit that comes up a dry hole. Under these circumstances, a contingency fee arrangement may be attractive.

Contingency fees are often viewed as outrageous or extreme. While ethical rules prohibit attorneys from charging or collecting an unconscionable fee, attorneys' fees are not unconscionable simply because they exceed what other lawyers in the community might charge for the same type of work. Whether a particular fee agreement is unconscionable is measured by the facts and circumstances existing at the time the agreement is executed, not when the case is won. A fee is unconscionable only if a competent lawyer could not form a reasonable belief that the fee is reasonable. In determining the reasonableness of contingency fee agreements, courts consider the fact that the attorney assumes a greater risk in such cases—that is, if collection efforts are unsuccessful, counsel might receive nothing. Thus, counsel's willingness to gamble on the outcome of the case is thought to merit an extra measure of compensation, when successful. A contingency fee contract that ultimately produces a fee larger than would have been permitted under an hourly rate or flat fee computation is usually upheld unless it is unconscionable. Typically, a one-third percentage of the total recovered is customary and reasonable in a contingency fee agreement. The liquidator should check local rules for guidance in setting contingency fees.

Understanding the appeal of a contingency fee arrangement to the estate and liquidator is not difficult. And yet one should be mindful of the tradeoffs. The largest tradeoff is in the ultimate cost of funding the litigation. A law firm is a business that must keep a careful eye on its bottom line. As a result, such firms only undertake contingency fee projects when they believe that their expected payment is substantially greater than the amount that they would earn on an hourly basis. Law firms typically expect to receive three times as much on a contingency fee basis as they would charge on an hourly basis. Moreover, with a contingency fee arrangement, the law firm usually wants the client to pay the out-of-pocket expenses associated with pursuing the case. They may also want a retainer.

In a flat fee arrangement, the liquidator may, for example, agree to pay a specified flat fee if recovery is obtained without suit and to pay an additional flat fee if a lawsuit is filed. Some flat fee agreements also provide for reversion to an hourly rate or contingent fee, if the debtor files an answer or cross-complaint.

Blended fee arrangements often involve discounted standard hourly rates that are "make whole," if the recovery equals a set amount, and a bonus, if the recovery exceeds that set amount. Consider the following arrangement: The liquidator has $2 million to fund litigation. A litigation fund is established in accordance with a budget for each suit, which includes a fraudulent transfer claim where the amount sought is $40 million, an accounting malpractice claim where the amount sought is $10 million, and 20 preference actions ranging from $6,000 to $145,000. The litigation budget is shown in table 8.1.

Consolidated expenses cover all out-of-pocket expenses for the litigations, including the costs of financial experts and consultants. Combined expert assignments are key to both efficiencies in expenses and consistency in cases. For every dollar of expenses invested over $500,000 the firm recovers two times the amount expended, as a first priority out of any litigation proceeds.

Under this scenario, the law firm agrees to cap its fraudulent transfer hourly fees at $1 million with a 40% discount off normal rates. If settlement or judgment produces a recovery, the firm would recoup its discount. The first half of the 20% discount is recovered out of the first dollars of the settlement or judgment (after recovery of expenses), the second half of the 20% is recovered 50-50 with the estate out of proceeds. The firm commits to fund the case to the end, even if the war chest runs out, in return for a priority recovery. There is also an incentive

Table 8.1

Fraudulent transfer	$1.0 million
Accounting malpractice	$0.5 million
Preferences	$0.0 million
Consolidated expenses	$ .5 million
Total	$2.0 million

component. The firm recovers 3% of the gross recovery from $20–25 million, 2% from $25.01–30 million, and 1% of amounts over $30 million.

The approach to the accounting malpractice case is similar but recognizes a lower amount in controversy. The fee cap is $0.50 million. Contingent fee thresholds would be 10% of the amount recovered from $5–7 million, 15% of the amount recovered from $7–9 million, 20% of amounts recovered over $9 million. Preferences are a straight 30% contingency fee on recoveries.

Such an arrangement could also provide that the fund is replenished with litigation recoveries as needed to insure prosecution and funding of cases. Small recoveries on preference actions could replenish the fund before distributions are paid to creditors.

Economic Assessment

Deciding whether or not to pursue a particular cause of action involves comparing the expected cost of the litigation with the expected result. Both the cost of the litigation and the expected benefit are uncertain in amount and timing. A similar problem appears frequently in the world of finance. The standard approach is a net present value (NPV) analysis. One first forecasts the net (i.e., positive and negative) cash flows going forward and then uses an appropriate discount rate to compute their present value. Those projects having a positive NPV are appropriate for funding, while those having a negative NPV are not. Clearly, this same approach should be applied to the litigation decision. Potential litigation represents an investment-like opportunity for the liquidator. A liquidator attempting to maximize the value of the estate must decide whether or not to invest the sum in litigation with anticipation of receiving a positive return on the sum invested.

To analyze which causes of action to pursue, a liquidator must consider the several basic questions:

1. How likely is the litigation to be financially successful?
2. How much is the litigation expected to cost?
3. How long is the litigation expected to take?
4. What is the probability of actual collection?
5. What discount rate should be applied to the net expected recovery?
6. How do the creditors view the litigation?

All of these questions have uncertain answers. Nonetheless, the liquidator must decide whether or not to proceed.

The Calculation

Consider a lawsuit expected to cost $1 million and to take at least two years to reach a conclusion. How much must the lawsuit be worth in terms of expected gain and likelihood of success to justify the expenditure? Assume the expected result, if successful, is a $5 million damage award. The probability of actual collection is 100%. Such a lawsuit would probably be worth pursuing if the chance of success was evaluated at 50% or better. One could probably justify risking $1 million expended over a two-year period for an expected payoff of $2.5 million (50% of $5 million). Further assume for simplicity that the litigation costs are all incurred at the end of the first year and the damage award, if the litigation is successful, is paid at the end of the second year. We have a projected outflow of $1 million in year one and an expected inflow of $2.5 million in year two. Applying a (very aggressive) 50% discount rate to this project, the present value of the estimated cost of litigation is $667,000 ($1,000,000 × [1/1.5]) and that of its expected recovery is $1,110,000 ($2,000,000 × $[1/1.5]^2$) for an NPV of $443,000 ($1,110,000 – $667,000). At a 30% discount rate, the NPV rises to $711,000. While litigants could differ over the appropriate discount rate for an estate expenditure of this risk level, most creditors who stand to gain from the estate's recovery would probably find it attractive. Even if a 100% discount rate is used, the NPV is a positive $125,000. However, if the probability of success was only 25%, the litigation's expected value might not be high enough to justify the risk. Repeating the analysis using a 50% discount rate yields an NPV of –$109,000, while a 30% discount rate yields –$29,000. Only with discount rates of less than 25% is the NPV positive. Given the risk inherent in such a case, the liquidator may well demand a higher return in order to proceed.

Potential litigation issues are sometimes realized through negotiation and settlement. Indeed, the vast majority of lawsuits eventually result in an out-of-court settlement. Thus, an analysis of litigation selection strategy should not ignore the possibility that the case will eventually settle. Assume in the above example that the case could be settled before incurring any litigation expenses by releasing the claim in exchange for a payment of $1 million. Should the liquidator accept the offer or spend $1 million of the estate's money on litigation with an upside of $5 million gross and $4 million net? If the probability of litigation success is estimated at 50%, the choice is to spend zero on litigation and receive $1 million now or to spend $1 million on litigation for an expected award of $2.5 million ($1.5 million net) received two years hence. Using a 30% discount rate, the present value of $1.5 million award is $711, 000. Clearly, at a 30% discount rate, a potential $1 million settlement dominates an expected NPV of $711,000 for litigation.

Determining the Inputs

Arriving at and quantifying answers to the first four basic questions and determining the appropriate discount rate is the most difficult part of the analysis.

The Probability of Success

Clearly, the most important factor in most decisions of whether or not to litigate is the probability that the contemplated litigation will succeed (i.e., the liquidator will prevail in court). What is the likelihood of success in achieving the estimated value of the litigation? This estimated probability is a subjective judgment; yet, the estimated probability can be approached systematically by separating the issues into components that can be estimated individually. These estimates can then be analyzed and the results combined into a composite forecast. Specifically, the probability of success can be viewed as a function of the plaintiff's and defendant's relative strengths in the following areas: the law, facts, equities, and receptiveness of the forum. An assessment of the relative importance of each of those factors and the litigant's relative strength in each is necessary.

For a case involving a single straightforward claim, estimating the monetary damages to be awarded if the litigation is successful is relatively simple. More complicated cases may involve several distinct claims, each with its own probability of success. The potential value of a successful litigation would vary depending on both the actual damage computation, as well as which claims are considered to be most solid. Those claims that would be viewed as highly speculative, such as punitive damages, would not be part of the calculation.

Some cases may also have secondary financial impacts. For example, winning a preference lawsuit against a defendant not only would result in a recovery for the estate but also in the defendant having a claim against the estate for the antecedent debt that was preferentially repaid. On the other hand, such a win may have the positive financial impact of improving the chances of obtaining a favorable settlement with another preference defendant because, for example, the defendant believes the court is aligned with the liquidator's view that all transfers made after a certain date were not made in the ordinary course. Assessing the financial impact of successful litigation versus unsuccessful litigation may require an analysis of these potential secondary impacts.

One useful approach to estimating the financial impact of litigation success is to begin with the maximum that could be achieved if the debtor prevailed on all of the claims and damages were awarded in the amounts requested. Next, subtract all the damages associated with claims that the liquidator believes he or she will likely be unsuccessful, even if the basic litigation is successful. Then, adjust downward the remaining claims and relief to reflect a realistic assessment of what the court would likely award, if the basic case were successful. In other words, if the litigant asserts a claim with an estimated maximum value of $2.5 million, a more realistic estimate may be some percentage of this sum. Finally, add or subtract the estimated financial impact on the estate of any secondary effects of the litigation.

This approach involves arriving at a single number for the estimated value of a successful litigation effort regardless of how long the case takes. For many cases, however, the base award is increased by prejudgment interest. A more sophisticated analysis would take this relationship into account. However, given the usual uncertainties present in all estimates, considering this additional complexity may not improve the analysis sufficiently to justify the effort. Furthermore, prejudgment interest is often an equitable award by the court and, like punitive damages, may be considered too speculative to include in the analysis.

Litigation Costs

Where estate funds are scarce and/or financing for litigation is difficult to obtain, contingency fees may be the debtor's only option. In this situation, the cost of litigation is simply a function of the contingency fee percentage times the expected award. In a more traditional hourly fee representation (or where a blend is applied), the calculation is more complicated. While a liquidator should request litigation budgets from counsel budgets are more often than not exceeded. A capped fee with a contingent upside is often the best route for the liquidator.

Once a case is filed, it can be resolved at various points thereafter (i) by settlement before any court decision, (ii) by agreed upon arbitration or mediation early in the case, (iii) by summary judgment, (iv) as the result of an unappealed decision from the trial court, (v) after the court rules on one or more appeals, or (vi) after further litigation to enforce collection. In a noncontingent fee arrangement, the liquidator must estimate the cost if the case is resolved at a particular stage and the probability that it will be resolved at that stage. Additionally, for some causes of action a prevailing plaintiff may recover attorney's fees, under state statute.

Time Required to Litigate

How long will the case take before the estate secures a final nonappealable judgment and collects the judgment? The speed at which a judge moves his or her docket is often unique to the judge. A liquidator in bankruptcy has the advantage of knowing in advance which bankruptcy judge has the litigation and thus is better positioned to make these estimates. While bankruptcy courts are generally quicker than federal courts to resolve disputes, an appellate level is added. The probability that the case reference may be withdrawn from the bankruptcy court to the district court must also be assessed. This places the suit before a district court judge whose identity is unknown until after suit is filed. A trial at the district court normally results in a longer trial but eliminates one appellate level. The ability to predict which judge will be assigned to a suit filed in state court is also frequently impossible.

The Probability of Ultimate Collection

Estimating the probability of ultimate collection requires evaluating the existence of insurance coverage for the claims and, if no insurance exists, the potential defendant's ability to pay the projected damage award. The potential defendant's financial ability to conduct meaningful settlement negotiations may also become an important question, if the liquidator intends to attempt to settle the case. The difficulty of this task depends on a number of factors, particularly whether the potential defendant has publicly reported financial information. If not, locating accurate financial information about the potential defendant is key. Once the information is obtained, the liquidator must assess the collectibility of the defined sum. First, the net resources of the potential defendant may be insufficient to pay the award because the potential defendant is insolvent or will be rendered insolvent by the judgment. The liquidator must assess the probability that the judgment would have such a significant impact on the defendant's financial circumstances that the defendant would file bankruptcy. The plaintiff seeking a judgment against a bankrupt defendant would, at best, be likely to be able to collect some percentage of the judgment, probably after experiencing a significant delay and incurring significant additional costs.

Second, the potential defendant, while having net resources in excess of the expected amount of the judgment or settlement, does not have those resources in a sufficiently liquid or accessible form to pay the judgment. For example, a defendant's gross assets could be largely in the form of undeveloped land, art, patents, start-up businesses, or any of a host of other types of holdings that have value but are not easily converted into cash.

Third, the potential defendant may seek to use various methods, legal or otherwise, to avoid payment. Such methods include attempting to transfer ownership or control of assets to third parties, attempting to conceal the existence of assets beneficially owned by the potential defendant, or placing those assets outside of the jurisdiction of the U.S. courts. In many circumstances, these efforts to protect assets from seizure may either succeed outright or discourage the plaintiff from proceeding with collection, due to the time and expense involved in recovering the assets. Estimating the probability of ultimate collection may be best expressed as a raw percentage of the judgment or settlement.

Determining the Appropriate Discount Rate

How creditors view the decision to litigate in large part depends on their perception of how the parameters of the particular proposed litigation would interact with the potential payout under Chapter 7 or the Chapter 11 plan. Some debtors are much better positioned than others to pursue and fund litigation. Thus, a given piece of potential litigation may have a risk-reward ratio that is attractive to the creditors of some debtors but not to others. In general, the more risk averse the creditors, the higher the appropriate threshold rate of return. The liquidator needs to establish what threshold rate of return would make pursuing the case worthwhile. To pursue the cause of action, the debtor must have and expend funds up front, unless a contingency fee arrangement has been made with the attorneys. Damages and other relief, if awarded, are not received until at least some, and in many situations almost all, of the costs associated with funding the case have been expended. To evaluate the overall financial impact of the litigation on the estate, one must choose an appropriate rate for discounting the expected cash flows. To do this, one must take account of the time value of money for the creditors; the riskiness of the project; and the risk tolerance of the liquidator, the United States Trustee, the creditors, the creditors' committee, and the bankruptcy judge.

The selected discount rate should include an appropriate premium to compensate the creditors for undertaking a project with this level of risk. Undertaking the project is likely to delay and, if unsuccessful, ultimately reduce their recovery by the amount spent on litigation. Most litigants are risk averse. As such, creditors only undertake a risky project if they can expect to be appropriately compensated (risk premium) for accepting the inherent risk. That risk premium is based on two factors: the degree of confidence that the liquidator has in the accuracy of the analysis and the probability of success. Potential litigation with a high probability of success and a relatively narrow range of financial outcomes (i.e., cost, awards, timing) would be classified as low risk. High-risk litigation has a very uncertain outcome and potentially negative financial impact on the estate.

Effect of Litigation on Creditors In addition to the risk of the litigation, the liquidator also needs to consider how litigation would affect the liquidation. How easy or difficult to absorb are the risks inherent in pursuing this case? For example, would the estimated cost of litigation reduce the creditor's expected recovery by 50%, but result in the expected financial impact of success that would triple the recovery for creditors? At the other extreme, the debtor may be engaged in many relatively small, separate relatively unrelated cases, each of which is likely to have only a modest affect on the ultimate distribution to creditors. Having many different cases under way tends to have an averaging affect on the distribution. Winning some of the cases tends to offset the adverse effect of losses in others. In this situation, the debtor has a diversified portfolio of causes of action to pursue. As long as only positive NPV projects are selected and the analyses are relatively accurate and unbiased, the net result of undertaking the litigation should be positive. Thus, a relatively low discount rate can be used to compute the NPVs. The one exception to this rule occurs when most or all of the cases turn on the same or similar legal issues. For example, preference litigation may stand or fall on how timing is judged to be ordinary course. Under this circumstance, having many different cases provides little or no diversification benefit. Thus, a high discount rate is usually indicated.

The Final Number The appropriate threshold rate for discounting the expected cash flows of potential litigation varies directly with three factors:(i) the expected dividend to creditors if the litigation is not pursued, (ii) the risk of the litigation itself, and (iii) the liquidator's perception of the creditor's willingness to absorb the risk.

Actual discount rates vary with the circumstances. Most major litigation is relatively unique, and if it is indeed major, its potential impact on the estate is likely to be substantial. Thus, such litigation is likely to be viewed as rather risky. Some idea of the appropriate return objective for projects such as these may be obtained by considering the return objectives of venture capitalists, who supply risk capital to promising start-up businesses. Their target rates of return are typically in the range of 30–35%. The liquidator might reasonably begin the effort to determine an appropriate threshold return objective for risky litigation by establishing a 30% benchmark. This benchmark would then be adjusted up or down, depending on the three factors enumerated above.

What If the NPV Is Negative?

Suppose after a careful analysis of the litigation potential, the liquidator concludes that the project has a negative NPV because the present value of the expected recovery from the case is less than the present value of the expected cost of undertaking the case. What should be done under these circumstances? The liquidator has two options: (i) abandon the cause of action or (ii) initiate the litigation notwithstanding its negative NPV and seek settlement on whatever terms may be available. Under option two, the liquidator must be prepared to abandon the case at some point in the future.

Initiate the Litigation

Without an actual lawsuit on file, the potential defendant typically refuses to discuss settlement. In the example, preparing the complaint is expected to cost a relatively modest $10,000. The liquidator believes that once the lawsuit is filed, the defendant will take the matter more seriously. Negotiations may then begin with an estimated 50% chance of resulting in a $200,000 settlement. If these negotiations fail, the liquidator would spend an estimated additional $300,000 to carry the litigation through the trial stage for a 40% chance of obtaining a

$1 million award. Given the time and risks involved, spending $300,000 for an expected award of $400,000 (subject to present value discounting) appears unattractive. If settlement efforts fail, the case is probably not worth carrying forward.

Under these circumstances, one might well choose to file the lawsuit, hoping that the defendant would then take the matter seriously enough to be willing to negotiate. With the above assumed parameters, the lawsuit would cost $10,000 to file, with an expected recovery of $50,000 (0.5 × $100,000). Thus, taking the case to this level looks like an attractive opportunity. If the attempt to force a settlement by filing a lawsuit succeeds, the liquidator has risked a small sum ($10,000) for a large potential recovery ($200,000). If it fails, the liquidator can abandon the case after an expenditure of $10,000, rather than spend $300,000 for an expected recovery of $400,000.

A similar situation arises if a case has a good chance of being resolved favorably by summary judgment. Suppose the case costs $30,000 to prepare for summary judgment and has a 50% chance of producing a $200,000 judgment. If summary judgment is denied, the case would cost another $100,000 to take to trial, with only a 50% chance of obtaining a $200,000 judgment. Thus, the case seems worth taking to the summary judgment stage but no further. At that stage, one spends $30,000 for an expected payout of $100,000 (0.5 × $200,000). To take the case to trial would, however, cost an estimated $100,000, with an expected subsequent payout of $100,000 (0.5 × $200,000), clearly an unattractive option.

The Abandonment Option

Thus, a cause of action that does not appear to be worth litigating to final judgment may be worth undertaking part way, if that is an option. The ability to abandon a project while it is under way allows one to cut one's losses. Clearly, this concept applies to all litigations and related projects. A liquidator can almost always have an existing lawsuit dismissed with prejudice any time after it is filed, provided the defendant has not asserted counterclaims. A litigant is not prohibited from filing a suit he does not expect to win under current law, as long as suit is warranted by a nonfrivolous argument for the extension, modification, or reversal of existing law or the establishment of new law. A cause of action may not be worth pursuing if one is restricted to considering either to undertake and carry it through to completion or not undertake it at all. If, however, one can chose to undertake the litigation in distinct stages with an option to abandon the litigation at any one of these stages, it may be worth beginning and moving forward at least part way even though, when viewed as a complete project, its NPV appears to be negative.

If the potential litigation evaluated from an all-or-nothing perspective has a negative NPV, one next evaluates strategies that assume the litigation will be abandoned if favorable resolution has not been achieved by a certain stage. One can begin by evaluating a plan to abandon the lawsuit if initial settlement efforts fail. If at that stage the litigation has a positive NPV, filing the suit is indicated. Similarly, if filing the suit and taking it to the summary judgment stage has a positive NPV, then taking it to that stage (assuming no new information is discovered along the way that changes the parameters) is indicated.

Circumstances Change

When litigation that appears to have a negative NPV if carried to the final stage (but having a positive NPV for at least the initial stages) is undertaken, yet another option arises. New information that emerges in the early stages of litigation may tip the balance in favor of continuing beyond the only stage (or stages) that initially looked attractive. Likewise, new information and the passage of time may lead to the conclusion that what had been viewed as a negative NPV case if carried to the trial stage has turned into a positive NPV case beyond the current stage. First, once a case has been carried to a certain stage, the funds expended prior to that stage become a sunk cost. At that point, one should consider only the additional costs of continuing the litigation relative to the potential payoff from success. Second, as time passes, the estimated time to complete the case from the current position has almost certainly shortened as compared to the time initially estimated (e.g., a year into the case is a year closer to going to trial). Thus, whatever payoff the case is expected to have is now discounted by a lesser present value factor. Third, the information learned from pursuing the case to the current stage may well have changed both the level of and the confidence in the estimated parameters. Therefore, a fresh analysis of the project may reveal that continuing the litigation through the trial stage has a positive NPV, even though the initial analysis found otherwise.

The option to abandon a case that initially looked promising, as well as the option to continue a case beyond the stage that was initially contemplated, tends to enhance the value of cases compared to an all or nothing approach. The availability of these options cannot, however, turn a clearly undesirable case into a worthwhile piece of litigation. In a close decision, however, it can tip the balance in favor of initiating the litigation.

Issues of Reputation

In evaluating the parameters of a cause of action that appears to have a negative NPV if carried to the trial stage, one should realize that the defendant could reach the same conclusion about its prospects. Able defendants and their counsel are very likely to realize that certain cases, even if filed, are not likely to be worth what it would cost the plaintiff to go to trial. Such defendants are, therefore, unlikely to be very impressed by such a filing. Thus, filing a case that is clearly a bluff designed to stimulate a more serious settlement posture from the defendant is likely to fail in this objective. Filing a case that is likely to be abandoned by the liquidator if not settled prior to reaching the trial stage is only likely to succeed in achieving a satisfactory settlement if the threat to go forward with the litigation is viewed by the defendant as credible. Indeed, a liquidator who has a reputation for abandoning lawsuits when settlement efforts fail is quite likely to achieve little advantage from such filings. Clearly, the strongest cases to pursue are those that are deemed worthwhile, even if they are litigated to the bitter end.

Managing Ongoing Litigation

The liquidator must closely monitor ongoing litigation, including costs as well as continued economic viability.

Monitoring Professionals

The liquidator must seek and obtain from counsel a candid assessment of the prospects of recovery in each case as it proceeds through discovery toward trial. The liquidator must also monitor fees and expenses. When attorneys are working on an hourly fee basis, the liquidator's duty to monitor their activity is heightened, because each dollar paid to the professionals directly affects creditor recoveries.

Assessing Continued Economic Viability

Once litigation has commenced, the situation changes, but the economic issues the liquidator must consider remain constant. Why does the situation change? First, because of the passage of time; second, because once funds have been expended they become sunk costs (which cannot be unspent); and third, because the ongoing legal process (i.e., discovery, briefs filed, motions ruled upon, initial decisions, etc.) is likely to change and often enhance the accuracy of the estimated inputs to the litigation analysis. The relative strengths of the parties' legal teams may be assessed and included as a factor in determining the probability of success. Also, prospects for settlement may well change over time. Accordingly, the liquidator should revisit his litigation analysis periodically, especially after a significant event (e.g., a ruling on summary judgment motions). As time passes, both sides' incentives to settle may increase, especially as the issues to be litigated are narrowed, each other's court filings are reviewed, and each side increases its understanding of the relative strengths and weaknesses of their respective positions. Thus, as each side acquires a more realistic viewpoint, both may see a meaningful gain from eliminating the delay, cost, and risk of further litigation.

In order to revisit the litigation decision, the liquidator again addresses factors, this time from the perspective of a case that is already under way. Thus, the questions now are:

- What is the current probability of success and the expected financial impact of success?
- How much more is the litigation expected to cost?
- How much longer is the case expected to take?
- What are the possible difficulties of ultimately collecting on the judgment?
- What is the current "temperature" of the creditors?

Once under way, the two sides are likely to have some idea of what they would be willing to offer or accept to resolve the case. As time passes and the issues are narrowed, the two sides' views on settlement are likely to move closer to each other. Quite frequently, the parties meet and discuss settlement several times during the course of the litigation. Indeed, local rules may require such meetings. Accordingly, when the litigation decision is revisited, the liquidator should consider options

- to continue the litigation (and make no further effort to settle);
- to offer to settle on aggressive terms;
- to offer to settle on terms that the other side is likely quickly to accept; or
- to abandon the litigation effort if no settlement is available.

To assess these various options, one would again compute the NPV of the litigation at the stage reached. One might or might not adjust the discount rate, depending on whether changed circumstances suggest a change. Quite possibly, the passage of time and the arrival of new information have reduced the uncertainty of the outcome. Thus, a somewhat lower discount rate may be indicated. Further adjustments may be indicated if the complexion of the bankruptcy has changed and the creditors have become more or less patient.

Once computed, the litigation project's new NPV should be compared with the sum that might be obtained from a settlement. If the NPV of continued litigation exceeds the expected sum available from settlement, continued litigation is indicated. Conversely, if the expected settlement exceeds the NPV of continued litigation, an attempt to settle on the best currently available terms is indicated.

Achieving the best settlement terms from negotiations is a matter of bargaining skills. While that issue is outside the scope of this analysis, one relevant point can be made here. In order to evaluate the strengths and weaknesses of the other side's position, one can also apply NPV analysis to the other side of the case.

When the two sides have similar views on the probabilities of winning and losing, the sum likely to be awarded if the estate wins, and the time frame, the NPV of continued litigation for the estate is almost always less than the

Tale from the Bankruptcy Trenches

On January 6, 1993, the trustee filed an action against BNEC's former auditors, (Defendant), its predecessor partnerships, and its present and former partners. Discovery was stayed, pending resolution of Defendant's motion to dismiss. The trustee filed an amended complaint on October 4, 1994, and formal discovery began. The amended complaint alleged that certain transfers of fees to Defendant were avoidable as preferential and fraudulent transfers under the Bankruptcy Code and that BNEC sustained damage as a result of Defendant's failure to properly audit the financial statements of BNEC and its numerous subsidiaries and its otherwise negligent accounting services to BNEC. Twelve years later, on January 10, 2005, the trustee's professional negligence lawsuit against Defendant went to trial.

The scope of the case was immense, in part because the allegations spanned three years of Defendant's audit work at BNEC, which, at the time, was one of the largest bank holding companies in the United States. Defendant defended the case very aggressively, leaving few, if any, legal issues unlitigated and assembling a large team of attorneys who generated a massive amount of adverse briefing to which the trustee had to respond.

Preparing for and Going to Trial

Documents

There was a large amount of documentary evidence that was relevant to the alleged negligence of Defendant in 1987, 1988, and 1989. BNEC, Defendant, and numerous third parties produced several million pages of documents during discovery. A huge database of documents was created, so documents could be reviewed and key documents selected and indexed. During the course of the litigation, documents were screened and rescreened in order to refine the set of exhibits to a workable number that could be presented to a jury of lay people.

Trial Time Limits

The court imposed strict limits on the amount of hours each side had to present its case, meaning, among other things, that the trustee's counsel Andrews Kurth, LLP (AK) was constantly challenged to pare and refine the trustee's presentation so that it could cover the wide range of issues that needed to be addressed within the time frame that the court had imposed.

Exhibits

Substantial time was spent culling the exhibits to a workable set that emphasized the most persuasive document for a particular issue and eliminated time-consuming redundancy. At the same time, counsel had to consider whether and how a particular document would be admitted into evidence, what kind of testimony or predicate would need to be laid in order to admit the document into evidence, and so on. As a result of these efforts, the trustee prepared, from a possible universe of millions of documents, 587 initial trial exhibits and 244 rebuttal exhibits, filling seven boxes.

As part of the trial presentation, the trustee projected the trial exhibits on a large screen in the courtroom, so that all jurors could see the docu-

(*continued*)

ment simultaneously. This involved a detailed prereview of each document to highlight the relevant sentence or paragraph to bring to the jury's attention.

Deposition

Over the course of years of discovery, the parties took 79 days of fact depositions. Selecting and editing the deposition excerpts was an extraordinarily labor-intensive project. Because the court set strict time limits and because long deposition presentations tend to strain the jury's attention, the lawyers devoted significant energies to streamlining, culling, and refining the trustee's deposition designations. Often, this involved strategic decisions over which topics to abandon in order to save time and avoid jury ennui and which witnesses to use to advance specific issues. In addition, the trustee was required to digest the impact of the deposition designations proffered by Defendant, and, based on the topics broached therein, reassess the universe of depositions to identify testimony to rebut Defendant's designations, followed by the lengthy refining and honing process described above.

Experts

The trustee had ten experts. Defendant had eight experts. Defendant filed motions to attempt to disqualify seven of the trustee's experts, and the trustee filed five similar motions against Defendant's experts. Preparing to argue and defend twelve such motions was itself a very significant undertaking. In addition, the level of importance attached to prevailing was high, because, if successful, Defendant's motions would have substantially challenged the presentation of the trustee's case, which rested very largely on expert testimony. Accordingly, considerable time was spent preparing for the hearing on these critical, detailed and complex motions.

Witness Presentation

A large amount of time was spent to meet with and prepare the witnesses the trustee expected to call at trial. Because the case relied substantially on expert testimony, and because the motions to disqualify experts had identified a large number of issues upon which the trustee's experts would likely be questioned, witness preparation was extremely time consuming and intense. AK met privately with each of the witnesses to prepare their testimony for trial.

Cross-Examination

In addition, the trustee's counsel outlined the anticipated cross-examinations of Defendant's key witnesses. This necessitated careful study of their depositions (from transcripts that not infrequently covered multiple days of testimony) and identification of the key documents the trustee would use to question those witnesses.

Jury Selection

The trustee was required to prepare voir dire questions to submit to the court for use in impaneling the jury. In addition, the trustee created profiles of the kinds of jurors who would tend to receive evidence favorably or unfavorably.

(*continued*)

Visual Aids

The trustee's counsel spent considerable time working with a consulting firm to prepare visual aids. These included things such as summaries of the key issues the trustee anticipated individual witnesses would raise, summaries of the trustee's claims and contentions, and charts and drawings depicting certain key concepts and transactions that the jury needed to understand in order to evaluate the evidence.

Trial

Because of the scope of the case and the demands of witness preparation, the trustee parceled out responsibility for various trial tasks among different attorneys. The trustee had six attorneys in Boston to work on the trial. The trustee was afforded an hour to present his opening statement to the jury. A considerable amount of work and energy had gone into the development of an opening statement that would both explain, in accessible terms, the key concepts the jury needed to understand to evaluate the evidence and present the trustee's case in the most favorable possible light. Defendant had assembled a large team of attorneys who attacked the trustee's case with an almost daily barrage of motions and briefs during trial.

Settlement

A month before trial, the parties met in Washington, D.C., with a third-party mediator. The mediation was unsuccessful but a dialogue continued between the parties. Settlement discussions culminated in the settlement of the case for $84 million at the end of the second week of trial. The trustee spent approximately $11 million in legal fees to achieve that result. Counsel worked at an hourly rate, which ultimately was to the estate's benefit. A standard 30% contingency would have cost the estate $25.2 million, over twice as much as the hourly rate. How was the decision made to settle?

Decision to Settle

Determining the number for which you are willing to settle and thus avoid the risk of an adverse verdict and forego the potential of a large verdict is not an exact science. A major factor in the BNEC trustee's decision to settle involved the looming expiration of the estate's net operating losses. If Defendant appealed a favorable verdict for the trustee, and the trustee did not actually collect the judgment before December 31, 2006, the taxes on the proceeds could have been 35%. By accepting the settlement, the trustee was able to use Net Operating Loss Carryforwards (NOLs) and significantly minimize the estate's tax liability.

Damages

Table 8.2 shows the estate's potential damages recoverable against Defendant.

The trustee was also entitled to mandatory statutory prejudgment interest. Since the events at issue occurred approximately 15 years before a projected verdict date, approximately 180% in interest would be added to the verdict

(*continued*)

Table 8.2

Bond proceeds downstreamed to subsidiary banks	$163,000,000.00
Cost of bond offering	1,997,590.00
Fees paid to auditor for work in 1987, 1988 and 1989	1,384,199.00
Preferential payments in 1990	561,010.00
Total	$166,942,799.00

amount on all claims, except the preferential payments. Interest on this claim would run from January 6, 1991, and would be at the lower federal pre-judgment rate.

Recovery of Fees

The claim for recovery of fees paid to Defendant in 1987, 1988, and 1989 was the simplest to prove, in part because it only required that the trustee show that Defendant was negligent. With interest, the trustee's recovery would have been approximately $3,878,557.20.

Preferential Payments

The claim for recovery of preferential payments was fairly straightforward; the only real issue was whether the payments were made in the ordinary course. However, the payments, totaling $561,010.00, were subject to an offset equal to the distributions made by the estate to unsecured creditors. As of that date, the trustee has distributed approximately $0.26 for every $1.00 of claims, giving Defendant the basis for an offset, reducing the preference claim against Defendant by $145,862.60 to $415,147.00.

Recovery of Downstreamed Bond Proceeds

The trustee's deepening insolvency claim for recovery of proceeds of a BNEC bond offering downstreamed by BNEC to its subsidiary banks in alleged reliance on Defendant's negligence was the trustee's largest and by far most challenging claim. This was in part because, in addition to the negligence question, there were many key issues on which the trustee had to prevail by a preponderance of evidence; a finding for Defendant on any one of those additional issues would have prevented any recovery.

Comparative Negligence

Not only was the trustee required to show negligence, insolvency, and causation, but the court intended to give the jury a comparative negligence instruction, meaning they would be asked to compare the negligence of BNEC (acting through its officers and directors) to the negligence of Defendant and assign a relative percentage to each. If the jury assigned over 50% negligence to BNEC, the estate would receive nothing. Table 8.3 illustrates the trustee's level of recovery based on the comparative negligence of BNEC's management.

The costs incurred by BNEC in connection with the bond offering were subject to the same analysis (see table 8.4).

(continued)

Table 8.3

Recovery on Proceeds Downstreamed	Comparative Negligence of BNEC	Interest (in millions)	Total (in millions)
163.00	0%	293.40	456.40
146.70	10%	264.06	410.76
130.40	20%	234.72	365.12
114.10	30%	205.38	319.48
97.80	40%	176.04	273.84
81.50	50%	146.70	228.20
0.00	51–100%	0.00	0.00

Note. BNEC—Bank of New England Corp.

Table 8.4

Costs	Comparative Negligence of BNEC	Interest	Total
1,997,590	0%	3,595,662	5,593,252
1,797,831	10%	3,236,095	5,033,926
1,598,072	20%	2,876,529	4,474,601
1,398,313	30%	2,516,963	3,915,276
1,198,554	40%	2,157,397	3,355,951
998,795	50%	1,797,831	2,796,626
0	51–100%	0	0

Note. BNEC—Bank of New England Corp.

Recovery Scenarios

A composite total recovery (see table 8.5) assumed full recovery bond proceeds ($456.4 million), fees ($3,878,557.20) and preferential payments ($415,147.00), and favorable jury findings on negligence, insolvency, and causation at various comparative negligence levels.

Alternative recovery scenarios were also possible (see table 8.6).

A recovery in the range of $0.00 to $4,293,704.00 was a more easily achievable outcome than a verdict for the highest possible damage recovery

Table 8.5

Comparative Negligence of BNEC	Total Recovery (in millions)
0%	466.286
10%	419.327
20%	373.889
30%	327.688
40%	281.489
50%	235.290
51–100%	4.293

Note. BNEC—Bank of New England Corp.

(*continued*)

Table 8.6

Jury Finding	Recovery by Trustee
No negligence by Defendant; Defendant prevails on ordinary course defense	$0.00
No negligence by accounting firm; trustee recovers on preferential payments	$415,147.00
Negligence by accounting firm; trustee recovers audit fees but no recovery for trustee on preference claim	$3,878,557.20
Accounting firm found negligent but subsidiary banks not yet insolvent or trustee fails to carry burden on causation; trustee recovers fees and preferential payments	$4,293,704.00

of $466 million, in part because to recover the highest possible sum, the trustee had to win not only the negligence issue, but all of the other key issues, including (as a result of the trial court's announced decision to submit a comparative negligence instruction) obtaining a 0% negligence attribution to BNEC (despite the trustee's prior suit alleging that BNEC's directors and officers *were* negligent). The $235,290,000.00 amount was a more easily achievable outcome than the $466 million maximum figure because it required less strenuous showing.

Expense of Continued Litigation

At the time of the settlement, the majority of legal expenses in connection with prosecuting the action had been incurred, but the trial was anticipated to continue at least another four weeks. Additionally, even if the trustee were successful, the expense of post-trial motions, an appeal, and possible retrial would increase the expense to the estate significantly.

Table 8.7

Recovery	Probability	Weighted Amount
0	10%	0
4,293,704	40%	1,717,481
235,290,000	45%	105,880,500
466,286,000	5%	23,314,300
		130,912,281
	Future fees	−4,000,000
		126,912,281
	Tax effected	× .65
		82,492,982
Actual settlement	84,000,000	
Tax effected using NOLs	× .98	
	$82,320,000	

(continued)

Tale from the Bankruptcy Trenches (*continued*)

The Bottom Line

Assuming the trustee believes there is (i) a 10% chance of a zero verdict, (ii) a 5% chance of a complete home run, (iii) a 40% chance that the jury will award only the audit fees and preferential payments, and (iv) a 45% chance that the jury will award all damages but assign BNEC's directors 50% negligence, a reasonable settlement number could be viewed as shown in table 8.7.

corresponding negative NPV to the defendant. In other words, if both sides estimate the same probability that the defendant will be ordered to pay the estate a certain dollar amount on a certain date, then from the trustee's perspective, the case has an NPV equal to the present value of the expected payment award less the estate's expected additional litigation costs. The defendant, however, faces a negative NPV from the case equal to the present value of the expected payment to the estate, plus the expected cost of continued litigation.

Conclusion

Often a great deal of time and money is required to obtain a substantial settlement or verdict. The BNEC litigation against its prepetition audit firm was no exception. The case was ultimately settled during trial for $84 million. However, multimillion-dollar settlements do not come easily.

9

Claims and Distributions

Dealing with claims, the "other side of the ledger," involves distributing money to those rightfully entitled to it. For cases pending in bankruptcy court, the Bankruptcy Code provides very specific rules concerning who gets what, when, and how. Before a claim is eligible to receive any payment, it must first be allowed. A claim is deemed allowed once it is filed, unless a party with standing in the case objects. To the extent that objections are successfully brought against priority claims, the pro rata payments to unsecured creditors are improved. The liquidator ensures that all legitimate claims are allowed and objects to and disallows all invalid claims. In performing this function, the focus of the liquidator is the maximization of the return to allowed creditors.

Absolute Priority under the Bankruptcy Code

Not all claims are treated equally. The Bankruptcy Code sets some very exact priorities of distribution. In general, secured creditors are paid first up to the fair market value of their collateral, followed by the expenses of administering the estate. Certain employee claims and taxes are paid prior to the general unsecured creditors who in turn are paid prior to holders who filed late claims, and claims for fines and penalties. Contractual subordination among creditor groups is upheld in bankruptcy.

These priorities reflect deliberate decisions by the U.S. Congress to favor certain groups who might withhold their goods and services if their claims were not given special treatment. In a Chapter 7 and, in most instances, a Chapter 11 liquidating plan, the order of payment of unsecured claims is as follows:

1. Costs of administration, including trustee's fees, professional fees, certain postpetition claims, and certain other costs and fees assessed by statute
2. Certain wage, salary, or commission claims
3. Certain claims for contributions to an employee benefit plan
4. Certain claims arising from purchase, lease, or rental deposits
5. Certain governmental claims for income, property, employment, and excise taxes, and for customs duties
6. Certain claims by a federal depository insurance regulatory agency
7. Unsecured claims in which a proof of claim is filed on time or in which a claim is filed late, but the creditor had no notice or actual knowledge of the case
8. Unsecured claims in which a proof of claim is filed late, with notice or actual knowledge of the case
9. Claims for any fine, penalty, or forfeiture; or for multiple, exemplary, or punitive damages to the extent the amounts are not for compensation for actual pecuniary losses
10. Interest on the claims paid above from the date of filing the petition at the legal rate

If all the foregoing are paid in full, any remaining value goes to equity holders of the corporate or partnership debtor, pursuant to the articles of incorporation or state law.

The Role of the Liquidator

No area of a liquidator's job is more vexing than the duty to object to improper or questionable claims and ensure the payment of proper claims. The concern with claims can result in a misconstruction of the role of the liquidator. The liquidator's job is not to minimize claims. Ensuring that creditors participate in the estate only to the extent that they are entitled to do so does not mean that he or she has the duty of reducing claims below the level of their legitimate participation. Effective liquidators avoid having their liquidations become claims litigation free-for-alls. Remember the goal: to get the maximum amount of money in the hands of entitled (and only entitled) creditors as quickly as possible.

Investigation of Claims

Each proof of claim must be read carefully. Often, objections to a given claim are discerned based on the claim as filed. Next, the claim is compared to the records of the debtor being liquidated. In appropriate circumstances, one or more employees of the debtor may be retained to help explore discrepancies in the records. Claims should be reviewed for appropriate documentation, accuracy, and timeliness. Judgments and liens listed in the schedules should be compared to claims that are filed.

Claim Objections

Claim objections have a substantial impact on recovery by every creditor having a valid claim. A dispute involving a secured claim should be addressed promptly if the claim equals or exceeds the value of the collateral in order to avoid expenditures on preservation of the collateral and to enhance unsecured creditor recovery.

The liquidator should review priority claims as early as possible in the liquidation process. The elimination of a defective priority claim provides a significant dollar-for-dollar addition to the pool of funds available for the group of unsecured creditors. Additionally, reserves held against priority claims must be in "100 cent" dollars. Eliminating the need for a large reserve against a defective priority claim results in more money being available for distributions to unsecured creditors.

Objections to unsecured claims should be filed promptly. This practice reduces the need to hold reserves and provides creditors with a more accurate idea of the amount of their recovery sooner.

Not resolving these disputes early is less critical in the rare case in which few unsecured claims are disputed. However, in the normal case where many claims are subject to objection, enough of those objections must be addressed promptly in order to make distributions meaningful. A court order is needed to resolve any claim objections filed by a Chapter 7 trustee.

Claim Objection Procedures

Another step preparatory to the initiation of claim objections is the fixing of procedures for handling claim objections. A bankruptcy court order should be sought establishing that to maintain their claim, the claimant must answer the claim objection. In almost any sizeable case, a claimant should be required to file an answer to a claim objection within a specified time frame. A large number of claimants will fail to answer the claim objection. Why? Frequently, creditors file a claim that they know or should know is false, notwithstanding the criminal penalties for filing a false proof of claim, but once an objection is filed they do not respond, which results in disallowance of the claim. In other situations, the claim might have been paid after it was filed by a third-party guarantor, or the claim was simply filed in error. As a result, requiring an answer to the claim objection can eliminate a substantial number of deficient claims. If the claimant fails to answer the objection, the claim is struck by default.

A claimant who expects a recovery of perhaps as little as 5–10% of the claim and who is asked to spend significant sums and time defending that claim is justifiably unhappy with the claims resolution process. Consistent with his or her fiduciary duty to each individual claimant, the liquidator should be cautious about asserting unfounded objections to claims and should try to resolve most claim objections informally. In a very real way, requiring an answer to claim objections facilitates out-of-court resolution of the objection, since an answer from a claimant provides the liquidator with a contact. The court may appropriately provide for mediation or other settlement procedures regarding claims.

Handling claim objections under a liquidating plan of reorganization is not much different from claim objections in a Chapter 7 case. Problems that arise in connection with discovery and trial involve the liquidator's relative unfamiliarity with the debtor's records, access to those records, and access to witnesses.

Omnibus Objections

Frequently, a group, or omnibus, objection is filed, even if the claims are each quite small. The most frequent reasons for objecting to a claim include: (i) insufficient documentation is provided; (ii) the claim amount is in error; (iii) the claim has been previously paid; (iv) the claim is not owed; (v) the claim is a duplicate of another claim; or (vi) the claim is filed late. Other grounds for objection may be found in the Bankruptcy Code. A second review for new, tardy, and/or amended claims should take place prior to a distribution of money to claimants. Other objectionable claims include contingent claims for indemnification, contribution, or reimbursement, and claims that include past due interest not allowable under the Bankruptcy Code.

Late Filed and Informal Proofs of Claim

The fact that a claim is filed late usually presents a simple objection for the liquidator. In a Chapter 7 case, the deadline or bar date for filing a proof of claim is absolute. In a Chapter 11 case, the standard for determining whether or not a claim may be filed late is excusable neglect. However, many courts consider factors other than excusable neglect, including potential prejudice to other creditors, in determining whether or not to grant a request to file a late proof of claim. In addition, a creditor who files a late proof of claim may not wait indefinitely to ask the court to permit that filing.

An informal proof of claim situation arises when the claimant has failed to file a proof of claim which complies with the official forms but has filed another paper or papers in the case sufficient to put parties on notice of the claim. A variety of filings have been held sufficient to support a finding that an amendable, informal proof of claim has been filed. An informal proof of claim, unless it is amended to comply with the official forms, presumably need not be objected to. Usually, the liquidator of the estate does not become aware of the existence of an informal proof of claim until the claimant first becomes aware that his or her participation in distributions is subject to serious question.

As might be expected, both late filed and informal proofs of claim create huge problems. First, a general fiduciary duty is owed to the claimant who hasn't followed the rules. If the claimant has a legitimate right to participate in the estate's distributions, the liquidator has a duty to ensure that the right is realized. Yet, those claimants who filed proper proofs of claim in a timely fashion benefit from the disallowance of any proofs of claim that were late or informally filed. Thus the liquidator experiences tension between pursuing the interests of one group of creditors versus that of another. The solution is for the liquidator to make certain that the court has before it all the facts and applicable law that may influence its determination as to whether or not to allow the claimant to participate. Court approval should be obtained in order to avoid later complaints from the claimants that followed proper procedures.

Strategy for Reducing or Eliminating Claims

One strategy for reducing or eliminating objectionable claims is to file a counterclaim where justified. For example, a lender-liability claim may be filed against a lender who (with questionable justification) withdrew credit availability shortly before the bankruptcy filing, thereby exacerbating the estate's financial distress. Similarly, a senior employee whose poor and/or conflicted management decisions contributed to the firm's distress may be vulnerable to a counterclaim. The firm's prepetition accounting firm and perhaps other professionals may be vulnerable to claims that an inadequate audit or other work contributed to or exacerbated the distress. The existence of counterclaims or the possibility of seeking equitable subordination may provide the estate with leverage to negotiate a reduction in the amount of or even the elimination of many disputed claims (see chapter 8).

Secured Claims

A secured claim is secured by either a consensual lien or a statutory lien. To be a secured claim the creditor must have appropriate documentation and proof of perfection. For example, a consensual lien on inventory requires a security agreement and Uniform Commercial Code–1 (UCC-1) financing statement filed for record. The trustee should verify that the lien was perfected at least 90 days prior to the bankruptcy filing (one year for insiders). The trustee may be able to avoid a lien perfected within 90 days (or one year) as a preference. Note that a secured creditor is not required to file a proof of claim. Therefore, prior to selling estate assets, the trustee ordinarily performs a lien search on the asset to be sold in order to verify that all liens have been identified.

From the standpoint of evaluating a secured claim, the most important issue (as it is in many areas of bankruptcy) is the value of the property securing the lien. The secured creditor is secured only to the extent of the fair market value of the property. A claim is unsecured to the extent that the value of the creditor's collateral is less than the amount of the claim. The creditor may collect interest on its secured claim to the extent set forth in the agreement between the creditor and the debtor, but only to the extent that the value of the creditor's collateral is greater than the amount owed to the creditor. As everyone is aware, valuation can be a very subjective matter. The U.S. Supreme Court has discussed the issue of valuation and stated that value is determined "in light of the purpose of the valuation and of the proposed disposition or use of such property." To many bankruptcy courts, this means that replacement value or its equivalent is the proper standard for valuing property.

With respect to a secured claim, the estate can recover from a secured creditor's collateral the reasonable and necessary costs associated with preserving or disposing of the collateral if those costs demonstrably benefited the secured creditor.

Tax Claims

Tax claims are filed by federal, state, and local taxing authorities. In most instances, a taxing entity files only one claim, which may include secured claims secured by tax liens as well as priority and general unsecured claims for taxes. The validity of all tax claims should be verified. In some instances, the liens may be subordinated to other classes of claims.

Employee Claims

The Bankruptcy Code caps an employee's priority claim for past due wages, salary, commissions, vacation pay, severance, and sick leave to $10,000. The amount over $10,000 is a general unsecured claim. Limitations also apply to breach of employment contract claims. The Bankruptcy Code limits the allowed claim of employees for damages arising out of breach of employment contracts to one year's compensation. Distributions made to employees with respect to wage related claims must be made net of applicable withholding tax (appendix 13). The liquidator may retain a service to facilitate employee distributions

General Unsecured Claims

Any claim not secured or otherwise entitled to priority status is considered a general unsecured claim. As previously noted, this category can include some tax claims and employee claims. It can also include claims of landlords, vendors, tort claimants, and other third parties. Each should be viewed by the liquidator with a healthy decree of skepticism. Distribution to vendors also triggers tax reporting obligations (see appendix 13).

Claims of Insiders

Claims of insiders are subject to intense scrutiny. The court determines the validity and amounts of claims of insiders for services rendered to the debtor. Such claims are disallowed to the extent that the amount of the claim exceeds the reasonable value of such services. They are also subject to equitable subordination.

Commercial Lease Rejection Claims

The filing of a bankruptcy petition affects the landlord-tenant relationship in many ways, notwithstanding the terms and conditions of the lease between the parties or other applicable law. This bankruptcy effect is particularly noticeable for a landlord that files a claim for damages resulting from a bankrupt tenant's rejection of its lease. The landlord may be surprised to discover that its damage claim arising from the rejection is ordinarily a prepetition general unsecured claim, not a postpetition administrative claim, even though the tenant's rejection occurred after the filing of the bankruptcy petition. The landlord may be even more surprised, and disappointed, to learn that the Bankruptcy Code places an arbitrary limit to the amount of its claim.

The Bankruptcy Code provision limiting the damages allowable to a landlord of a debtor for lease rejection is designed to compensate the landlord for his or her loss while not permitting a claim so large (based on a long-term lease) as to dominate the claims of other general unsecured creditors. The damages that a landlord may assert against a debtor can have three components (i) unpaid prepetition rent, (ii) rent for postpetition use of the property, and (iii) lease rejection damages. The Bankruptcy Code does *not* limit administrative expense claims for a debtor's postpetition use of the leased premises to which the landlord is otherwise entitled. A formula set out in the Bankruptcy Code must be applied in order to determine the damages suffered as a result of the lease rejection. Unpaid rent due and owing as of the earlier date of rejection or surrender of the premises is added to this amount in order to arrive at the final allowable amount.

Tort Claims

Tort lawsuits filed against the debtor prior to bankruptcy are stayed by the automatic stay. The tort claimant is then forced to either (i) seek to have the stay lifted (which is hard to do) and proceed with the litigation or (ii) file a proof of claim and either mediate or have a mini-trial conducted in the bankruptcy court on the claim. Tort claims are fact intensive. Facts necessary to try a tort claim are not ordinarily based on documentary evidence and the problem of access to eyewitnesses can be acute. As a result, in recent years an alternative dispute resolution (ADR) procedure has been commonly used. ADR procedures for tort claims let the parties confront each other outside of court and usually shorten the process.

The ADR procedures usually involve (i) requiring the claimant to furnish any added information as the procedures may require; (ii) setting a period during which both sides exchange settlement offers (most claims are settled during this phase); (iii) a provision for mandatory, nonbinding mediation; and (iv) a provision for arbitration before the matter goes to a court. The procedure may provide for sharing various costs, including the fees of adjusters as well as those of mediation and arbitration services representing y both sides.

The estate's insurance carriers are also likely to play a role in designing the ADR procedures. Absolutely nothing should be done that adversely affects insurance coverage. Prudence dictates consulting with any of the estate's carriers at every step in order to avoid a denial of coverage for violation of any policy provision.

Environmental Claims

During the past two decades, environmental claims have become a prominent issue in many bankruptcy cases. Debtors subject to substantial environmental claims are disadvantaged by the conflict between the Comprehensive Environmental Response Compensation and Liability Act (CERCLA) and the Bankruptcy Code governing the discharge of environmental claims arising prior to the bankruptcy filing. This set of circumstances requires a court to determine the nature of the environmental obligation and the time that it arose.

Reclamation Claims

A reclamation claim is essentially a procedure that allows the claimant/creditor to reclaim property it sold to the debtor for which it was not paid. The seller must comply with the UCC requirements for reclamation. Additionally, to reclaim property from a debtor in bankruptcy, the creditor/seller must also make a written demand for the goods. These claims arise in the early days of a case and are subject to strict time limits set forth in the Bankruptcy Code.

Subordination of Claims

The bankruptcy court can subordinate certain claims to other claims for purposes of distribution. Subordination agreements can be enforced to the extent that they are enforceable under nonbankruptcy law. Claims arising from rescission of a purchase or a sale of stock, or the purchase or sale of stock, are subordinated to all claims or interests that are senior or equal to the claim or interest represented by such security. Subordination of a claim under principles of equitable subordination is also a possibility.

Contractual Subordination

The concept of contractual subordination is expressly recognized in the Bankruptcy Code and contractual subordination arrangements are honored in bankruptcy cases. Accordingly, one class of creditors (junior creditors) may agree by contract (subordinated indenture) that distributions otherwise payable to them will instead be turned over to the beneficiaries of the contract (the senior debt), until these senior creditors have been paid in full.

Contractual subordination generally arises in situations involving the public debt of the debtor. In light of the numerous other contractual rights that are subject to avoidance in the bankruptcy court, this recognition is notable. This type of treatment is also essential for subordination to be meaningful. If subordination provisions were avoidable in bankruptcies, they would not accomplish the task for which they were devised, namely, to allow a debtor access to additional capital while affording superior protection to those existing creditors who demand it. Most of the publicly traded investment opportunities in debtors with high-yield obligations have outstanding multiple layers of publicly held indebtedness. These obligations frequently contain provisions subordinating certain of those obligations to others under a variety of circumstances. Thus, one is likely to encounter terms like "senior subordinated" and "junior subordinated debentures" to reflect the various degrees of contractual subordination. (Appendix 8 calculates the impact of subordination.)

Equitable Subordination

The Bankruptcy Code also recognizes but does not spell out the ability of the bankruptcy judge to subordinate claims based on equitable considerations. Equitable subordination is generally applied to a creditor who has committed fraud or other inequitable conduct that has given that creditor an unfair advantage over other creditors. A three-prong test is typically employed by the bankruptcy court to determine whether a claim should be equitably subordinated: (i) the claimant must have engaged in some type of equitable misconduct; (ii) the misconduct resulted in injury to the creditors of the bankrupt or conferred an unfair advantage on the claimant; and (iii) equitable subordination of the claim must not be inconsistent with the provisions of the Bankruptcy Code. The claim of an insider or some other party owing a fiduciary duty to the debtor is much easier to subordinate. Claim(s) are subordinated only to the extent necessary to offset the harm that the debtor and its creditors suffered as a consequence of the inequitable misconduct.

Distribution Mechanics

A number of questions arise in connection with distributions. How often should they occur? Should a threshold size for distributions be established? To the extent that a creditor holds a disputed claim, should the creditor receive interest on distributions withheld, pending allowance of the claim? What should be done with unclaimed distribution funds?

Timing

The easy answer to the question of how often distributions should occur is that they should occur as often as makes sense. What makes sense? Well, for the Chapter 7 trustee distributions are left to his or her business judgment. Typically, distributions are made at the end of a Chapter 7 case; however, limited circumstances sometimes support one or more interim distributions to creditors. Interim distributions should occur only after most claims are resolved and sufficient assets have been reserved to administer the estate. The United States Trustee must review and approve the trustee's proposed interim distribution of funds.

Distributions under a liquidating plan are made in accordance with the terms of the plan. Often the plan provides for interim distributions if cash on hand exceeds a specified threshold dollar amount. Alternatively, interim distributions may be left to the discretion of the liquidator after a reserve for anticipated future expenses has been established. The Chapter 11 creditors may not wish to give this much latitude to their liquidator. To require a distribution on a specific schedule generally does not make sense.

Reserved Funds

How much should be held back from distributions? The amount to be reserved must cover 100% of asserted priority claims, potential tax liabilities, and an amount to cover the anticipated costs of operation. In addition, a sufficient amount must be reserved in the estate to ensure that dividends equal to those being paid to valid claimants can be paid to the holders of disputed claims, if each of those claims is resolved. A separate litigation reserve is required if the estate includes substantial causes of action that will be litigated; the object of setting up the reserve is to avoid having to settle valuable causes of action for less than what is appropriate because the estate cannot fund the cost of the litigation.

In setting up a reserve, the liquidator must consider future proceeds to be gleaned through liquidation of remaining property, the likelihood of success in pending litigation, and the likely amount in which disputed claims will ultimately be allowed. To facilitate the process, the liquidator may need to seek estimation of disputed claims in court. It is better to err on the side of caution. The proceeds of the interim distribution are either disbursed to holders of

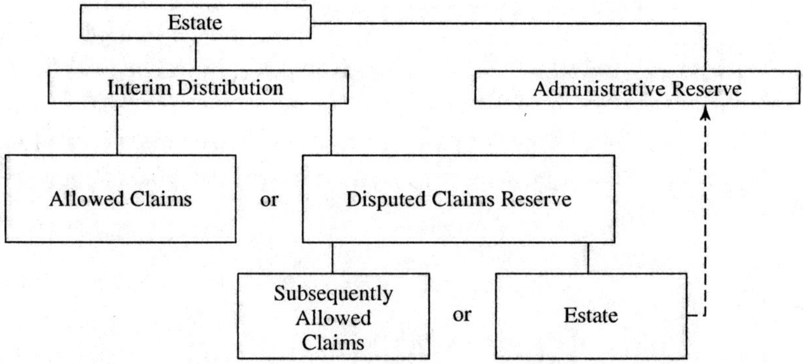

allowed claims or deposited into a disputed claims reserve (see figure 9.1). Creditors whose claims have not been resolved as of the date of the interim distribution have an opportunity to participate fully in the interim distribution, should their claims subsequently be allowed.

Payment Procedure

A Chapter 7 trustee must submit all proposed distributions of funds to the United States Trustee for approval. Court orders are necessary for interim distributions but are not necessary for the final distribution of funds to creditors, if no objections have been filed to the trustee's final report. The final distribution to creditors must be paid within 30 days of the entry of the final orders on compensation and expenses. Payment of the trustee's final compensation and expenses cannot be made until the final dividends are paid to creditors. Checks should be mailed to the addresses furnished by the creditors on their proofs of claim or on any subsequent change of address information reflected in the court records.

All dividends of less than $5 must be turned over to the clerk of the bankruptcy court. The trustee must furnish the name of the creditor, the creditor's last known address, and the amount of the dividend to the clerk. If more than one such dividend is due, only one check made payable to the clerk is necessary. The appropriate claim numbers should be listed on an accompanying report.

Unclaimed Funds

If any checks are not negotiated by creditors within 90 days, a Chapter 7 trustee must issue a stop payment request on the checks. (The exact method for stopping payment depends on the procedures established with the trustee's bank). In addition, the trustee must make a good faith effort to locate creditors who do not cash their checks within 90 days or whose checks are returned as undeliverable. If efforts to locate the creditor fail, the amounts represented by the checks are treated as unclaimed dividends and deposited with the clerk of the bankruptcy court with a transmittal document indicating the last known address of the creditor. When a creditor returns funds to the trustee because the creditor has been paid from another source, the trustee should redistribute the funds to other creditors.

Absent contrary provisions, unclaimed funds under a plan of reorganization go back to the debtor, or the party who acquired the debtor or its assets under the plan of reorganization. However, liquidating plans should be drafted to ensure that unclaimed funds are recycled for distribution to the creditors who can be found. For example, when most of the property of the debtor is acquired by a third party, the plan of reorganization should make clear that the estate that pays creditors is the entity to receive unclaimed funds.

Claims Registers

The court prepares a claims register of all proofs of claim filed in a particular case. Each claim is given a number. There is an active claims trading business in the United States. Investors often monitor cases and, based on their analysis of ultimate payout, seek to purchase claims in a particular case. The burden is on the purchaser and claimant properly to notify the court and liquidator when a claim has traded hands so that distributions can be properly made.

Record Dates

The record date is the date on which the liquidator looks at the claims register to determine which of the claimants are entitled to participate in the distribution. In a case involving publicly traded debt, a record date may also be set by the indenture trustee. On this date, the indenture trustee looks at its records to see who owns the bonds as of that date. A bondholder must be listed as a holder of record (i.e., the registered owner of a security) to insure the right of a payout.

Substantive Consolidation

Substantive consolidation is an equitable remedy whereby the assets and liabilities of two or more entities are pooled, and the pooled assets are aggregated and used to satisfy the claims of creditors of all the consolidated entities. Substantive consolidation eliminates intercompany claims and issues concerning ownership of assets among the consolidated entities. It also eliminates guaranty claims against a consolidated entity that guaranteed the obligations of another consolidated entity. The sole purpose of substantive consolidation is to ensure the equitable treatment of all creditors. Where a bankruptcy trustee is liquidating multiple entities in a corporate family, substantive consolidation simplifies the claims process and the accounting for liquidation proceeds. A Chapter 11 liquidating plan that provides for substantive consolidation likewise makes the liquidating trustee's job much easier. Receivers and assignees can each reach a similar result under state alter-ego laws.

Bankruptcy courts apply a two-prong test for substantive consolidation. Did creditors deal with the entities as a single economic unit and not rely on their separate identity in extending credit such that consolidation is fair from the vantage point of creditor expectations, taking into account any prejudice to particular creditors resulting from the consolidation? Alternatively, are the assets and liabilities of the entities in question sufficiently entangled such that the process of untangling them would be so time consuming and costly that it is not in the interest of the creditors to complete that process? Whether substantive consolidation is appropriate in a case is fact intensive, requiring an understanding of the relationships and transactions among the entities and each entity's statements to and transactions with creditors.

The liquidator in the position of determining whether substantive consolidation should be recommended should make the following inquiries:

- Was each of the debtors able to prepare and file separate schedules listing their prepetition assets and liabilities?
- Were separate books and records maintained for each of the debtors' prepetition?
- Were consolidated federal and state tax returns filed prepetition?
- Did each of the debtors observe corporate formalities, prepetition, including conducting periodic board meetings and annual shareholder meetings?
- Were the meetings by written consent rather than in person and did they involve debate and discussion?
- Did substantial overlap exist as to the officers and directors of each debtor and the officers and directors of other debtors?
- Did all of the debtors directly or indirectly participate in a centralized cash management system?
- Did the debtors receive direct or indirect credit support through intercompany loans (whether directly to the debtor or indirectly to the debtor through the debtor's parent[s]), guaranties, indemnities, or other means of support?
- Did the debtors disseminate financial information to creditors or potential creditors or otherwise make available such information other than the consolidated financial statements of the parent and its subsidiaries?
- Did the debtors have separate credit ratings by the major domestic rating agencies?
- Did the parent absorb substantial overhead costs for the subsidiary debtors?
- Did all of the debtors utilize centralized services for risk management, insurance procurement, legal services, benefits, and similar services?
- Did accounting policies permit noncash settlements of intercompany obligations by transferring intercompany receivables? For example, Sub

Tale from the Bankruptcy Trenches

BNEC was the parent corporation of an affiliated group of corporations which filed consolidated federal income tax returns and combined income and/or excise returns in various states prior to seizure. In 1989, the BNEC Consolidated Group recognized net operating losses for federal income tax purposes, which could be carried back to previous years allowing for a tax refund. In July 1990, BNEC through its existing management filed Form 1139, Corporation Application for Tentative Refund under a request for expedited processing due to hardship conditions which enabled it to receive a refund on an expedited basis for the carryback to prior tax years of its 1989 losses (the 1989 carryback return). "Quickie" refunds are frequently sought by troubled companies. The local office of the IRS authorized payment, and in August 1990 BNEC received a federal tax refund totaling approximately $85,000,000 (the 1989 carryback refund).

Because the size of the 1989 carryback refund exceeded $1 million, the Congressional Joint Committee on Taxation was required to review and approve the refund. During the summer and early fall of 1990, IRS agents from local IRS offices examined the 1989 BNEC consolidated U.S. federal income tax return and the associated 1989 carryback return. Upon completion, the local IRS agents sent a report to the joint committee reviewer in New York City with a recommendation to approve the refund.

The IRS has three years following its receipt of a return to assess tax for that return year. Based on a presumed filing date of July 1990, the statute of limitations for the 1989 tax year would have expired in July 1993. In May 1991, four months after BNEC filed bankruptcy, the trustee was first requested to execute Form 872—Consent to Extend the Time to Assess Tax (the consents)—to extend the statute of limitations to December 31, 1992, for the tax years 1985, 1986, 1987, and 1988. At that time, the IRS advised the trustee that execution of the consents would allow for favorable resolution of the items under examination and the trustee executed these consents. The bar date for filing proofs of claim against BNEC was in June 1991, and the IRS filed a contingent claim pending resolution of the refund issue.

In October 1992, the trustee was again requested to execute consents extending the assessment period to March 31, 1994, for the tax years 1985, 1986, 1987, 1988, and 1989. At the time of the request, the IRS office in Boston advised the trustee that any assessment with respect to the 1989 refund was unlikely, and the trustee executed these consents.

Subsequently, the joint committee reviewer disagreed with the IRS. The case was then sent back to the IRS to compute the amount of the 1989 carryback refund based on the joint committee's review. In October 1993, the trustee was notified by the IRS case manager that, according to IRS recalculations, BNEC had been over-refunded $14,154,710. (This amount did not include interest which had accrued since the time the 1989 refund was paid.)

The IRS advised the trustee that if the new consents extending the assessment deadline to March 31, 1995 were not executed, the IRS case manager would (i) no longer entertain the trustee's arguments as to the merits of the 1989 carryback refund, (ii) not allow the trustee to review their calculations of the refund claim, (iii) be unable to consider the impact of years after 1989 on the amount of refund correctly due the BNEC Consolidated

(*continued*)

Group, (iv) determine the entire amount of the refund to have been given in error, and (v) turn the matter over to the IRS' collection branch. Once turned over to the collection branch, the amount of refund determined to have been given in error would be treated by the IRS as a debt owed by the debtor's estate, and the trustee's avenues to argue the case on the merits at the procedural level of the IRS without requiring court action would be foreclosed. All BNEC's subsidiaries, which were part of the consolidated group and were not in bankruptcy (and thus not protected by the automatic stay), would be at risk. Their assets, including their bank accounts, would be subject to seizure. The trustee executed new consents.

In June 1994, representatives of the trustee's accounting firm met with the IRS to review factual discrepancies with regard to the 1989 carryback claim. In June 1994, the IRS issued to the trustee notices of proposed adjustments reflecting the IRS' position that BNEC had been over-refunded approximately $9.2 million out of the original 1989 refund. In September 1994 BNEC filed a written protest to the proposed adjustments. Following lengthy negotiations the trustee reached a settlement with the IRS pursuant to which a deficiency of $6,262,252 (including interest), with respect to BNEC's prepetition tax years was accepted. The settlement funded in June 1995.

A had a $1 million receivable from Sub B., Sub A exchanged its receivable from Sub B for a $1 million receivable from the parent, and Sub B exchanged its payable to Sub A for a $1 million payable to the parent. Sub B then had no liability to Sub A (and Sub A no receivable from Sub B); Sub B had a $1 million payable to the parent, and parent had a $1 million payable to Sub A.

Answering these questions requires a review of the debtors' books and records, public filings, key contracts, and other documents. In addition, interviews of current and former employees and evaluation of the relationships between certain of the debtors and their largest creditors is necessary.

Substantive consolidation is an equitable doctrine that is not easily quantifiable. No single factor is dispositive as to whether substantive consolidation is appropriate in a given circumstance. Such an assessment is inherently subjective and the relevance of the underlying data may be subject to differing interpretations (see the Friede case study in chapter 4).

Conclusion

The final step in a liquidation is the distribution of the proceeds derived from the liquidation to the claimants. That process, however, occurs only in the context of identifying which claims to allow and at what level of priority. How much is to be distributed to each creditors class depends not only on the total size of the pot (the numerator) but also on the size of the claims (the denominator). Priority claims require very close attention because they must be paid off the top. Many tax claims are priority claims and the IRS is a frequent visitor to bankruptcy courts. In the BNEC case, resolution of the IRS claim took approximately four years and countless hours of the trustee's and his professionals' time. This is not uncommon, and in the end, it was worth it. Through persistence and preparation, the trustee reduced the original $14 million claim by more than half.

10

Receiverships and Assignments for the Benefits of Creditors

For many years, state-court equity receiverships were quite common, but as business practices became more national, they fell out of favor because the orders of the state court supervising the receivership could not be enforced beyond the state's borders. Occasionally, a business is small and local enough for a state-court receivership to work. Assignments for the benefit of creditors are even more limited, as they are conducted out of court. Federal equity receiverships are available to government agencies that seek liquidation of companies violating federal laws. State receivers, federal equity receivers, and assignees are all liquidators. (See appendix 11 for state statutes governing receiverships and assignments for the benefit of creditors.)

State Court Receiverships

Receiverships are governed by state law. Usually, a receiver is appointed when a corporation has been dissolved, is insolvent or in danger of becoming insolvent, or has forfeited its corporate rights. In most states, the corporation is not allowed to petition the court for a receiver. Usually, one or more stockholders, a creditor, or other party with interest in the corporation files the petition.

The Receiver

The receiver is a neutral person who must act for the benefit of the receivership estate, not on behalf of any particular creditor. Persons eligible for the appointment are defined by state statute. In many states, the receiver must be a citizen and qualified voter in the state at the time of appointment. Some states also allow business entities to act as receivers. A party, attorney, or other person interested in the action may not be appointed. A creditor or stockholder may recommend an individual for that position; however, the judge is not required to accept the recommendation. If grounds exist for terminating the appointment of the original receiver and appointing a new receiver before conclusion of the case, the appointing court may do so.

The Receiver's Duties and Powers

The administration of a receivership is governed by state statute, case law, and court order. A detailed order should be prepared appointing the receiver, specifying the receivership property, giving the receiver precise instructions and powers, and fixing the amount of the receiver's bond. The order is the most important initial document, and if well drafted, can eliminate many potential problems.

At the outset, the receiver must swear an oath to perform his or her duties faithfully and post bond in an amount fixed by the court. The bond ensures that the receiver will obey the court's orders and faithfully discharge his or her duties.

The order should fully specify the receiver's powers. To carry out the assigned tasks, the order should allow the receiver to (i) take and keep possession of specified property, (ii) make transfers, (iii) receive rents, (iv) collect and compromise demands, and (v) bring and defend actions. The order should be carefully tailored to cover these circumstances so that the receiver knows how to deal with likely contingencies without returning to court for further instructions. For example, the receiver may be specifically authorized to make payments on encumbrances and liens in the order of their priority, pay taxes, pay for necessary repairs to the property, obtain insurance, collect or if necessary sue on receivables for rents and so on. The receiver is obliged to perform the tasks specified in the appointment order but no more without obtaining instructions from the court. If the powers and duties are vaguely formulated in the order of appointment or do not cover a point in issue, the receiver may ask the court for further instructions.

Dealing with the Assets

The receiver must take possession and file a detailed inventory of the property as soon as possible after appointment. Supplemental inventories of subsequently obtained property must also be promptly filed. Property in the possession of a receiver may not be taken from the receiver by judicial process, unless specifically authorized by the court in which the receivership is pending. Likewise, no one has authority, even under a prior deed of trust or execution, to sell property held in *custodia legis* by a duly appointed receiver, unless the court in which the receivership is pending authorizes the sale. A receiver does not have to sell the property to realize its value. Unlike a trustee in bankruptcy, a receiver does not have the status of a good faith purchaser for value, and a receiver stands exactly in the shoes of the debtor.

Pursuing Litigation

Typically, receivers can file suit without obtaining court approval. Also, they may be sued without leave of court, because there is no automatic stay equivalent.

Handling Claims and Creditors

To obtain payment on a judgment against a receiver, the owner of the judgment may apply to the court that appointed the receiver to order the receiver to pay the judgment. Often, the receiver asks the court to approve a claims resolution process similar to that in bankruptcy court. A deadline is set for filing claims, and the receiver reviews the claims.

Investing Funds

A receiver should invest funds in an interest-bearing account. The initial order should grant this authority.

Reporting to Creditors

Upon termination of the receivership, the receiver must make a final report and account to the court. At the final hearing, the court determines any objections or claims made against the receivership and approves or disapproves the report and account. After approval, the receivership is complete and the receiver is discharged. The bond is released upon completion of disbursements and other requirements, in accordance with the order approving the final report and account.

Compensation of Receiver

The court must approve the receiver's fees and costs. The initial order should set forth the basis of compensation at an hourly rate, percentage of recovery, or blended rate.

Priority of Payment

The receiver's costs and fees are first deducted from the receivership property or its earnings or proceeds. The receiver then applies the earnings of property and sale proceeds held in receivership to the payment of claims in the order established by the applicable state receivership statute. The priority typically is as follows:

- Fees and costs of receiver
- Wages of employees due by the receiver
- Debts owed for materials and supplies purchased by the receiver for the improvement of the property held as receiver
- Debts due for improvements made during the receivership to the property held as receiver
- Claims and accounts against the receiver on contracts made by the receiver and tort claims against the receiver accruing during the receivership
- Creditors holding claims arising before the receiver was appointed

Subsequent Bankruptcy

If, after the appointment of a receiver, a bankruptcy petition is filed by or against the debtor whose property is the subject of the receivership, the receiver as a custodian under the Bankruptcy Code, must turn over the receivership property to the bankruptcy trustee. The Bankruptcy Code may allow the receiver to continue to manage and possess the property, notwithstanding subsequent bankruptcy, if the interests of creditors would be better served. If the receiver is doing an effective job, the United States Trustee often appoints the receiver to be the bankruptcy trustee.

Termination of Receivership

A company may not stay in receivership forever. Generally, a corporation may not remain in receivership for more than a statutorily prescribed period of time (e.g., three years). However, the court may extend the receivership if it is in the best interest of all concerned parties, and (i) litigation prevents the court from winding up the affairs of the corporation within the prescribed time, or (ii) the receiver is operating the corporation as a going concern. Generally speaking, a receivership terminates upon completion of the duties for which the receiver was appointed or at any other time upon court order.

Federal Equity Receiverships

A federal court equity receivership is typically commenced by a federal agency filing a complaint in the federal district court where a business is located together with a motion to appoint a receiver for the business. Federal agencies can seek the appointment of an equity receiver for a business that has violated federal law. The SEC frequently seeks the appointment of a receiver for businesses that have engaged in fraudulent accounting practices or have fraudulently induced people to invest. The Federal Trade Commission has sought receivers for companies that violated consumer protections laws. Entities such as Housing and Urban Development, the Commodity Futures Trading Commission, and the Small Business Administration have also sought receiverships. A receivership order typically provides for divestiture of the business. The receiver may operate the business and ultimately sell the business as a going concern or sell assets of the business separately.

The Receiver

The federal district judge who orders the receivership also appoints the receiver. The federal agency seeking the receivership typically recommends an individual to act as receiver, who frequently, but not always, is appointed by the judge. The receiver is not a government employee.

The Receiver's Duties and Power

A federal district court's power to supervise an equity receivership and to determine the appropriate action to be taken in the administration of the receivership is extremely broad. At the commencement of the receivership, an order is entered giving the receiver broad powers to take charge of the assets belonging to the business, to manage those assets, and to see to the proper administration, and when appropriate, eventual sale of the assets and distribution to creditors. Receivership powers can include (i) conducting the receivership bidding process (which may be private, depending upon the circumstances); (ii) staying litigation against a company's past or present officers, directors, managers, agents or general or limited partners, unless specifically permitted by court order; and (iii) establishing claim resolution procedures. Receivers can pursue litigation on behalf of the business including the recovery of fraudulent transfers under applicable state law.

Compensation of the Receiver

Typically, receivership fees and costs cannot be assessed against the government agency seeking the receivership. Prior to accepting the appointment, the receiver should be satisfied that there are sufficient receivership assets to cover costs and expenses. The receiver is paid first out of proceeds from the disposition of receivership property. The amount of the fee is determined by the district court.

Priority of Payment

The federal agency that sought the receivership typically comes up with a plan to distribute proceeds of the liquidation. Because equity demands equal treatment of victims in factually similar cases, the plan typically distributes the funds to defrauded customers on a pro rata basis. Creditors' attempts to trace their money to a particular receivership asset, and to assert priority rights to that asset, are normally unsuccessful.

Subsequent Bankruptcy

Attempts by the owner of the business or by individual creditors to convert the receivership into a bankruptcy proceeding do not typically succeed. The petitions are dismissed for lack of good faith.

Assignment for Benefit of Creditors

An assignment for the benefit of creditors is another tool that can be utilized to liquidate a business. An assignment is a business liquidation device that provides an alternative to bankruptcy. It is an old common law tool that could be used more often as an effective alternative to bankruptcy. Assignment can save time and expenses and is often beneficial to principals who have personally guaranteed company obligations or have personal liability on tax claims. It may be of substantial benefit to secured creditors by relieving them of the costs and risks of liquidation where the creditor wishes to avoid foreclosing on its collateral for other reasons. The significant difference from a formal bankruptcy proceeding is the ability of assignment to avoid following all the administrative procedures that govern bankruptcy court proceedings. Assignments lessen the time required to sell assets, increase the liquidation options, and keep the costs substantially lower, often resulting in a greater return for creditors. A variety of factors, including the flexibility in the method of sale, the ability to act quickly and the greater time the assignee will generally devote to the liquidation effort help to explain the enhanced results.

The Assignment Contract

An assignment is simply a contract whereby the troubled entity (assignor) transfers legal and equitable title, as well as custody and control of its property, to a third party (assignee) in trust, to apply the proceeds to the payment of the assignor's debts. The assignee liquidates the property and distributes the proceeds among the assignor's creditors, in accordance with priorities established by state law.

Virtually any transfer to a trustee, by which the debtor seeks to divest itself of both title and control of *all* assets and intends to create an absolute conveyance for the purpose of distributing proceeds among its creditors, is in legal effect an assignment, (no matter what the parties call it). An assignment must vest *all* interest in the property transferred to the assignee; however, the assignee takes only that property that the assignor may legally convey or assign. When the business is solvent and the property's value exceeds the amount of the total debts, the excess is held in trust by the assignee and returned to the assignor.

An assignment is most successful when the debtor, the secured creditors, and the assignor cooperate. For example, an assignee of a manufacturing business may, with the cooperation of the secured parties and the principals, operate the business for a limited time in order to complete work in process and maximize recovery of accounts receivable. An assignee often employs the principal of the assignor, who is likely to be invaluable in clarifying business records and liquidating assets at the highest possible price. A Chapter 7 trustee seldom is in a position to avail the bankruptcy estate of this option, tending instead to liquidate in bulk or mass, rather than employ what might be more rewarding methods.

The Assignor

An assignor can be any individual, partnership, or corporation that owes anything to anyone. Any debtor owning property has, as an incident of ownership, the inherent common law right to make an assignment. The general rule is that any insolvent debtor may make an assignment. An assignment is not feasible (and thus discouraged) for individuals, because individuals do not receive discharges as they would in a Chapter 7 bankruptcy.

Under certain circumstances, a general partner may assign the partnership property. The partner usually needs the express consent and authorization of other partners in order to make an assignment. An assignment is not within the contemplation of an ordinary partnership or the usual course of business and therefore is beyond the scope of agency arising from the partnership. Corporations may make assignments unless restricted by their articles or some statutory provisions. A corporate resolution is required because an assignment is a disposition of all of the corporation's assets.

The Assignee

The assignee generally is selected by the assignor, although a court may remove an assignee for violations of the assignment contract or for nonfeasance. Prior to making a distribution to creditors, the assignee may not give up his or her duties under the assignment without court order.

The Assignee's Powers and Duties

The exact duties depend on the type of case but typically include protecting the assets of the estate, administering them fairly, and representing the estate. In this respect, although the assignee may be a trustee and the creditors may be considered the beneficiaries of the assignment, the assignee is no more than a representative of the assignor and does not technically represent the creditors.

The standard of care for an assignee is an ordinary prudent person who would make the same decisions in similar circumstances. The assignee may be liable for losses occasioned, if the standard is not met or for failure to observe statutory priority given debts owed to the United States government.

Dealing with Assets

Any property that the debtor can sell or convey or would be subject to execution may be assigned. When a corporation makes an assignment, all corporate property—real, personal, tangible, and intangible—is transferred to the assignee, including causes of actions, customer lists, bank accounts, and rights and credits of all kinds, both in law and equity. A cause of action in tort, such as a business tort, that survives to a personal representative can be enforced in the name of an assignee. The assignee represents the assignor and is not a bona fide creditor; thus, the assignee acquires no greater right in the property than the assignor had at the time it was assigned. Many states have detailed statutes setting forth the rights of the assignee with respect to the property he or she holds.

The goodwill of a business (even one closed and in liquidation) is an asset that an assignee not only recognizes but also attempts to utilize, when liquidating the assets of a business. Goodwill is seldom of any value in a Chapter 7 trustee's liquidating sale. Goodwill may be a significant asset whose value can be realized through a turnkey sale to someone interested in the assignor's business. While going-concern value seldom is obtained, an assignee could keep the assignor's assets in place for a period while seeking to find a purchaser. An assignee thus may attempt to operate a business for a short time in order to sell it as a going concern and realize the goodwill value.

Pursuing Litigation

An assignee is often able to pursue causes of action that a Chapter 7 trustee could not or would not. The assignee is free to enter into contracts to recover assets or liquidated claims. Thus, an assignee may hire an attorney on a contingent fee basis to pursue claims that may be theoretically possible but impractical for a Chapter 7 trustee to pursue in a bankruptcy. The assignee has the flexibility to contract with one or more creditors or even shareholders to fund the cost of pursuing a valuable cause of action without requesting court approval.

Handling Claims and Creditors

A conditional sale vendor, lessor, or secured creditor elects whether to retake its property or collateral or utilize the assignee to undertake the liquidation. Such creditors, in fact, are often the greatest beneficiaries of the assignment and usually consent to the proceeding, as assignment generally realizes more value on their collateral or property than does a Chapter 7 bankruptcy. These obligations nearly always are personally guaranteed by the company's principals who benefit from the improved liquidation results.

While no formal consent is required, secured creditors often must agree to an assignment in advance, because their active cooperation frequently enhances the values derived from the liquidation of the assets. The acceptance of an assignment by unsecured creditors is not necessary. Under common law, the proceedings are deemed to benefit them through equality of treatment.

The funds realized on liquidation by an assignee cannot be claimed by a single creditor or jointly by all creditors since the assignee holds the funds in trust. Creditors who file claims under an assignment thereby waive all objections to the validity of the assignment.

Investment of Funds

The assignment should contemplate how funds are handled. The assignor should not continue to have access to business accounts, and the assignee should open new accounts for operating the business. To the extent possible, funds should be placed in interest-bearing accounts. Applicable state law should be reviewed for more specific requirements.

Reporting to Creditors

An assignee must render an accounting to creditors within a reasonable time and generally does so when the estate is closed. In many instances, periodic bulletins are sent to creditors.

Compensation of Assignee

The assignee is entitled to compensation either as stated in the contract of assignment or as negotiated with creditors. Even if the contract is silent on the assignee's fees, a court has equitable power to grant the assignee reasonable compensation. The compensation issue should be resolved in advance and in the contract.

Priority of Payment

The parties contractually agree to payment priorites.

Subsequent Bankruptcy

If a creditor or creditors file an involuntary bankruptcy petition, the bankruptcy court may abstain from accepting jurisdiction. To do so, the court must find that the assignment essentially treats creditors in a manner similar to a Chapter 7 bankruptcy and that acceptance of jurisdiction brings no additional benefits to creditors. Where bankruptcy court jurisdiction may be beneficial to prevent fraud or injustice, an assignment may be avoided by a bankruptcy trustee.

Termination of Assignment

The contract setting up the assignment should specify when the arrangement terminates and what happens to any residual amounts or liabilities.

Distribution Priorities

Secured creditors usually retain their collateral, or its value, as a lien on the proceeds. The costs and expenses of the assignment, including the assignee's fees, legal expenses, and costs of administration, are paid first, just as in a Chapter 7 bankruptcy. Accordingly, in situations where the assets are overencumbered, the subordination of the secured creditor(s) to such expenses must be obtained. This matter is resolved by agreement prior to acceptance of the assignment. Thereafter, distribution is generally made in accordance with the priorities established by state law. They typically are as follows:

- Obligations owing to the U.S. government
- Labor wages and benefits
- State income sales and use taxes
- Employment insurance contributions
- Unsecured creditors arising from deposits for specified purposes
- General unsecured claims

Interest is paid only after the principal is paid for all claims filed. Interest rates are computed according to the original agreement between the vendor and the assignor. Thereafter, interest claims are computed and prorated if necessary. Surplus is returned to the assignor after nonparticipating creditors have had an opportunity to reach surplus.

State Avoidance Laws

Receivers and assignees do not benefit from the avoidance powers under the Bankruptcy Code. However, receivers and assignees often can recover preferential payments to insiders and fraudulent transfers under state fraudulent transfers laws. The degrees to which receivers and assignees can bring avoidance actions vary. Forty-one states and the District of Columbia have enacted some version of the Uniform Fraudulent Transfer Act of 1984. Three states still have in effect the Uniform Fraudulent Conveyance Act of 1918. Leaving only six states that do not have either but which recognize a common law fraudulent transfer. The Uniform Fraudulent Transfer Act, similar to the Bankruptcy Code, allows recovery of transfers for less than reasonably equivalent value or fair consideration at a time when the debtor was insolvent, undercapitalized, or unable to pay debt as they became due.

Conclusion

While most liquidations involving companies of any significant size are accomplished through a bankruptcy proceeding, either Chapter 7 or Chapter 11, advantages over bankruptcy do exist under certain limited circumstances. Understanding the options is the key. Two other approaches, receiverships and assignments, provide alternatives, particularly for smaller, more localized liquidations. Both approaches are more informal and less restrictive than a bankruptcy proceeding, but both are difficult to apply in most situations. For example, as a practical matter an assignment requires unanimous consent from the creditors. Similarly, state court receiverships are governed by state court law and thereby limited to actions that do not need to be enforced beyond state borders. Federal court receiverships are typically controlled by the government agency seeking it. Moreover, neither receiverships nor assignments provide the liquidator with many of the important powers accorded in bankruptcy, such as the automatic stay or the ability to sell assets that have been cleansed of claims by the bankruptcy process. Nonetheless, in those situations where the bankruptcy powers are not needed and the estate is small and local enough to be handled in state court, the more informal receivership or assignment may well be appropriate and is sure to be less costly.

11

Closing Down

Inevitably, the day arrives when the liquidation is complete. All assets have been sold, all monies distributed, and it is time to close down. Whether an insolvent company was liquidated through bankruptcy, receivership, or assignment for the benefit of creditors, or a solvent company was liquidated by its shareholders, closing down involves providing for the retention and ultimate destruction of business records and dissolving the business entity. For the liquidator, it also involves preparing a final report. In this chapter, we address record retention requirements under federal and state law, dissolution of the business entity under applicable law, and final reporting by the liquidator.

Record Retention

Absent a Bankruptcy Court order to the contrary, the business records of a company must be retained for a period of time that adheres to the federal regulations and the regulations for each state in which the company is transacting business. As a rule of thumb, maintaining records for six years appears to be sufficient. Generally, a company must retain documents related to regulated activities, which include accounting, sales and tax records; employment and personnel records; and industry-specific records, such as medical records for a physician's practice group. Records belonging to a former organization may be the responsibility of the surviving or the former organization depending upon the terms of the merger or acquisition. A company must comply with federal laws affecting the records and the state laws for each state in which the organization is doing business. Each state has different regulations regarding the retention of records; therefore, a company will be required to retain records for different periods of time depending upon the various states in which it is incorporated and doing business.

Federal

Table 11.1 summarizes selected federal regulations regarding document retention.

State

State laws affecting record retention vary widely. For example, Delaware does not provide strict guidance to corporations regarding the retention of business records. Records retention specialists at the Delaware Public Archives recommend that corporations (in addition to adhering to all federal requirements for record retention) use the Delaware state agencies record-retention schedule as a guide in deciding how long to retain corporate records. The Delaware records retention and disposition schedules regarding the division of corporations and employment/personnel records can be found at their Web site. In contrast, the State of Texas has specific laws covering matters such as state franchise tax records, employment records, and sales tax records. It also has a general record-retention statute covering documents to be retained for unspecified periods. The liquidator must determine which state laws apply and comply accordingly.

Liquidating Trustees

A liquidating Chapter 11 plan should include procedures for the destruction of records that are no longer needed by the liquidator. For example, a plan provision such as the following is helpful:

> The estate representative shall take possession of all books and records of the debtor. The estate representative may from time to time, upon approval of the bankruptcy court and after notice to those persons specifically requesting notice under this section, destroy such records; provided, however, that any person objecting to records being destroyed must make arrangements for storage of such records including payment of all costs associated with such storage.

Additionally, it is advisable for the liquidator at the beginning of the assignment to formulate a document retention policy (appendix 12). If the policy is followed, criticism of the liquidator can be minimized.

Bankruptcy Trustees

Specific rules apply to a bankruptcy trustee's records related to the liquidation itself. A bankruptcy trustee is required to retain the paper and electronic case

Table 11.1

Type of Document	Statute or Rule	Time for Retention
General retention period, if not stated in other statute or rule	44 U.S.C. '3507(g) (Paperwork Reduction Act of 1980)	Three years
Section 10(a) prospectus for Form S-8, Registration Statement	17 CFR '230.428(a)(2) (SEC)	Five years after documents used as a part of prospectus to offer or sell
Employment records of hiring, promotion, transfer, layoff, termination, rates of pay, and selection for training	29 CFR '1910.1020(d)(i) (OSHA)	Five years
Employee exposures, medical records, and analyses of such exposure or medical records	29 CFR '1910.10210(d)(i) (OSHA)	30 years unless others OSHA rule specifies different period. For example, records of exposure to bloodborne pathogens must be kept for duration of employment, plus 30 years.
General income tax requirement for books of account and records to establish gross income for tax purposes	26 CFR '1.6001-1 (IRS)	"So long as contents may become material in administration of any internal revenue law"
Records of property acquisition if material to income-tax determination	26 CRF '1.6001-1 (IRS)	Until taxable disposition made
Records of income, deduction, and credits (including gains and losses)	26 CFR '1.6001-1 (IRS)	At minimum, until statute of limitation for return expires. Generally taxes shall be assessed within three years after filing return. Claims for refund or credit must be filed within three years of filing or two years after payment whichever later. Six-year statute of limitations if substantial omission of income; seven years if claim is for credit for bad debts or securities losses. No statute of limitations for fraud or for no return (other exceptions possible).
Employment tax records	26 CFR '31.6001-1(e)(2)	Four years after due date or paid
Payroll records and other unemployment contracts	26 CFR '516.5 (Wage & Hour DOL)	Three years
Earnings, wage tables, and other employment payment records	26 CFR '516.5	Two years
Records of employee benefit plans subject to ERISA	29 U.S.C. '1027	Six years after filing documents

Table 11.1 (*continued*)

Type of Document	Statute or Rule	Time for Retention
Records of employment evaluation, seniority, month of birth descriptions, or any other documents that explain the basis for wage payment differential between sexes	29 CFR '1620.32(c) (Equal Pay Act)	Two years minimum
Employment and payroll records containing name, address, date of birth, pay rate, compensation for a week, and other materials pertinent to enforcement of age discrimination	29 CFR '1627.3(a)	Three years
Resumes from other applicants, promotions, test papers, and physical exams of other individuals	29 CFR '1627.3(b)	One year

Note. OSHA—Occupational Safety and Health Administration; ERISA—Employer Retirement Income Security Act.

files and estate accounting records for a period of at least two years after the date on which the trustee was discharged and during which a proceeding on the trustee's bond may be commenced. The following is a representative, not exhaustive, list of items that must be maintained for each case:

- All documents relating to the financial transactions of the estate (e.g., cash receipts log; receivables ledger; copies of incoming checks, bank statements, cancelled checks, transmittal letters, and other supporting documentation for receipts; bills or invoices for estate expenses; tax returns or waivers, etc.)
- All documents relating to the possession and maintenance of assets (e.g., receipts for property turned over to the trustee, appraisals, inventories, casualty insurance, etc.)
- All documents relating to the supervision of relevant professionals
- All documents relating to the disposition of assets (e.g., lien documentation; collection letters; notices or advertisements of sales or abandonments; court orders regarding the disposition of assets and the payment of expenses; offers received, auctioneer's reports, etc., and all supporting documentation relating thereto)
- All notes and internal memos created in connection with the above, including case notes contained in the memo and note fields of the trustee's Chapter 7 computer system, notations written on correspondence or memos to the file, records of telephone conversations, and time records

Records available electronically from the court (e.g., bankruptcy petitions, schedules, statements; court orders for sales and disbursements) do not need to be kept in the estate files.

Postclosure Storage

Liquidators can contract with document repositories, such as Iron Mountain or Safeguard, who will, for a lump-sum prepayment, store and ultimately destroy records. The repository must be given a schedule of the retention periods for the documents (typically, on a box-by-box basis). Once the retention period has expired, the box is destroyed. Meanwhile, a third party needing and having a right to access the records can pay the repository to access them. In a lengthy liquidation, the liquidator may be allowed to destroy records prior to closure of the estate, if the applicable retention periods have been met. A bankruptcy trustee or other court-supervised liquidator should obtain court approval for the destruction of records as a matter of self-protection. Identifying which records to maintain over the long term and which to destroy is a difficult and uncertain task.

Dissolution of Business Entities

The three basic methods of dissolution are: (i) dissolution of a bankrupt debtor or debtor in receivership done pursuant to court supervision, (ii) voluntary dissolution of a company pursuant to state law, and (iii) involuntary dissolution of a company pursuant to state law.

Dissolution of a Bankruptcy Debtor

When a corporation or other business entity enters bankruptcy, the state laws governing voluntary dissolution are modified. The trustee or any other individual designated by the court to act on behalf of the debtor can dissolve the entity without action by or notice to the board of directors, managers, members, or the shareholders. Likewise, the state or federal court supervising a liquidation can enter a decree of dissolution when the liquidation is complete.

Voluntary Dissolution of a Nondebtor

For a company dissolving outside a court-supervised liquidation, state law of incorporation applies. State corporate laws differ with respect to voluntary dissolutions of a company organized under the laws of that state (see appendix 9). The majority of states have adopted statutes based on the Model Business Corporation Act of 1984. Voluntary dissolution of a corporation may be implemented by unanimous written consent by the shareholders, or a proposal by the board of the directors, which is submitted for action at a meeting of the shareholders. For the proposal by the board to be adopted, (i) the board must "recommend" dissolution; (ii) the corporation must have furnished notice to each shareholder, whether or not entitled to vote; (iii) the notice must state that the purpose of the meeting is to "consider dissolving the corporation"; and (iv) unless the articles of incorporation provide otherwise, the proposal to dissolve must be approved by two-thirds of all votes entitled to be cast, but in no event less than a majority vote.

After dissolution is authorized, either by written consent of shareholders or approval of the board's proposal, the corporation may be dissolved by filing articles of dissolution with the state office in which the corporation's articles of incorporation are filed and the unanimous consent or resolution passed by the board.

Articles of dissolution must contain (i) the name of the corporation; (ii) the date dissolution was authorized; (iii) if dissolution was approved by the shareholders, the number of votes entitled to be cast on the proposal to dissolve and either the total number of votes cast for and against dissolution or the total number of undisputed votes cast for dissolution and a statement that the number cast for dissolution was sufficient for approval; (iv) if voting by voting groups was required, the information required by the prior subdivision must be separately provided for each voting group entitled to vote separately on the plan to dissolve; (v) if dissolution was approved by written consent of all shareholders, a statement to that effect in lieu of the information required by (iii) and (iv), and a copy of the written consent or consents signed by all shareholders of the corporation.

A dissolved corporation continues in existence but may not conduct business except that required to wind up or liquidate its business and affairs. Dissolution does not affect the limited liability of its shareholders, change the standard of conduct of the corporation's officers and directors, prevent the commencement of suits by or against the corporation, transfer title of the corporation's property, or abate or suspend proceedings against the corporation.

A dissolved corporation may handle known claims by providing written notice to claimants of the mailing address where claims should be sent, the final date that the corporation will accept receipt of claims (at least 120 days from the effective date of the notice), and that the claim will be barred if not received by the deadline. A corporation that publishes notice of dissolution in a newspaper of general circulation in a county in which its principal office is located is not subject to unknown claims and certain other claims, unless the claimant commences a proceeding to enforce its claim within two years of publication of such notice. The notice must include information that must be set forth in the claim, the mailing address where the claim may be sent, and state that the claim will be barred if an action is not commenced within two years after the publication of the notice.

Involuntary Dissolution of a Nondebtor

The secretary of state in the state where the debtor is incorporated may dissolve involuntarily the corporation for failing to (i) file reports, (ii) pay fees, franchise taxes, or penalties, or (iii) maintain a registered office in the state. Many defunct corporations are dissolved involuntarily each year. While simple and cheap, using this method of dissolution is not good business practice.

Final Reports

Chapter 7 Trustee

A trustee in a Chapter 7 case must file the final report (TFR) and final account of the administration of the case. The TFR must be prepared when all monies have been collected, all claims have been reviewed or determined by the court, and the bar date has expired for creditors to file claims. In addition, any required tax returns must have been filed and resolved. The report must be filed prior to any distribution of funds to creditors, unless the court previously ordered an interim distribution.

The TFR summarizes all actions taken by the trustee to administer the case and enables parties in interest to understand how the trustee plans to disburse the funds. Each report must

- describe specifically the disposition of each estate asset (as listed in the debtor's schedules or otherwise discovered).
- report all financial transactions by the trustee.
- request final payment of the trustee's compensation and expenses and any unpaid professional fees and expenses.
- report the trustee's actions on claims or their disposition.
- propose the details of the final distribution to creditors.
- attach original bank statements and canceled checks (from estate accounts) received by the trustee during the case.
- file all outstanding applications for professional compensation and expenses.

Estate funds should generally be maintained in an interest-bearing account until the trustee is ready to distribute the funds to creditors. Funds should not be invested after the final tax return is prepared, if the cost of preparing an additional tax return would exceed the interest earned. Normally, this situation only becomes an issue in corporate or partnership cases. The United States Trustee reviews the TFR to assess whether the trustee has properly and completely administered estate property.

If the net proceeds realized in an estate exceed $1,500, a notice must be sent to all creditors with a summary of the final report before actually making the distribution to the creditors. The notice informs creditors of the following: (i) the trustee's final report for the case is on file with the clerk of the bankruptcy court; (ii) the trustee and other professionals have applied for compensation in given amounts; (iii) the money on hand will be distributed to creditors in accordance with the bankruptcy priority laws; and (iv) the creditors have a right to object to the trustee's report. If no objections are lodged to the notice of intent to distribute or to the report of distribution, then the trustee may make the distribution according to the final report.

Within 125 days after the entry of an order allowing final compensation and expenses, a trustee submits to the United States Trustee for review a final account, signed under penalty of perjury, certifying that the estate has been fully administered. The trustee certifies that all funds have been disbursed consistent with the distribution report and that all checks have been negotiated or any remaining checks have been paid into court and that the estate has been fully administered.

Other Liquidators

As discussed in chapter 10, state receivers and assignees for the benefit of creditors have similar final reporting requirements that cover monies received and distributed. The reporting obligations of a liquidator under a Chapter 11 plan are typically written in the plan or trust agreement.

Conclusion

The liquidation approaches completion after all assets have been sold and most or all monies have been distributed. But the liquidator may not be able simply to close shop and move on. One of the key after-liquidation issues, record retention, requires the retention and appropriate destruction of records over a specified period of time. In addition, final reports summarizing the trustee's administrative activities and an account of distributions and disposition of claims must be prepared.

Appendix 1

Guidelines for Employment and Supervision of Professionals

Definition of "Professional"

A liquidator may employ attorneys, accountants, appraisers, auctioneers, brokers, underwriters, farm managers, private investigators, and so on. If the person to be employed is a "professional person" employed in a bankruptcy, the liquidator must obtain court approval of the employment. A "professional person" is defined in the Bankruptcy Code as someone who

- plays a central role in the administration of the estate,
- possesses discretion or autonomy over some part of the estate,
- has special knowledge or skill usually achieved by study and educational attainments, and/or
- operates under a license or governmental regulation.

When in doubt, seek court approval of the employment. To be compensated from the estate, a professional must be employed with court approval.

Employment Standards

The liquidator must determine at the outset whether the services of a professional are needed, the level of work required, estimated costs and benefits associated with the work, and whether the cost is warranted. Accounting services normally are required when the debtor is a corporation engaged in business, or when liquidated assets generate tax consequences and require the filing of a tax return on behalf of the estate. Accounting services commonly include reviewing the debtor's books and records for preferences and fraudulent transfers, preparing and filing tax returns, and determining whether a tax refund is due to the estate.

As a rule, professional persons employed by a trustee must be disinterested and must not have an interest adverse to the estate. The employment of a professional with a conflict of interest can result in denial of compensation to that professional.

Employment Procedures

Notice and hearing is not required to hire professionals, only court approval. The trustee must provide a copy of the employment application to the United States Trustee, which must include the following information:

- Specific reasons for employment
- Name of the person to be employed
- Reasons for selecting the firm or individual
- Professional services to be rendered
- Proposed arrangements for compensation
- Professional's connections with the trustee, debtor, creditors, and other parties in interest

The application should be accompanied by a verified statement of the person to be employed setting forth the person's connections with the debtor, creditors, any other party in interest, including the trustee, their respective attorneys and accountants, the United States Trustee, or any person employed by the United States Trustee.

Fee-sharing arrangements are prohibited. The trustee and the professional person should discuss and agree upon the terms and conditions of employment, including the manner of compensation, with the understanding that the court ultimately sets the fees for professional persons, which may be increased or decreased depending on the circumstances, even to the extent of recapturing monies paid as interim fees.

Supervision of Professionals

The trustee under Chapter 7 or Chapter 11 is a fiduciary and representative of the estate. A trustee cannot avoid or abdicate responsibilities by employing professionals and delegating to them certain tasks. The trustee must exercise appropriate business judgment on all key decisions; supervise estate professionals to ensure their prompt and appropriate execution of duties, compliance with required procedures; and ensure that professional fees and expenses are reasonable and necessary.

The trustee must pay particular attention to the activities of professionals who are not closely regulated by state authorities or who take physical possession of estate property and funds, such as auctioneers, brokers, collection agents, and property managers. The standards for supervising auctioneers apply equally to other professionals who take possession of estate funds and property.

Compensation of Professionals

Applications for compensation and reimbursement of expenses filed by professionals hired during a Chapter 7 or Chapter 11 must be prepared in accordance with the procedural guidelines adopted by the United States Trustees. The United States Trustee reviews professional fee applications and, when appropriate, objects to the requested fees and expenses.

Unless otherwise permitted by the court, the professional may make application for interim compensation and reimbursement of expenses not more than once every 120 days. The trustee has a fiduciary obligation to review professional fee applications and to object when appropriate. Reasonable and necessary legal services are those that require professional legal skills and expertise beyond the knowledge and skills of a trustee. A trustee who also serves as an attorney or accountant in a case must be careful to avoid double-dipping.

Practical Aspects of Retaining Professionals

Rules vary from jurisdiction to jurisdiction, but under the cannons of ethics, a lawyer or law firm is not supposed to represent a client in a proceeding that is adverse to another client or former client. So, for example, if a law firm has a particular bank as a client or former client and the liquidator thinks that the estate may pursue a claim against that bank in court, the law firm would probably not be allowed to represent the estate in that matter. Similar conflicts may arise with accounting firms and with certain other professionals. When such a conflict arises, the liquidator retains a different set of professional for that specific work. Prior to retaining a professional, the liquidator should identify likely litigation targets and then ask each professional firm to run a conflicts check.

In a large liquidation case, the liquidator is likely to retain one law firm as the estate's general counsel. Then, to the extent that representation is needed in a jurisdiction foreign to that general counsel, the estate is likely to retain a second law firm as local counsel. In addition certain types of legal work may require legal specialists and the retention of one or more additional law firms (e.g., special litigation counsel, special regulatory counsel, special ERISA counsel). Having several sets of lawyers working for the estate is not unusual. Some efficiency is lost and some duplication and extra cost is incurred when the legal work is parceled out among a number of firms. The same point applies to accounting firms. Accordingly, the liquidator is advised to carefully select his general counsel.

Most liquidators of large estates have a substantial amount of legal work to be performed: processing claims, preparing contracts, tax work, pension plan work, and so on. This type of work tends to be relatively straightforward. To the extent that the estate's employees can do some of these tasks, the trustee should only assign the most demanding, expertise-requiring work to lawyers and other high hourly-rate professionals. Most liquidators undertake the vast majority of the estate's legal and other professional work under this hourly fee-for-service arrangement.

As discussed in chapter 8, a different type of arrangement may be appropriate for handling litigation. Some form of contingency fee arrangement is the usual alternative. With a contingency fee arrangement, the law firm agrees to undertake the project and share the risk for a piece of the action. The estate provides the cause of action and the law firm provides the legal work.

Appendix 2

Investment Guidelines for Chapter 7 and Chapter 11 Trustees

A depository (e.g., bank) account for the estate must be opened as soon as funds are received. The account should be maintained under the direction and control of the trustee at all times. In Chapter 7 or absent a specific court order to the contrary, accounts may only be maintained at depositories that have agreed to abide by the requirements established by the United States Trustee, including specific account security requirements at the bank above the norm. As a rule, liquidators should deposit funds in an interest-bearing account to maximize the return to creditors. Under no circumstances should monies of separate estates be aggregated or commingled into the same account or deposited to the liquidator's general business, personal, or trust account.

One of the advantages of using a liquidating Chapter 11 plan is the ability of the estate administrator of a post-bankruptcy liquidation to escape the strictures of the consequences of the United States Trustee's investment and deposit restrictions. Reasonably safe bank accounts and investments can be used by non–Chapter 7 and Chapter 11 trustees, which yield substantially greater returns. This appendix addresses those restrictions for trustees operating under Chapter 7 and any trustees appointed during the pendency of Chapter 11.

Types of Accounts

Interest-Bearing

Bankruptcy trustees should invest the estate's monies in a way that produces the maximum, safe net return. Absent a specific court order to the contrary, interest-bearing estate accounts are restricted to either government guaranteed securities, money market accounts, or savings accounts. The interest rate should be no less than that available for other similar accounts. Bankruptcy trustees may be held personally liable for failure to collect interest on the estate's funds.

Non-Interest-Bearing Accounts

Under limited circumstances, the trustee may maintain money of the estate in a non-interest-bearing checking account. For example, (i) the interest-bearing account available only allows a limited number of withdrawals each month, and the trustee needs to make payments in excess of the monthly limit; (ii) the trustee will be making an interim distribution to creditors; or (iii) the trustee is directed by court order to make an immediate distribution.

Investment Accounts

When the estate receives a substantial amount of funds that will not be distributed for an extended period of time (e.g., six months), the trustee should consider investing in higher yield investments such as certificates of deposit or treasury bills. In general, the trustee's investments should be as risk free as possible. The trustee should exercise care that no withdrawal of funds results in a loss to the estate. The trustee should not make an investment that will predictably delay closing. Investment vehicles must be opened, issued, or purchased in the name of the trustee as trustee of the estate.

Prohibited Investment Accounts

The bankruptcy trustee cannot invest estate funds in certain types of instruments. For example, estate funds cannot be invested in repurchase agreements, reverse repurchase agreements, non-bank money market accounts, mutual funds, stocks, corporate bonds, and commercial paper unless such investments are government guaranteed.

Bond Recovery Account

Some banks offer a concentration account, or bond recovery account, to expedite the payment of bond premiums for trustees. This type of account is permitted for this limited purpose, if authorized by the United States Trustee in writing. The trustee must keep detailed records concerning the calculation, allocation, and payment of the premium, and must not allow a balance to accumulate uninvested. In addition, the bank must list the account on its monthly or quarterly bank balance report to the United States Trustee.

Opening the Account

Most large banks are extremely eager to obtain trustee accounts. The reason is simple. Because of the restrictions normally imposed by the United States Trustee, these accounts earn a very low rate of interest compared to the rates of interest demanded by other large depositors. More important, the deposits tend to sit for a long period of time. Many large banks have become familiar with the rather technical and complicated requirements and are generally quite helpful to trustees. Small banks typically do not have the experience necessary to manage these accounts. Accordingly, these accounts usually go to the same banks in a particular area. Of course, the trustee needs to be very careful to avoid the appearance of impropriety in accepting anything from a bank that is seeking to secure the trustee's banking relationship.

In order to open the account, the bank may require some proof of the trustee's appointment to the case and a tax identification number for any interest-bearing account. When the debtor is a corporation or partnership, the trustee should use the debtor's tax identification number. Failure to provide the tax identification number to the bank results in backup withholding being assessed and remitted to the Internal Revenue Service by the bank institution.

Estate bank accounts are free of any service charges for maintaining the accounts, supplying check stock, providing monthly bank statements and canceled checks, and providing computer hardware and software. Subject to United States Trustee approval, service charges may be assessed under certain circumstances, such as for a Chapter 7 operating case.

All bank statements, deposit slips, and checks should be readily identifiable as pertaining to a bankruptcy estate. They should be captioned with the bankruptcy case name and number and the Chapter 7 trustee's name. The terms "debtor" and "trustee" should appear, unabbreviated, in the caption, as follows: Case Number 02-12345; ABC Corp., debtor; John Doe, trustee. (Each item in this example is required, in no particular order. The term "case number" is desirable, but may be abbreviated or omitted.)

The check stock used by the trustee must be capable of being digitally reproduced in a legible image. In addition, if the check stock is preprinted with the check number or preprinted serial number, adequate precautions must be instituted and maintained to ensure that the check stock, including voided checks, is accounted for and that every check in each estate account is consecutively numbered.

Requirements for Depositories

A bankruptcy trustee may only use a depository that has agreed to comply with the requirements of the United States Trustee. The United States Trustee can provide the trustee with a list of depositories that meet these requirements. If a bank wishes to be added to the list, it should contact the appropriate United States Trustee for a list of current requirements. If a depository fails to comply with the United States Trustee requirements, the trustee should promptly notify the United States Trustee and arrange to move the funds to another depository.

The trustee is responsible for ensuring that the banking institution is in compliance. If the estate's aggregate funds on deposit in a single institution exceed the $100,000 FDIC insurance limit, the excess funds must be bonded or be collateralized by securities deposited with the appropriate Federal Reserve Bank. The trustee must notify the United States Trustee if the amount on deposit in any individual estate in any single depository exceeds or is expected to exceed $100,000.

Securities used as collateral must be government obligations valued at par. A government obligation is a public debt obligation of the United States government with principal and interest that is unconditionally guaranteed by the government. Public debt obligations include U.S. treasury bills, bonds, and notes. Zero-coupon treasury bonds are not acceptable collateral. While not public debt obligations, banks may also pledge a limited number of other bonds issued or guaranteed by the government that contain an unconditional government guarantee of principal and interest. The Treasury Department's Web site lists acceptable collateral. The United States Trustee may request an opinion from bank counsel or contact the executive office before accepting bonds that purportedly contain an unconditional government guarantee. If a bond in favor of the United States is filed to protect the deposit of estate funds, the United States Trustee is required to approve the corporate surety securing the bond. The United States Trustee can only select a surety listed in Treasury Circular 570.

The United States Trustee obtains summaries of the amounts on deposit from each bank being used by a trustee in order to assist in monitoring trustee accounts and bonding requirements. The United States Trustee also receives a report from the Federal Reserve Bank in order to review the sufficiency of the collateral posted by the banking institutions. The bankruptcy trustee must assist the United States Trustee in obtaining bank statements and summaries of amounts on deposit. An authorization for the bank's release of information to the United States Trustee may be required from a bankruptcy trustee.

An Investment Strategy

With all the strictures set forth above in mind, how does a liquidator earn the most attractive but secure rate of return on a lot of cash? One can assign the task to a portfolio manager but doing so would reduce the yield, by perhaps 25 basis points. Twenty-five basis points on a holding of $10 million, for example, is

Tale from the Bankruptcy Trenches

In the BNEC case, the Chapter 7 trustee purchased only U.S. government guaranteed investments, including treasury bills, certain agency securities, and FDIC-insured CDs. Agency securities backed by the full faith and credit of the U.S. government generally offered the highest yield. The trustee used two different brokers at two different firms in order to allow them to compete in offering the estate the best rates. Maturities were limited to a maximum of one year, thereby limiting any adverse impact from interest fluctuation risk. They were spread out on a monthly basis, so that funds from periodic maturities would be available to pay administrative expenses as needed, and were concentrated to occur on a date just before any expected interim distributions. The trustee also used a government-only money fund to hold very short-term funds. As a result, BNEC earned a top money-market rate with essentially zero risk, and the trustee always had the funds available when needed to pay bills on time.

$25,000 per year. Moreover, the estate loses some flexibility by using a money manager. Managing a portfolio of several tens of millions of dollars is a relatively straightforward do-it-yourself task. In the BNEC case, the Chapter 7 trustee employed the following strategy.

Appendix 3

Asset Category Definitions

account—a right to payment of a monetary obligation, whether or not earned by performance, (i) for property that has been or is to be sold, leased, licensed, assigned, or otherwise disposed of; (ii) for services rendered or to be rendered; (iii) for a policy of insurance issued or to be issued; (iv) for a secondary obligation incurred or to be incurred (i.e., obligation of a person who (a) has a stake in the proper enforcement of a security interest because he/she has an obligation to pay the secured debt (i.e., a guarantor) or (b) has a right of recourse against the debtor or another obligor with respect to an obligation secured by the collateral); (v) for energy provided or to be provided; (vi) for the use or hire of a vessel under a charter or other contract; (vii) arising out of the use of a credit or charge card or information contained on or for use with the card; (viii) as winnings in a lottery or other game of chance operated or sponsored by a state, governmental unit of a state, or person licensed or authorized to operate the game by a state or government unit of a state; or (ix) health-care-insurance receivables (i.e, an interest in or claim under a policy of insurance that is a right to payment of a monetary obligation for health-care goods or services provided).

aircraft—any vehicle or structure intended for use as a means of transporting passengers or goods in the air, including airplanes, helicopters, blimps, hot-air balloons, and all engines and avionics attached thereto.

boats and vessels—various types of structures that float on water, including boats, barges, dredges, and offshore drilling rigs.

chattel paper—a record or records that evidence both a monetary obligation and a security interest in specific goods, a security interest in specific goods and software used in the goods, a security interest in specific goods and license of software used in the goods, a lease of specific goods, or a lease of specific goods and license of software used in the goods. The monetary obligation is secured by the goods or owed under a lease of the goods and includes a monetary obligation with respect to software used in the goods. A record is inscribed on a tangible medium or stored in an electronic or other medium and is retrievable in perceivable form. If records of a transaction include an instrument or series of instruments, the group of records constitutes chattel paper. The category includes retail installment sales contracts, sales contracts and security agreements, conditional sales contracts, chattel mortgages, and personal property leases. It also includes car-rental agreements by a car-rental agency, and promissory notes and security agreements evidencing credit sales of goods by an appliance dealer.

copyright—a right granted by the federal government under copyright law to the creator or owner of an original work of authorship (e.g., a painting, play, book, database, advertisement, certain types of computer programs) that is in a tangible medium of expression (e.g., recorded on magnetic tape, written or typed on paper, etc.).

deposit accounts—demand, time, savings, passbook, or similar accounts maintained with a bank. The category includes a nonnegotiable certificate of deposit, which is a written document issued by a bank, savings and loan association, credit union, or similar financial organization that (i) states on its face that it is a certificate of deposit or receipt for a book entry; (ii) contains an acknowledgment that a sum of money has been received by the issuer, with an express or implied agreement that the issuer will repay the sum of money; and (iii) is not a negotiable instrument. The category does not include investment property or accounts evidenced by an instrument.

documents: warehouse receipts and bills of lading—receipts issued by a person engaged in the business of storing, transporting, or forwarding goods for hire, which act as evidence of title to such goods. A warehouse receipt is a document that describes goods stored in a warehouse and, generally, (i) entitles the person in possession of it to receive, hold, and dispose of the document and the goods that it covers and (ii) is a commitment by the issuer to deliver the described goods to the owner of the receipt and to use reasonable care to protect the goods from damage. A bill of lading is a document of title issued by a carrier in connection with the shipment of goods. It enables a remote buyer and a remote seller to consummate a transaction with limited risk to either party.

equipment—all tangible personal property used or bought for use primarily in business, including use in farming operations or in a profession (e.g., computers, file cabinets, etc.). On a balance sheet, this is typically noted as FF&E.

farm products—goods other than standing timber that are used in a farming operation and that are (i) crops grown, growing, or to be grown, including crops produced on trees, vines, and bushes; and aquatic goods produced in aquacultural operations; (ii) livestock, born or unborn, including aquatic goods produced in aquacultural operations; (iii) supplies used or produced in a farming operation; or (iv) products of crops or livestock in their unmanufactured states.

fixtures—goods so tied to particular real estate that the law considers them to be part of the real estate.

general intangibles—any personal property (including things in action) other than accounts, chattel paper, commercial tort claims, deposit accounts, documents, goods, instruments, investment property, letter-of-credit rights, letters of credit, money, and oil, gas, or other minerals before extraction. The category includes payment intangibles and software. Payment intangible is the account debtor's principal monetary obligation. Software is a computer program and any supporting information provided in connection with a transaction relating to the program. The category does not include a computer program that is included in the definition of goods. The category is quite broad and includes things such as the following items:

- intellectual property (i.e., patents, trademarks and copyrights)
- goodwill
- literary rights
- rights to the repayment of unsecured loans not evidenced by promissory notes
- rights to payment to dealers for retroactive volume discounts
- assignments of beneficial interests in trusts
- interest in a limited liability company
- tax refunds
- rights to performance
- payments under the federal payment-in-kind program
- payments under non-negotiable promissory notes
- reversionary interests under true leases of goods
- customer lists and trade names
- unearned extended warranty charges
- newsletters
- membership in an agricultural coop
- interest in an annuity

instrument—any negotiable or other instrument that evidences a right to the payment of a monetary obligation. It is not itself a security agreement or lease and is of a type that in the ordinary course of business is transferred by delivery with any necessary endorsement or assignment. The category does not include (i) investment property, (ii) letters of credit, (iii) writings that evidence a right to payment arising out of the use of a credit or charge card or information contained on or for use with the card, or (iv) nonnegotiable certificates of deposit. Examples of negotiable instruments include (i) a promissory note, (ii) a draft, (iii) a negotiable certificate of deposit, and (iv) a check.

inventory—goods leased by a person as lessor or held (i) for sale, (ii) for lease, (iii) to be furnished under a service contract, (iv) as raw materials, (v) as work in process, or (vi) as materials used or consumed in a business. Goods held for sale include the finished suits of a clothing manufacturer, the spare parts of an auto parts dealer, and the stock in trade of a retail merchant. Leased goods include the fleet of cars held for lease by a car rental agency and similar goods that a leasing company provides to customers. Goods furnished under a service contract include any goods used to perform a service contract. It does not matter whether the goods are sold. For example, paint is inventory of a house painter whether or not a homeowner is billed for the paint separately. Raw materials and materials used or consumed in a business include any raw materials that are manufactured or processed into finished goods. During the production process, they are work in process. These materials are inventory at all times, from their acquisition as raw materials to their completion as finished goods. The stage of manufacturing or processing, however, can affect their value. While the value or collateral usually increases during the manufacturing process, some specialty goods with a limited market can decrease in value if the market dries up. Goods that are incorporated into a finished product (e.g., steel, lumber, nails), goods that are used up in business operations (fuel), and goods that are used in conjunction with finished goods (e.g., cartons, packages, wrappings) are inventory of the manufacturer.

leasehold improvements—tenant's improvements in connection with a commercial lease of office or retail space and improvements such as office buildings and retail shopping centers on ground leases of real property.

letter of credit rights—a right to payment or performance under a letter of credit, whether or not the beneficiary has demanded or is at the time entitled to demand payment or performance. The category does not include the right of a beneficiary to demand payment or performance under a letter of credit.

motor vehicles—every kind of motor-driven or propelled vehicle, including trailers, house trailers (other than house trailers that are manufactured homes), and semitrailers; motorcycles, motor-driven cycles, and mopeds (excluding those motorcycles, motor-driven cycles, and mopeds designed for and used exclusively on golf courses); and four-wheel all-terrain vehicles designed by the manufacturer for off-highway use, whether required to be registered or not.

oil and gas—interests in oil, gas, and other minerals in the ground or produced and saved, leasing rights, and rights to share in production and royalties.

patent—a 17-year right to exclude others from making, using, or selling products that are covered by a U.S. patent.

real estate—land and any improvements (i.e., any buildings or other structures, including fences, driveways) constructed or installed on the land in a permanent manner. Real estate includes not only the ordinary building materials (e.g., brick, mortar, doors, windows, etc.) that were used to construct a building, but also goods that were installed in and have become an integral part of the building, such as light fixtures, elevators, and heating and air-conditioning equipment.

rolling stock—locomotives, railroad cars (e.g., hopper cars, boxcars, tank cars), and other portable or movable machinery or apparatus of a railroad.

securities and security entitlements—a security, whether certificated or uncertificated, security entitlement, securities account, commodity contract, or commodity account. This category includes obligations of an issuer or a share, participation, or other interest (including corporate stocks and bonds) in an issuer or in property or an enterprise of an issuer which:

- is represented by a security certificate in bearer or registered form, or the transfer of which may be registered upon books maintained for that purpose by or on behalf of the issuer;
- is one of a class or series or by its terms is divisible into a class or series of shares, participation, interest, or obligation; and
- is or is of a type dealt in or traded on securities exchanges or securities markets; or is a medium for investment and by its terms is a security governed by Article 8 of the UCC.

tort claims—a civil wrong arising in torts for which a remedy may be obtained in the form of damages.

trademark—common-law rights to a logo, name or other mark established by use of the mark and federal or state statutory trademark registrations of the mark.

Appendix 4

Internal Control Guidelines

A liquidator must establish and maintain an appropriate system of internal controls in order to safeguard estate funds and property, ensure the integrity of financial record keeping and reporting, and discourage employee theft. This includes segregation of duties and internal controls over banking, receipts, receivables, disbursements, computer operations, and files. While these guidelines focus on bankruptcy trustees, they are strongly recommended for any liquidator.

In addition to the cash receipts log, the liquidator should utilize a receivables ledger or other tracking mechanism for monitoring collections and following up on delinquent payments. A receivables ledger is used whenever numerous receivables or other assets (i.e., monies due from installment sales) with multiple payments are received over time. An acceptable receivables ledger identifies the customer or payer, the balance due, amounts collected, and the status of collection efforts. This log may be kept electronically or on paper.

Segregation of Duties

The liquidator oversees the entire liquidation and must actively supervise employees and independent contractors in the performance of their cash-management and accounting duties. The operation is normally conducted in a single location in order to facilitate adequate supervision, to maintain strong internal controls, and for ease of administration. Where the liquidation involves a company operating at multiple locations or with subsidiaries at multiple locations, supervision is more challenging.

In accordance with good business practice the liquidator must at a minimum (i) verify, on a test basis, that incoming receipts are promptly and properly deposited by comparing the cash receipts log to the bank statements; (ii) review and sign all checks; (iii) authorize stop-payment requests and cancellations in writing; (iv) review, date, and initial the monthly bank-account reconciliations; (v) receive the monthly bank statements, unopened; review the statements and canceled checks for errors, unusual transfers and endorsements, alterations, and forged or unauthorized signatures within 10 days of receipt; and immediately report discrepancies to the bank. Evidence of alterations, forgeries, and similar concerns must be reported to the United States Trustee. If a canceled check image is illegible, the trustee should request a clearer image or a substitute check. (The trustee is not required to initial and date every bank statement.); (vi) ensure that unique case-management system and electronic case file (ECF) passwords are established for each authorized employee. Passwords should be changed at least annually and when an employee leaves or no longer works on the liquidation. (Additional password controls are appropriate for certain functions, such as initiating bank account transfers or generating disbursement checks.); and (vii) have sole responsibility for setting up passwords and access rights within the computer system used for management, record keeping, and reporting. Access to sensitive data fields, such as creditor name and address, distribution amounts, and so on should be limited to employees who need access to these fields to perform their assigned job duties.

Clearly, the larger the liquidation, the more tasks the liquidator delegates. Wherever possible, cash-handling duties should be separated from record-keeping functions. In other words, the person who maintains the records of receipts and disbursements should not have access to cash receipts and disbursements. Internal controls are strengthened when the following duties are divided among the liquidator and several employees: receiving and logging receipts in the cash receipts log; restrictively endorsing checks; preparing deposit slips; making deposits; reconciling bank statements; maintaining records; reconciling the cash receipts log to bank statements; preparing interim reports, and having custody of check stock. When small staff size precludes segregating duties, the liquidator must be more actively involved. Documenting routine staff procedures and developing written job descriptions are important internal-control measures that help ensure consistent staff performance.

Monitoring Bank Accounts and Check Stock

The liquidator or an assistant should reconcile all bankruptcy estate accounts before the end of the following month. The reconciliation may be documented on the face of the bank statement or on another form created for this purpose, but it should not be done electronically. The bank statement balances must be shown and all differences explained on the reconciliation. Multiple debits for the same amount, unauthorized debits and credits, and other unusual entries on the bank statements should be identified and promptly investigated. Errors should be reported to the bank within 30 days of receiving the statements. The liquidator should ask the bank to reverse any service charges and back-up withholding taxes that appear on the statements. The preparer and the liquidator should each initial and date bank reconciliations. The reconciliations may be kept with the bank statements in the estate file or in a separate folder or notebook.

Only the liquidator and, at most, one employee should be authorized to (i) open and close bank accounts and (ii) transfer funds between accounts. These actions may be handled by letter, telephone, or computer. Care should be taken to ensure that estate bank accounts are promptly closed once the bank account has a zero balance. Only intra-estate transfers between accounts should be permitted. All other transfers should be by estate check.

Check stock and deposit slips should be kept in a secure location to prevent unauthorized access and use. If checks are drawn on more than one account, the consecutive sequence of the checks should be unique for each account (e.g., 101, 102, 103, etc. for the interest-bearing checking account; 10001, 10002, 10003, etc., for the money-market account).

Blank check stock, if preprinted with a bank logo, account number, and other identifying information, should contain a control number. The liquidator should maintain a log of these control numbers and account for every check used. At a minimum, the log should indicate the control number and, if applicable, the bankruptcy case number/name. If the blank check stock is completely blank (i.e., the account number, bank logo, and other identifying information are printed when the trustee prints the check), a control number is not necessary. The liquidator should, however, keep both types of check stock in a limited access, secure area.

Generally, voided checks should be kept in the estate files. However, checks that bear a control number and are used for printer alignment, damaged, or rendered useless during the check-printing process should be voided and retained with the check-control log. If there is no no control number or other identifying information on the voided check, the useless check paper should be shredded and thrown away. The numbers of voided checks may not be re-used.

Checks that have been outstanding for more than 90 days or checks returned by the U.S. Post Office (e.g., for inadequate address) should be processed by an individual uninvolved with authorizing and/or preparing those checks. The checks should be voided and the cause of the problem researched and corrected before the checks are reissued. These efforts should be documented.

Stop-payment requests and check cancellations must be approved by the liquidator. Either the liquidator or an employee may initiate the telephonic or electronic request regarding a stop payment, but the request must be followed up in writing either by (i) the liquidator's written confirmation to the bank (with a copy maintained in the estate file) or (ii) by the liquidator's initialing and dating the computer system's transmission log (which serves as evidence of the electronic transmittal of the stop-payment or cancellation request).

Receipts

Immediately upon receipt, checks must be restrictively endorsed by writing or stamping "For deposit only to account ________," and both currency and checks should be recorded in the cash receipts log. Payers should be instructed to makes checks payable to the trustee or the trust, for example, Jane Doe, trustee or to the ABC Liquidating Trust. Currency and checks must be kept in a safe or locked cabinet until deposited. Funds should be deposited as soon as possible after receipt (generally mailed or taken to the bank within two business days). Nonsufficient funds checks should be formally recorded and monitored until resolved. Supporting documentation for receipts, such as copies of checks and transmittal letters, should be kept in the file. Sale orders or notices and reports of sale should also be kept in the file, if not available electronically from the court or if they contain other information that supports the receipt, such as the liquidator's handwritten notations about the sale. Supporting documentation should contain the related docket entry number or date, when applicable.

Handling Currency

The liquidator should discourage the receipt of payments in currency (i.e., cold hard cash). When a liquidator cannot avoid accepting currency, careful procedures should be followed. First, provide a duplicate, numbered receipt to the payer and immediately deposit the funds in the estate account. Both the payer and liquidator should keep a copy of the receipt. If the funds cannot be deposited immediately, either because the liquidator uses a remote bank or because an estate account has not been opened, immediately convert the currency to a cashier's check or money order and place it in a secure location until it can be deposited. When possible, the liquidator should attempt to obtain the cashier's check or money order free of charge. If this is not possible, the service charge may be deducted from the funds received, with the cashier's check or money order issued for the net amount. If currency is received so late in the day that it is impossible or impractical to deposit or convert the cash, secure the funds in a safe or locked drawer until the next business day when these procedures can be carried out. The liquidator also may want to investigate the possibility of using the bank's night depository or 24-hour services if the bank is not in a remote location.

All supporting documentation in connection with handling currency should be kept in the file in order to provide an audit trail. When an employee handles currency, the liquidator needs to verify that the amount of the check or money order matches the amount of funds initially turned over to the employee, less any applicable service charge.

Earnest Monies

In connection with the sale of assets, the liquidator may occasionally receive and hold earnest monies. These funds are held in trust until the sale is consummated in accordance with applicable law. The funds should be deposited to the account immediately upon receipt. They should not be held in the liquidator's office or commingled with a law firm's trust account. Alternatively, the liquidator may deposit earnest monies into a separate trust account established specifically for this purpose. A separate account for each estate that the liquidator is handling is necessary. Specific accounting and record-keeping requirements have been established for trustee accounts of this type. A bankruptcy trustee should discuss this option and obtain approval from the United States Trustee prior to opening such an account.

Handling Undeposited Funds

Funds are to be deposited to the estate bank account promptly after receipt (generally mailed or taken to the bank within two business days) and must not be placed in a file while the trustee waits for subsequent events to occur. However, in rare instances, funds may be received which cannot or should not be immediately deposited. Such instances may include, but are not limited to (i) receipt of a deposit or settlement offer, the acceptance of which will be deemed acceptance of the terms of the proposed settlement; (ii) garnished funds received from court clerks or employers in cases with nominal or no other assets; and (iii) funds paid in settlement of sanctions imposed in petition-preparer cases.

When a liquidator cannot or should not immediately deposit funds received, the following procedures apply: (i) note receipt of the funds in the cash receipts log and place the funds in a safe place until deposited or turned over to the debtor or other party; (ii) immediately convert any currency received to a cashier's check or money order; (iii) dispose of the funds within 30 days after receipt or, in cases requiring a court order for disposition, 21 days after entry of a final order; (iv) if a court order for disposition of the funds is required, the bankruptcy trustee must obtain such order without undue delay; and (v) record the final disposition of the funds in the cash receipts log.

Receivables

A receivables ledger or other tracking mechanism should be maintained when multiple payments are being collected (e.g., accounts receivable, notes receivable, installment sales). The tracking system should reflect a running balance of amounts owed and should be updated as payments are received.

If a third party is employed to collect the receivables, the liquidator should send the first demand letter. In addition, the liquidator should retain a control copy of the receivables turned over and should request a periodic status report and accounting of the collection efforts undertaken, monies collected, and remaining balances due.

Disbursements

All disbursements should be made by checks drawn on the estate account (with the exception of items discussed below) and be fully supported by appropriate documentation (e.g., invoice, fee application, court order). The liquidator should review all supporting documentation and personally sign all checks. No signature stamp should be used. Checks should not be presigned by the liquidator before the date, payee, and amount are entered. Checks must be made payable to a specific payee and not payable to cash, bearer, or currency. The supporting documentation should indicate the liquidator's review and approval, which may be recorded electronically or by hand. As an additional control, the liquidator should consider asking the bank to obtain verbal approval from the liquidator when checks over an established dollar amount (e.g., $50,000) are presented for payment.

The supporting documentation should be kept in the estate file. Court orders for disbursements (when required) do not need to be kept in the file, if available electronically from the court. But if the amount on the invoice or fee application differs from the amount approved in the court order, an explanation of the difference must appear on the supporting documentation. If the only supporting documentation is the court order electronically available from the court, a copy of the check may serve as supporting documentation. The supporting documentation should contain the related docket entry number or date, when applicable.

Cashier's checks and wire transfers should only be used to make a payment under extraordinary circumstances, which include but are not limited to (i) an immediate payment necessary to prevent loss to the estate or injury to a person or property and the service provider will not accept a check; (ii) a wire transfer required by applicable law or regulation (e.g., tax deposits in excess of $50,000); and (iii) a payment that must be made to an overseas creditor or a foreign corporation. A copy of the cashier's check or wire transfer bank advice and related documentation should be maintained in the file. Counter checks may never be used.

All checks must be captioned with the bankruptcy case name and number and the Chapter 7 trustee's name. The terms "debtor" and "trustee" should appear, unabbreviated, as illustrated in the following example: Case Number 02-12345; ABC Corp., debtor; John Doe, trustee. (Each item in this example is required, in no particular order. The term "case number" is desirable, but may be abbreviated or omitted.) The checks also must include a statement that the check will be void if not cashed within 90 days.

Computer System

The litany of requirements and strictures in connection with the day-to-day operations might seem daunting, but the software industry has provided excellent computer systems that simplify an otherwise extraordinary responsibility. Without the computer systems, jumping through the regulatory hoops would prove to be an intolerable burden.

The data within the case-management system and all electronically maintained estate files must be backed up daily. A copy of the backup disk(s) or tape(s) should be maintained in a secure offsite location at least weekly. The liquidator is responsible for ensuring that the data and files are protected and recoverable. If the software provider backs up the data, the liquidator should obtain written assurances from them regarding data integrity, security, and recovery within a reasonable amount of time (e.g., 24–48 hours). The liquidator may want to keep local backups in the event that the service provider cannot restore the data within the necessary time frame. The liquidator should ensure that the backup and recovery procedures are tested periodically and should routinely back up those computer files that are not part of the daily back up described above.

The liquidator also ensures the continued availability of the software needed to access the files. If the liquidator upgrades computer software or hardware, or converts to a new system, continued access to archived electronic case information must be ensured. This may require retention of the retired hardware and/or software. As a security matter, unused out-of-date software should not be retained on the new system. Only authorized users should be allowed access to the computer programs and data via the terminal, network, or modem.

The computer system and data should be protected from viruses, intrusion via the Internet, and power disruptions. Virus protection software should be updated at least monthly. The software should contain a tamper-proof feature that consecutively numbers estate-account checks as the checks are created or printed by the computer system. The number sequence on manually written checks should not duplicate the computer-generated numbers. The software should prevent any changes to the date, check number, payer/payee, and amount of a transaction, the re-use of numbers on voided checks, and the deletion of a transaction, after the check has been printed or deposit has been made.

Appendix 5

Discounted Cash-Flow Valuation

To use the income approach in valuing an estate or an asset held by the estate, the liquidator must make appropriate adjustments for the time value of money. Suppose, for example, an asset is expected to produce an income of \$1,000 per year for 10 years and then cease to exist. Such an asset would throw off total payments of \$10,000 over the 10-year period. But no buyer would want to pay \$10,000 for it. That is because a sum of money to be paid in the future is worth less than that same sum of money to be paid today. The first payment of \$1,000 is to be paid a year from now. If you had that \$1,000 today, it could be invested at some rate of return (e.g., 5%) and a year later would have grown to a higher amount (\$1,050). Looked at from the other direction, \$1,000 received a year hence is equivalent to $\$1{,}000/(1.05) = \$952$ today (using a 5% discount rate). Similarly, using a 5% rate of return, \$1,000 to be received two years from now is worth $\$1{,}000/(1.05)^2 = \$907$, and so on. In general \$1,000 to be received a year from now is worth $\$1{,}000/(1 + r)$ where r is the appropriate rate of discount for the passage of time. If the sum is to be received in two years, the discounted sum is $\$1{,}000/(1 + r)^2$ and if it is to be received in year n, the discounted value is $\$1{,}000/(1 + r)^n$. Accordingly, the value of an asset that is expected to produce an income of \$1,000 per year for 10 years is equal to

$$\mathrm{V} = \frac{\$1,000}{(1+r)} + \frac{\$1,000}{(1+r)^2} + \frac{\$1,000}{(1+r)^3} + \cdots + \frac{\$1,000}{(1+r)^n}$$

If the set of expected payments were valued using a 5% discount rate, the asset would have a present value of \$7,722. If, however, the appropriate discount rate were higher, the estimated value would be lower. For a 10% rate, the estimated present value would be \$5,650.

Conceptually, the income approach is rather straightforward to apply. One simply forecasts the payment stream, selects an appropriate discount rate, and the rest is arithmetic. Software for performing the calculations is available. Indeed bonds, mortgages, and other assets with easily forecasted income streams are often valued in just this way. And yet most assets are very difficult to value using the income approach in its pure form.

The first problem encountered in applying the income approach to an asset which does not have a contractually fixed income stream is the difficulty of forecasting these cash flows. One can start with the current levels and look back at past fluctuations and forward with some idea about future conditions. Using such information, one may be able to generate cash-flow forecasts for one or a few years into the future. The reliability of such forecasts, however, is very likely to drop off quickly as the distance to the anticipated cash flow is increased. Moreover, selecting the appropriate discount rate is itself a challenge.

Mindful of these drawbacks, the financial profession has devised a couple of shortcuts that, given the uncertainty of most of the numbers being used, rarely sacrifices much reliability compared to the more detailed approach. The first of these goes under the name of the dividend discount model. It was designed for stock market valuation but it can be applied to any type of asset. The basic valuation formula is

$$\text{Value} = \frac{\text{Initial Cash Flow}}{(r-g)}$$

where

$$r = \text{appropriate discount rate}$$

and

$$g = \text{expected average growth rate in cash flows.}$$

The initial cash flow (most recent 12 months) is known. Accordingly, the valuation formula only requires estimates for r and g. The appropriate discount rate r is not necessarily easy to forecast, but the process is not too difficult to grasp. The appropriate formula is

$$r = \text{RFR} + \text{RP}$$

where

RFR the risk-free rate in the market place

and

RP is the risk premium appropriate for this asset.

The RFR number is easy to obtain. Most financial economists view the rate on U.S. government bonds as close to risk free. The 10-year treasury-bond rate (available in the newspaper) will do for most purposes. The more serious problem arises in the effort to come up with an appropriate value for the risk premium. One could read a book on the subject and still not know how to target a reliable number in specific cases. Look for assets that the market has priced that have similar risks to the asset you are trying to value. Then derive an estimate for the risk premium on those marketable assets and apply that value to your own asset. As an example, you might rate the investment as having a risk comparable to an A-rated corporate bond. If such bonds were priced to yield 1.5% more than government bonds, the risk premium (RP) would equal 1.5%.

An even greater difficulty arises in trying to estimate the future growth rate. Again, books are written on the subject. General advice on how to forecast a growth rate is rather limited. The history of past growth rates may provide some guidance, but the future is not always like the past.

Fortunately, we have another shortcut to consider that can be used to produce reasonable valuations, which is even easier to apply. This shortcut is called the market multiple approach. The formula for the market multiple is

$$\text{Value} = (\text{earnings})(\text{market multiple}).$$

The earnings number may be any of several different measures of current (last 12 months) earnings, including profit (before or after taxes), earnings before interest, earnings before interest, taxes, depreciation and amortization (EBDITDA), or free cash flow (EBDITDA–CAPEX, where CAPEX stands for required capital expenditures). Each of the earnings numbers has an associated market multiple. That market multiple is derived from valuations of similar businesses in the market (either purchase-and-sale transactions or active trading of public securities). Such market multiples can be derived from publicly available information. A stock's price-earnings ratio (PE) is an example of a market multiple. So, for example, if a similar publicly traded company has a PE of 15 and the business to be valued is generating earnings of $1 million dollars a year, its value would be estimated at $15 million.

Appendix 6

Evaluation of Preference Payment Claims

The bankruptcy liquidator's duties involve assessment of the debtor's preference claims. In general every payment made by the debtor during the 90-day preference period prior to the bankruptcy filing is considered a preference payment that is subject to certain defenses. The three primary defenses include: (i) new value provided by the vendor to the debtor after the alleged preferential payments for which the vendor was not paid that offsets the amount of these payments; (ii) the payment was made in the ordinary course of business; and (iii) the transaction was a contemporaneous exchange or otherwise not a payment on account of antecedent debt. The liquidator and/or accounting staff must analyze each of these payments and determine whether suit should be brought. The initial assessment of potential preference claims should be approached systematically.

The first step is to identify all payments made by the debtor during the 90-day preference period from the debtor's accounts payable disbursement records. Payees can be grouped into certain categories in order to exclude payments made to employees, bankruptcy-related professionals, government agencies and taxing authorities, and vendors whose contracts were assumed in bankruptcy.

Second, calculate new-value amounts and subtract these offset amounts against the preference-period payments. This represents the maximum net preference recovery, (i.e., total payments minus new-value offsets), before any payments are excluded for ordinary-course-of-business defenses.

Third, perform an ordinary-course-of-business analysis. Payments which were clearly made in the ordinary-course-of-business should be completely eliminated from the maximum net preference value.

Where ordinary course status is less certain, potential recovery percentages should be assigned based on an estimate of the strength of the ordinary course of business defense. For example, vendors with preference-period payment patterns generally consistent with prepreference period patterns are estimated to have a stronger defense, thus yielding lower estimated recovery percentages. Vendors with less consistent patterns are estimated to have weaker defenses and thus higher estimated recovery percentages. These recovery percentages are then applied to the lesser of the maximum net preference value or high case ordinary-course value to calculate an estimated range of preference payment recoveries.

This preliminary analysis reflects the impact of various potential defenses to a preference action, but it obviously does not predict the possible outcome of preference actions. Defenses in addition to those whose impacts are estimated above may be raised.

Data Gathering

Electronic data can be extracted from the debtor's information system and organized into four sets: (i) payment information, (ii) payment invoice detail, (iii) unpaid invoices, and (iv) vendor information.

The payment-information data set includes the payment detail for payments made within the approximate 12-month period prior to the petition date. This information is used in determining preference-period payments as well as determining the trends and assumptions used in estimating potential new-value and ordinary-course-of-business defenses.

The payment-invoice data specify exactly which invoices were paid with each payment. These data are used in the analysis to estimate new value and ordinary-course-of-business defenses.

The unpaid-invoices data set includes all of the invoices that remained unpaid as of the petition date. This data set is used to facilitate the compilation of the new-value information required to estimate new-value defenses. The invoice detail associated with the payment detail discussed above includes the invoice history of a vendor except for those invoices that were not paid. Therefore, this data set completes the invoice activity for each vendor during the approximate 12-month period prior to the petition date.

Finally, the vendor information data set contains general information associated with each vendor such as vendor names, vendor numbers and types.

Analysis

Typically, the debtor's payment information contains the disbursement date (payment dates) regardless of the date such payments actually cleared the respective bank accounts (clearing dates). The clearing date is a key fact required to establish which payments were made during the 90-day preference period. Accordingly, payment-information records must be updated to include clearing dates based on information obtained from bank accounts utilized by the debtor during the 12-month period. Some disbursements may have never cleared a bank account. Unrecorded disbursements may be identified in bank statements. These differences result from several causes, including the existence of certain transactions that are processed directly to the general ledger rather than through the accounts payable and disbursements ledger. Investigation of these items with debtor's management is necessary, so that they can be updated to represent the actual disbursement history based on clearing dates.

Often, open credit memos and invoices in a debtor's books and records are recorded as offsetting transactions, one a debit or series of debits, and the other a credit or a series of credits. This type of situation occurs when a debtor adjusts its accounts payable records to correct errors and record accounting adjustments. These open credit memos and invoices net to $0.00. Since, however, the credit memos and invoices have different dates in the system, they can affect the preference calculation. A systematic process of matching credit memos and invoices must be performed to eliminate from the preference calculation the open credit memos and invoices that net to $0.00. This adjustment is necessary in order to eliminate accounting adjustments and isolate the true economic substance of each transaction.

Vendors should be excluded from the preference analysis if the vendor's contract(s) were either already assumed or the debtor plans on assuming the contract(s) at confirmation. It is possible that these vendors received payments for goods and/or services not related to these contracts. However, unless the effort has been taken to match invoices and payments to specific contracts, all invoices and payments made to these vendors should be excluded from the preference analysis. Also, vendors holding cash collateral at the petition date, vendors holding letters of credit at the petition date, and vendors holding reclamation claims typically have additional defenses not considered in the new-value or ordinary-course calculations.

New-Value Analysis Amount

The new-value analysis is the maximum difference between the amounts paid and the amounts shipped per vendor within the preference period. This analysis is performed by developing a list of total payments by day (based on check clearing date) and the total amount invoiced per day (based on invoice date). The maximum positive difference between the amounts paid and the amounts invoiced is considered to be the maximum amount of the net preference claim, which is also subject to further reduction based on the ordinary-course-of-business defenses.

Appendix Table 6.1

Days Prior to Petition Date	Payments ($)	Shipments	Pay to Ship Per Day Difference	Maximum Net Preference
90	—	100	(100)	—
75	100	—	100	100
70	100	—	100	200
60	100	—	100	300
45	—	200	(200)	100
40	—	300	(300)	—
30	500	—	500	500
20	500	100	400	900
	1,300	700	600	

*Number in thousands.

To serve as "new value," new products or services must be delivered subsequent to a preference payment; otherwise it is not new value. In other words, if a vendor provided goods or services two days prior to a preference payment, this would not qualify as new value as it occurred prior to the payment. The date in which the maximum difference between the amounts paid and the amounts invoiced is identified for purposes of determining the preference payments net of new value offsets. Appendix table 6.1 is designed to illustrate this point.

The maximum net preference from the table is $900,000. Although the total difference between the amounts paid and amounts shipped during the entire preference period was only $600,000, some of these shipments did not qualify as subsequent new value. The maximum net preference amount of $900,000 results from $1,000,000 of payments and $100,000 of shipments in the last 30 days prior to the petition date. All other activity in the preceding 60 days is not considered, because new-value shipments had offset payments prior to this point in time. To understand this new value concept fully, consider the following:

- The shipment made 90 days prior to the petition date arrived before any payments were made during the preference period and, therefore, had no effect on the maximum net preference. This is value that was provided by the vendor, but it arose prior to any payments, and it was not subsequent new value.
- The next three transactions are all payments within the preference period that increase the maximum net preference. Therefore, a $300,000 maximum net preference amount exists 60 days prior to the petition date.
- The $200,000 shipment made 45 days prior to the petition date reduces the maximum net preference amount from $300,000 to $100,000 and qualifies entirely as a new-value reduction.
- The $300,000 shipment made 40 days prior to the petition date reduces the maximum net preference from $100,000 to $0. Therefore, only $100,000

of this shipment qualifies as subsequent new value. The other $200,000 of shipments has no impact on the preference calculation.

- The $500,000 payment made 30 days prior to the petition date increases the maximum net preference from $0 to $500,000.
- The $400,000 difference between the $500,000 payment and the $100,000 shipment made 20 days prior to the petition date increases the maximum preference from $400,000 to $900,000.

As illustrated in the example, the maximum net preference amount for each vendor represents the largest dollar difference between the amounts paid and the amounts shipped between a certain date within the 90-day preference period and the petition date.

Ordinary-Course Analysis Value

Three primary analyses can be performed as ordinary-course-of-business tests: (i) scattergrams, (ii) a weighted average comparison, and (iii) standard deviation. A scattergram analysis compares the number of days between the invoice date and payment date for the historical period and the preference period (see appendix table 6.2). As can be seen from this example, the historical payments were made anywhere from 19 to 41 days after the invoice date, while all of the payments during the preference period were made more than 41 days after the invoice date. Note that this example depicts a clear difference between historic-period and preference-period payments. Data indicates the payments made during the preference period were made outside of the ordinary course of business, as the payment timing was different from historical patterns. Payment patterns related to a debtor's vendors are generally wider and more sporadic, thus making an ordinary course of business more difficult.

Appendix Table 6.2

	Preference		Preference Period	
Days to Clear	Paid Inv Count	Paid Inv ($)	Paid Inv Count	Paid Inv ($)
19	16	1,440		
21	1	1,305		
24	21	1,800		
26	1	1,350		
27	1	1,215		
30	1	2,430		
36	1	720		
41	2	4,230		
49			1	2,025
52			1	945
69			1	95,990
>90			1	1,350
	44	14,490	4	100,310

The weighted average number of days to pay during the historical nine-month period should be calculated based on the number of days between invoice date and payment date, with the average weighted by the invoice amounts. For example, if it took 100 days to pay an invoice in the amount of $100,000 and 50 days to pay an invoice in the amount of $10, the weighted average would approximate 100 days, as the $100,000 invoice would impact the weighted average substantially (10,000 times) more than the $10 invoice.

Based on the weighted average days to pay comparison, a standard deviation calculation can be performed to identify those historical weighted averages that have a large deviation. A large standard deviation indicates that the historical-payment timing was sporadic. Therefore, no ordinary-course-of-business pattern exists.

A specified range of days can then be identified as ordinary-course payment timing for each vendor, based on a review of the results of these analyses, particularly the scattergrams. Payments made within the specified range should be considered payments made in the ordinary course of business. Payments outside this range less new value represent the estimate of the high end of the recoverable amounts. Payments that were made prior to invoice date (prepayments) or on the same date as the invoice date (cash on delivery) should also be excluded. These payments are not payments made on account of antecedent debt, which is a necessary condition for establishing a preference payment claim.

A review of the payment history is necessary in order to determine how to treat wire payments made to vendors. Vendors should be separated into two groups: (i) vendors with wire payments treated as the normal method of payment and (ii) vendors with wire payments treated as preference payments. Vendors with wire payments treated as the normal method of payment have a consistent history of wire payments before and during the preference period. Wire payments (and invoices paid by these payments) for these vendors should be eliminated from the estimated recoverable amount, if the wire payment was made in the ordinary course of business, based on the payment history for that vendor. A wire payment to be classified as preference will exhibit a change in the method of payment from checks to wires just preceding or during the preference period.

Appendix Table 6.3

Estimated Recovery Percentages			
Grade	Low %	High %	Grade Criteria
A	40%	60%	Completely different timing differences
B	20%	40%	Significant timing differences
C	5%	20%	Slight to moderate timing differences
D	0%	5%	No to slight timing differences

Such wire payments for these vendors should be considered a preference payment, regardless of whether the wire payment was made in the ordinary course of business.

Conclusion

In summary, the high case ordinary-course analysis results in a total potential preference payment amount calculated as follows: amount of total payments less new value and less payments that have been treated as payments made in the ordinary course of business or were contemporaneous exchange payments. Recovery estimates can be based on a grading system used in connection with reviewing the ordinary-course patterns for each vendor. Grades can be assigned to each vendor based on a manual review of the vendors. Appendix table 6.3 presents a possible grading system, the percentage recovery range per grade, and general criteria used for assigning each grade.

Obviously, these recovery percentages must be assigned without the benefit of testimony and documents that might be gathered in a more in-depth analysis. Such an analysis might yield a more meaningful estimate the value of preference claims. Upon assigning a grade to each vendor, the recovery percentages can be applied to calculate the low and high case preference recovery estimates for each vendor. Questions as to collectibility can further reduce these estimates.

Appendix 7

Litigation Net-Present-Value Exercise

The following exercise assists the liquidator in calculating the net present value of an estate cause of action using the components of (i) probability of success, (ii) litigation cost, (iii) time required to litigate, and (iv) probability of ultimate collection. Instinct, or gut feeling, is an important overlay to the value derived from this exercise.

Probability of Success

In appendix table 7.1, the person conducting the analysis believes that the decision will depend 30% on the law, 40% on the facts, 20% on the equities, and 10% on the receptiveness of the forum in which the case is heard. The litigant assesses his or her position in relation to the law at 80% (versus 20% for the other side) and 60%, 50%, and 50% on the facts, equities, and forum, respectively. These inputs yield a composite forecast for success of 63%. This percentage must be applied to the estimated financial impact of success.

Litigation Cost

Assume the cost forecasts shown in appendix table 7.2 for the six identified stages of litigation.

Note that this sum is approximately what is estimated if the case goes to trial, but not appealed ($289 versus $350). Most of these costs would be incurred at the summary judgment or trial phase.

Appendix Table 7.1

Factor	Relative Importance (I)	Relative Strengths (S)	Product (I × S)
Law	0.3	0.8	0.24
Facts	0.4	0.6	0.24
Equities	0.2	0.5	0.10
Forum receptivity	0.1	0.5	0.5
Total	Sum to 1.0		0.63

Appendix Table 7.2

	Total Cost (in $1,000) (C)	Probability (P)	Cost Factor (C × P)
Early settlement	10	.1	1
Arbitration	30	.1	3
Summary judgment	100	.1	10
Trial no appeal	350	.4	140
Appeal	400	.2	80
After collection efforts	450	.1	45
Total	450	Sum to 1.0	289

Time Required to Litigate

The time forecast is constructed in the same fashion as the cost forecast. To estimate the time likely to be required to resolve the litigation, one would first estimate the length of time required to resolve the issue for each of the six events. Then, one would estimate the likelihood of the resolution occurring at that time frame. Assume the estimates shown in appendix table 7.3 were made.

With these inputs, one would forecast that the case is expected to take 1.83 years with a 90% chance that it would be resolved by the end of the second year.

Probability of Ultimate Collection

The value of the defined sum from a potential judgment or settlement may be viewed as follows:

$$(\mathrm{VDS}) = \mathrm{GVDS} - (\mathrm{DI} + \mathrm{DE} + \mathrm{DA})$$

where

(VDS) = net value of defined sum
(expected amount of judgment or settlement),

GVDS = gross value of defined sum,

Appendix Table 7.3

	Length in Years (L)	Probability (P)	Product (L × P)
Early settlement	.3	.1	.03
Arbitration	.5	.1	.05
Summary judgment	1.0	.1	.10
Trial no appeal	1.5	.4	.60
On appeal	2.0	.2	.80
After collection efforts	2.5	.1	.25
Expected length	2.5	Sum to 1.0	1.83 years

DI = discount applicable,
if potential defendant is or may
be rendered insolvent,

DE = discount applicable,
if a large portion of the potential
defendant's assets are illiquid, and

DA = discount applicable, if the potential defendant
is likely to attempt to avoid making payment
by trying to put his or her assets beyond
the reach of the plaintiff.

Discount Rate

$$NPVp = PV(YX) - PV(PLC)$$

where

NPVp = expected value of continued litigation for the estate,

PV(YX) = present value of expected payment YX awarded on Z date,

PLC = estate's expected additional litigation costs,

Y = probability of success,

X = expected judgment, and

Z = date on which judgment is expected to be paid.

$$NPVd = PV(YX) + PV(DLC)$$

where

NPVd = expected cost of continued litigation for the defendant,

$$\text{PVC XY} = \text{present value of expected payment YX awarded to plaintiff on Z date,}$$

$$\text{DLC} = \text{defendant's expected additional litigation cost,}$$

$$\text{NPVd} > \text{NPVp and NPVd} - \text{NPVp} = \text{PV(DLC} + \text{PLC),}$$

$$\text{PV(YX)} - \text{PV(PLC) to PV(YX)} + \text{PV (DLC), and}$$

$$\text{NPVp} < \text{NPVd.}$$

A conservative trustee will apply a somewhat higher risk premium to compute the present value of the potential award. The resulting higher discount rate will make the present value of the award smaller. A conservative defendant will, in contrast, want to prepare for an adverse outcome and therefore have a somewhat lower discount rate. Such a discount rate will result in a higher present value of the expected award from the viewpoint of the defendant. Thus, if the litigants are conservative in their analyses, the plaintiff will generally compute a lower present value for the expected award.

A More Sophisticated Analysis

In the preceding discussion, the potential litigation is evaluated first on an all-or-nothing basis. If that analysis produces a negative NPV, it is then evaluated for the initial stages. Thereafter, the NPV of continued litigation is recomputed as the case evolves. Given the uncertainty of the estimated parameters, this approach is as reliable as possible under the circumstances, and yet it does involve some shortcuts that may introduce errors. If neither the all-or-nothing nor the initial stage NPV is positive, the litigation would undergo a separate stand-alone analysis with parameter estimates for each subsequent stage of the litigation. In particular, separate estimates would be made for the likely amount to be received from litigation success for each stage. Thus, prejudgment interest and any other relevant variables would be incorporated into the award amount estimated for each stage. The NPV of each stage could then be computed from the parameters of that stage.

With this more sophisticated analysis, one would compute the all-or-nothing NPV at each stage of the litigation. The liquidator would estimate each of the four parameters (cost, time, probable success, and collectibility) for the initial stage (early settlement). An appropriate discount rate would be chosen, and the NPV for this stage as a stand-alone project would be computed. The analysis would be repeated for each successive stage (i.e., arbitration, summary judgment, trial with no appeal, on appeal, and after collection efforts). If the NPV is positive for any stage, the litigation should be undertaken, unless settlement offers a still higher value. As with the earlier analysis, this analysis would, and usually should, be reviewed as the case progresses.

Appendix 8

Calculating the Impact of Subordination on Distributions

As part of working out who gets what in a liquidation, the parties have to deal with which unsecured creditor is subordinate to whom. These theories apply equally in Chapter 7 and Chapter 11 liquidations. The subordination issue typically arises in larger cases involving publicly held debt issues (bonds).

Most trust indentures (i.e., the stated contract between the issuer/borrower and the creditor) involving publicly issued subordinated debt provide for inchoate forbearance; that is, the subordinated debt may be paid according to the terms thereof, unless a default exists with respect to senior creditors. Senior creditors typically include bank debt or other particularly designated categories of debt owed by the borrower. In the real world, senior creditors typically do not include trade debt. Trade debt is neither senior nor junior to the bond debenture issue, but rather is characterized as neutral, even though its proper place usually is more with the senior than the junior unsecured debt holders.

Just who is senior to whom is often in dispute. For example, the trade creditors want to claim seniority to the subordinated debt while the junior bondholders want to claim the contrary. The indenture may not be totally clear on the matter of to what the subordinated debt is subordinate. If, for example, the trade debt is clearly *pari passu* with the senior unsecured bank debt, but the junior debt is only subordinated to senior bank debt, a complicated payout formula is required.

First, the available proceeds are allocated to the three categories of debt holders as if they were of equal standing. Then the value that is, in the first pass, allocated to the subordinated debt, is usually reallocated to the senior bank debt up to the amount of their shortfall. Any remaining monies are to be distributed to the junior bondholders. The trade debt distribution is not impacted by the transfer from the junior to the senior creditors. Other formulae are applicable for other classifications.

An example may help clarify this scheme (see appendix table 8.1). First, assume there is no subordination and everyone is *pari passu.*

Appendix Table 8.1

	Claims ($ million)	Available for distribution
Bank debt	$ 50	$99 million
Trade debt	50	
Subordinated debt	50	
Total	$150	

	Initial Allocation ($ million)	% of Recovery on Claim
Banks	$33	66%
Trade	33	66%
Subordinate	33	66%
Total	$99	

Now, consider the result if the subordinated debt is subordinated to the bank debt: The bank's shortfall is $17 million, which is taken from the subordinate

Appendix Table 8.2

		% of Recovery on Claim
Banks	$50 million	100%
Trade	33 million	66%
Subordinate	16 million	32%
Total	$99 million	

holders' initial allocation. The final allocation is shown in appendix table 8.2. Now contrast this result with other possibilities. Suppose, for example, both trade and bank debt were classified as senior with the debenture debt subordinated to both. In that situation, the initial allocation of the subordinated holders would be allocated pro rata to both trade and bank debt (see appendix table 8.3).

Appendix Table 8.3

		% of Recovery on Claim
Banks	$49.5 million	99%
Trade	49.5 million	99%
Subordinates	0.0 million	0%
	$99.0 million	

Now suppose both trade and debenture debt is subordinated to bank debt but the trade and subordinated debt are *pari passu* (an unlikely situation). The bank's initial $17 million shortfall would be taken pro rata from both the trade and subordinate debt holders (see appendix table 8.4).

Appendix Table 8.4

		% of Recovery on Claim
Banks	$50.0 million	100%
Trade	24.5 million	49%
Subordinate	24.5 million	49%
Total	$99.0 million	

Finally, suppose the bank debt is senior to both and the trade debt is senior to the subordinated debentures (see appendix table 8.5).

Appendix Table 8.5

		% of Recovery on Claim
Banks	$50 million	100%
Trade	49 million	98%
Subordinated	0 million	0%
Total	$99 million	

Clearly, the way a subordination clause applies can have a major impact on the payout for the various classes of creditors.

The results shown in the example represent possible outcomes from subordination provisions in bond indentures. The payment provisions in a consensual plan of reorganization generally reflect the legal impact of the subordination clause, but in the give and take of plan negotiations, the juniors tend to fair a bit better and the seniors a bit worse than strict application of the subordination provisions provide. If the case is converted to Chapter 7, the subordination provisions will be strictly enforced. This threat is a potent weapon for the senior creditors in the Chapter 11 plan negotiation process.

Discussions often become heated over the classification of subordinated debt in workout scenarios, both pre- and postbankruptcy. Clear answers to the powers of the absolute priority rule are often absent. In determining the position of unsecured debt under a liquidation analysis, investment bankers sometimes allocate relative values to subordinated debt, particularly when multiple layers of subordinated debt exist. This analysis may assign value to subordinated debt issues even though all subordinated debt is out of the money (presumably, based on an analysis incorporating the results of the workout/ bankruptcy dynamics). So, despite accounting results to the contrary, the dynamics of bankruptcy often yield returns to deeply subordinated and deeply out-of-the-money paper.

Appendix 9

State-by-State Dissolution Requirements

Appendix Table 9.1

State	Statute	Based on Model Business Corporation Act 1984
Alabama	Ala. Code § 10-2B-14.02 (2005)	Yes
Alaska	Alaska Stat. § 10.06.605 (2005)	No
Arizona	Ariz. Rev. Stat. 10-1402 (2005)	Yes
Arkansas	Ark. Code Ann. § 4-27-1402 (2005)	Yes
California	Cal. Corp. Code §§ 1900, 1903 (2005)	No
Colorado	Colo. Rev. Stat. Ann. § 17-114-102 (2005)	Yes
Connecticut	Conn. Gen. Stat. § 33-881 (2005)	No
Delaware	Del. Code Ann. tit. 8, § 275 (2005)	No
District of Columbia	D.C. Code Ann. §§ 29-101.77-.78 (2005)	Patterned after
Florida	Fla. Stat. Ann. 607.1402 (2005)	Yes
Georgia	Ga. Code Ann. § 14-2-1402 (2005)	Yes
Hawaii	Haw. Rev. Stat. § 414-382 (2005)	Yes
Idaho	Idaho Code Ann. § 30-1-1402 (2005)	Yes
Illinois	Ill. Comp. Stat. Ann. 5/12.10, 5/12.15 (2005)	No
Indiana	Ind. Code § 23-1-45-2 (2005)	Yes
Iowa	Iowa Code § 490.1402 (2005)	Yes
Kansas	Kan. Stat. Ann. § 17-6804 (2005)	No
Kentucky	Ky. Rev. Stat. Ann. § 271B.14-020 (2005)	Yes
Louisiana	La. Rev. Stat. Ann. § 12:142 (2005)	No
Maine	Me. Rev. Stat. Ann. tit. 13-C, §§ 1402, 1403 (2005)	Yes
Maryland	Md. Code Ann., Corps. & Assn'ns § 3-403 (2005)	No
Massachusetts	Mass. Gen. Laws Ann. ch. 156D, § 14.02 (2005)	Yes
Michigan	Mich. Comp. Laws Ann. §§ 450.1801, .1804 (2005)	No

Appendix Table 9.1 (*continued*)

State	Statute	Based on Model Business Corporation Act 1984
Minnesota	Minn. Stat. Ann. §§ 302A. 701, 302A.721 (2005)	No
Mississippi	Miss. Code Ann. § 79-4-1402 (2005)	Yes
Missouri	Mo. Rev. Stat. Ann. § 351.464, 351.466 (2005)	Yes
Montana	Mont. Code Ann. § 35-1-932 (2005)	Yes
Nebraska	Neb. Rev. Stat. Ann. § 21-20, 152 (2005)	Yes
Nevada	Nev. Rev. Stat. Ann. § 78.580 (2005)	No
New Hampshire	N.H. Rev. Stat. Ann. § 293-A:14.02 (2005)	Yes
New Jersey	N.J. Stat. Ann. §§ 14A:12-3, 12-4, 12-4.1 (2005)	No
New Mexico	N.M. Laws Stat. Ann. § 53-16-2 to -3 (2005)	Yes
New York	N.Y. Bus. Corp. Law §§ 615(a), 1001 (2005)	No
North Carolina	N.C. Gen. Stat. Ann. § 55-14-02 (2005)	Yes
North Dakota	N.D. Cent. Code §§ 10-19.1-105, 10-19.1-107 (2005)	No
Ohio	Ohio Rev. Code Ann. § 1701-86 (2005)	No
Oklahoma	Okla. Stat, tit. 18, § 1096 (2005)	No
Oregon	Or. Rev. Stat, §§ 60.624, 60.627 (2005)	Yes
Pennsylvania	Pa. Cons. Stat. Ann. § 1972 (2005)	No
Rhode Island	R.I. Gen. Laws §§ 7-1.2-1302, 7-1.2-1303 (2006)	No
South Carolina	S.C. Code Ann. § 33-14-102 (2005)	Yes
South Dakota	S.D. Codified Laws § 47-1A-1402 (2006)	Yes
Tennessee	Tenn. Code Ann. § 48-24-102 (2005)	Yes
Texas	Tex. Corps. & Ass'ns Code Ann. §§ 6.02, 6.03 (2005)	Partially
Utah	Utah Code Ann. § 16-10A-1402 (2005)	Yes
Vermont	Vt. Stat. Ann. tit. 11A, § 14.02 (2005)	Yes
Virginia	Va. Code Ann. §§ 13.1-742 to -743 (2005)	Yes
Washington	Wash. Rev. Code § 23B.14.020 (2005)	Yes
West Virginia	W.Va. Code § 31D-14-1402 (2005)	Yes
Wisconsin	Wis. Stat. § 180.1402(1)(a) (2005)	Yes
Wyoming	Wyo. Stat. Ann. § 17-16-1402 (2005)	Yes

Appendix 10

Asset Purchase Agreement

This Asset Purchase Agreement (the "Agreement") is made and entered into as of this [___] day of _______, 200_ by and between [____________________], a [_______________] (the "Buyer"), on the one hand, and Friede Goldman Halter, Inc., a Mississippi corporation, and Debtor and Debtor-in-Possession (the "Seller") under Case No. __________ (collectively, the "Case") in the United States Bankruptcy Court in the [__________] District of [__________] (the "Bankruptcy Court").

Recitals

A. Seller is engaged in a variety of businesses related to the design, manufacture, conversion and modification of offshore drilling rigs, marine vessels and engineered products for the maritime and offshore energy industries. The relevant line of business for the purposes of this Agreement is the Seller's business segment specifically involved in the design, construction and repair of small to medium-sized ocean going vessels for commercial and government markets, known within the Seller's operations as Halter Marine or the Vessels group (the "Business").

B. Seller wishes to sell to Buyer substantially all the assets it uses in connection with the Business at the price and on the other terms and conditions specified in detail below and Buyer wishes to so purchase and acquire such assets from Seller.

NOW, THEREFORE, for good and valuable consideration, the receipt and sufficiency of which is hereby acknowledged, the parties agree as follows:

1. *Transfer of Assets*

1.1 *Purchase and Sale of Assets.* On the Closing Date, as hereinafter defined, in consideration of the covenants, representations and obligations of Buyer hereunder, and subject to the conditions hereinafter set forth, Seller shall sell, assign, transfer, convey and deliver to Buyer, and Buyer shall purchase from Seller all of Seller's right, title and interest as of the Closing Date in and to the following assets, wherever located (collectively, the "Property");

1.1.1 *Leases and Contracts.* Seller's right, title and interest (i) as lessee under those real property leases described on Exhibit "A-1" to this Agreement (collectively, the "Real Property Leases"), (ii) as lessee under those equipment, personal property and intangible property leases, rental agreements, licenses, contracts, agreements and similar arrangements described on Exhibit "A-2" to this Agreement (collectively, the "Other Leases"), and (iii) as a party to those other contracts, leases, orders, purchase orders, licenses, contracts, agreements and similar arrangements described on Exhibit "A-3" (collectively, the "Other Contracts" and together with the Other Leases, the "Other Leases and Contracts").

1.1.2 *Real Property and Improvements.* Seller's fee simple ownership interest in that certain real property described in Exhibit "A-4" and all improvements located thereon (collectively, the "Real Property"), but in all events only to the extent, if any, Seller's interest in the same (collectively, the "Improvements").

1.1.3 *Personal Property.* All of those items of equipment and tangible personal property owned by Seller and listed in Exhibit "B" attached to this Agreement and any other tangible personal property acquired by Seller after the date hereof but prior to the Closing Date exclusively in connection with the Business, (collectively, the "Personal Property"). As used in this Agreement, the Personal Property shall not include the Inventory.

1.1.4 *Intangible Property.* All intangible personal property owned or held by Seller and used exclusively in connection with the Business, but in all cases only to the extent of Seller's interest therein and only to the extent transferable, together with all books, records and like items pertaining exclusively to the Business (collectively, the "Intangible Property"), including, without limitation, the name [____________] and the items identified on Exhibit "C" hereto. As used in this Agreement, Intangible Property shall in all events exclude, (i) any materials containing privileged communications or information about employees, disclosure of which would violate an employee's reasonable expectation of privacy and any other materials which are subject to attorney client or any other privilege or requirement to maintain confidentiality (including any rights to assert privilege), and (ii) Seller's corporate books and records relating to its organization and existence.

1.1.5 *Receivables.* All accounts receivable arising out of the operation of the Business and, subject to Section 1.2, all causes of action relating or pertaining to the foregoing (collectively, the "Receivables").

1.1.6 *Inventory.* All supplies, goods, materials, work in process, inventory and stock in trade owned by Seller exclusively for use or sale in the ordinary course of the Business (collectively, the "Inventory").

1.1.7 *Stock.* All stock in the following subsidiaries: ____________ [list subsidiaries to be acquired] (the "Purchased Subsidiaries").

1.2 *Excluded Assets.* Notwithstanding anything to the contrary in this Agreement, the Property shall not include (i) those items excluded pursuant to the provisions of Section 1.1 above; (ii) all cash and cash equivalents; (iii) Inventory transferred or used by Seller in the ordinary course of the Business prior to the Closing Date; (iv) any lease, rental agreement, contract, agreement, license or similar arrangement ("Contracts") terminated or expired prior to the Closing Date in accordance with its terms or in the ordinary course of the Business; (v) [any right, property or asset listed on Exhibit "D" hereto]; (vi) all preference or avoidance claims and actions of the Seller, including, without limitation, any such claims and actions arising under Sections 544, 547, 548, 549, and 550 of the United States Bankruptcy Code; (vii) the Seller's rights under this Agreement and all cash and non-cash consideration payable or deliverable to the Seller pursuant to the terms and provisions hereof; or (viii) insurance proceeds, claims and causes of action with respect to or arising in connection with (A) any Contract which is not assigned to Buyer at the Closing, or (B) any item of tangible or intangible property not acquired by Buyer at the Closing.

1.3 *Instruments of Transfer.* The sale, assignment, transfer, conveyance and delivery of the Property to Buyer and the assumption of liabilities provided herein by Buyer shall be made by assignments, bill of sale, deed, stock power and other instruments of assignment, transfer and conveyance provided for in Section 3 below and such other instruments as may reasonably be requested by Buyer or Seller. None of the foregoing documents shall increase in any material way the burdens imposed by this Agreement upon Seller or Buyer.

2. *Consideration.*

2.1 *Purchase Price.*

2.1.1 The cash consideration to be paid by Buyer to Seller for the Property (the "Purchase Price") shall be $[________________].

2.1.2 Concurrently with the mutual execution and delivery of this Agreement (the date of such mutual execution and delivery is sometimes referred to herein as the "Execution Date"), Buyer shall deposit into escrow (the "Escrow") with an escrow agent or company (the "Escrow Holder") reasonably designated by Seller $[___________] (the "Deposit") in immediately available, good funds (funds delivered in this manner are referred to herein as "Good Funds"), pursuant to joint escrow instructions to be delivered to and acknowledged by the Escrow Holder on or before the Execution Date. Such escrow instructions shall include the provisions set forth in this Section 2.1. Upon receipt of the Deposit, the Escrow Holder shall immediately deposit the Deposit into an interest-bearing account. The Deposit shall become nonrefundable upon the earlier of (x) the approval of Buyer as the approved Buyer at the hearing on the Sale Motion (as defined in Section 8.4.2 below), or (y) the termination of the transaction contemplated by this Agreement by reason of Buyer's default (a "Buyer Default Termination"). At the Closing, the Deposit (and any interest accrued thereon) shall be delivered to Seller and credited toward payment of the Purchase Price in the manner specified in Section 2.1.3 below. In the event the Deposit becomes non-refundable by reason of a Buyer Default Termination, Escrow Holder shall immediately disburse the Deposit and all interest accrued thereon to Seller to be retained by Seller for its own account. If the transactions contemplated herein terminate by reason of (A) Seller's default, (B) the failure of a condition to Buyer's obligations, or (C) the consummation of a sale to a third party as described in Section 8.4.1 below, the Escrow Holder shall return to Buyer the Deposit (together with all interest thereon). The Escrow Holder's escrow fees and charges shall be paid one-half by Seller and one-half by Buyer.

2.1.3 On the Closing Date, Buyer shall (i) pay and deliver to Seller, by wire transfer in Good Funds, the Purchase Price less the Deposit (and interest accrued thereon) and (ii) instruct the Escrow Holder to deliver the Deposit (and any interest accrued thereon) to Seller, by wire transfer of Good Funds.

2.2 *Assumed Liabilities.* Buyer shall, effective as of the Closing Date, assume and perform all liabilities accruing under the Real Property Leases and under the Other Leases and Contracts on and after the Closing Date and or otherwise required to be performed with respect to the property on or after the Closing Date; provided that Buyer shall pay all cure amounts owing under any of the Real Property Leases, Other Leases and Contracts as of the Closing which the Bankruptcy Court may order to be paid as a condition to the Seller's assumption and assignment of any Real Property Lease or Other Lease or Contract. Other than the liabilities and obligations of Seller expressly assumed by Buyer hereunder, Buyer is not assuming and shall not be liable for any liabilities or obligations of Seller.

3. *Closing of Transactions.*

3.1 *Closing.* The Closing of the transactions provided for herein (the "Closing") shall take place at the offices of [Andrews & Kurth LLP, 600 Travis, Suite 4200, Houston, Texas 77002].

3.2 *Closing Date.* The Closing shall be held within five days after satisfaction or waiver of the conditions to closing in Section 4 (the "Closing Date") but in no event later than [________________] (the "Outside Date"); provided, however, that the Outside Date shall automatically be extended for consecutive 30 day periods if the only condition remaining to be satisfied is the condition specified in Section 4.1.7 and 4.2.4. In the event the conditions to Closing (other than the condition in Section 4.1.7 and 4.2.4) have not been satisfied or waived by the Outside Date, then any party who is not in default hereunder may terminate this Agreement. Alternatively, the parties may mutually agree to an extended Closing Date. Until this Agreement is either terminated or the parties have agreed upon an extended Closing Date, the parties shall diligently continue to work to satisfy all conditions to Closing.

3.3 *Seller's Deliveries to Buyer at Closing.* On the Closing Date, Seller shall make the following deliveries to Buyer:

3.3.1 An Assignment and Assumption Agreement substantially in the form and content attached as Exhibit "E" hereto, duly executed by Seller, pursuant to which Seller assigns the Real Property Leases and the Other Leases and Contracts (the "Assignment Agreement"); provided, however, that the Assignment Agreement need not be delivered by Seller if the Bankruptcy Court has issued an order prior to the Closing Date authorizing the assumption and assignment of the Real Property Leases and the Other Leases and Contracts.

3.3.2 A bill of sale, duly executed by Seller, in the form and on the terms of the bill of sale attached hereto as Exhibit "F," pursuant to which Seller transfers the Property other than the Real Property Leases and the Other Leases and Contracts to Buyer (the "Bill of Sale").

3.3.3. A special warranty deed or deed of trust, duly executed by the Seller, in respect to the Real Property.

3.4 *Buyer's Deliveries to Seller at Closing.* On the Closing Date, Buyer shall make or cause the following deliveries to Seller:

3.4.1 That portion of the Purchase Price to be delivered by Buyer directly to Seller at the Closing under Section 2.1 (and Buyer shall cause Escrow Holder to deliver the Deposit and accrued interest to Seller).

3.4.2 The Assignment Agreement, duly executed by Buyer.

3.5 *Prorations.* Rent, current taxes, prepaid advertising and other items of expense (including, without limitation, any prepaid insurance under the Real Property Leases or Other Leases and Contracts, or any of them) and income relating to or attributable to the Business and/or the Real Property Leases or the Other Leases and Contracts shall be prorated between Seller and Buyer as of the Closing Date. All obligations due in respect of periods prior to Closing shall be paid in full or otherwise satisfied by Seller and all obligations due in respect of periods after Closing shall be paid in full or otherwise satisfied by Buyer. Rent shall be prorated on the basis of a thirty (30) day month. Buyer shall pay to Seller in cash on the Closing Date the amount of any security or similar deposits with the landlords or other contracting parties under the Real Property Leases and the Other Leases and Contracts and the amount of any other deposits made by Seller relating to the Real Property or the property to which the Other Leases and Contracts relate.

3.6 *Sales, Use and Other Taxes.* In accordance with Section 1146(c) of the Bankruptcy Code, the making or delivery of any instrument of transfer, including the filing of any deed or other document of transfer to evidence, effectuate or perfect the rights, transfers and conveyances contemplated by this Agreement, shall be in contemplation of a plan or plans of reorganization to be confirmed in the Case, and as such shall be free and clear of any and all transfer tax, stamp tax, motor vehicle title transfer tax or fee or similar taxes. The instruments transferring the Property to Buyer shall contain the following endorsement, or an endorsement of similar effect:

"Because this [instrument] has been authorized pursuant to Order of the United States Bankruptcy Court for the Southern District of Mississippi, in contemplation of a plan of reorganization of the Grantor, it is exempt from transfer taxes, stamp taxes or similar taxes pursuant to 11 U.S.C. § 1146(c)."

In the event that, notwithstanding the above provisions, any (a) real estate transfer taxes or similar taxes or charges are required to be paid in order to record the deeds to be delivered to Buyer in accordance herewith, or in the event any such taxes are assessed at any time thereafter, or (b) sales, use, transfer or other similar taxes or charges are assessed at Closing or at any time thereafter on the transfer of any other Property, then in each instance such taxes or charges incurred as a result of the transactions contemplated hereby shall be paid by Buyer.

3.7 *Possession.* Right to possession of the Property shall transfer to Buyer on the Closing Date. Seller shall transfer and deliver to Buyer on the Closing Date such keys, lock and safe combinations and other similar items as Buyer shall require to obtain immediate and full occupation and control of the Property, and shall also make available to Buyer at their then existing locations the originals of all documents in Seller's possession that are required to be transferred to Buyer by this Agreement.

4. *Conditions Precedent to Closing.*

4.1 *Conditions to Seller's Obligations.* Seller's obligation to make the deliveries required of Seller at the Closing Date shall be subject to the satisfaction or waiver by Seller of each of the following conditions.

4.1.1 All of the representations and warranties of Buyer contained herein shall continue to be true and correct at the Closing in all material respects, all covenants and obligations to be performed by Buyer prior to the Closing shall have been performed in all material respects and Buyer shall have certified the foregoing to Seller in writing.

4.1.2 Buyer shall have executed and delivered to Seller the Assignment Agreement and each other document reasonably requested by Seller pursuant to Section 1.3.

4.1.3 Seller shall have received the total Purchase Price in immediately available funds.

4.1.4 Buyer shall have delivered to Seller appropriate evidence of all necessary action by Buyer in connection with the transactions contemplated hereby, including, without limitation: (i) certified copies of resolutions duly adopted by Buyer's Board of Directors approving the transactions contemplated by this Agreement and authorizing the execution, delivery, and performance by Buyer of this Agreement; and (ii) a certificate as to the incumbency of officers of Buyer executing this Agreement and any instrument or other document delivered in connection with the transactions contemplated by this Agreement.

4.1.5 Concurrently with or prior to the Execution Date, Buyer shall have caused an entity satisfactory to Seller (in Seller's sole and absolute discretion) to execute and deliver to Seller a guaranty of all of Buyer's obligations under this Agreement and under any documents executed by Buyer in favor of Seller pursuant hereto.

4.1.6 No action, suit or other proceedings shall be pending before any court, tribunal or governmental authority seeking or threatening to restrain or prohibit the consummation of the transactions contemplated by this Agreement, or seeking to obtain substantial damages in respect thereof, or involving a claim that consummation thereof would result in the violation of any law, decree or regulation of any governmental authority having appropriate jurisdiction.

4.1.7 The Bankruptcy Court shall have entered the Procedure Order in accordance with Section 8.4.1 below and the Approval Order in accordance with Section 8.4.2 below and the Approval Order shall not have been stayed as of the Closing Date.

4.1.8 All applicable waiting periods relating to the Hart-Scott-Rodino Antitrust Improvements Act of 1976 (the "HSR Act") shall have expired or been terminated and any proceedings that may have been filed or instituted thereunder shall have been satisfactorily concluded.

4.2 *Conditions to Buyer's Obligations*. Buyer's obligation to make the deliveries required of Buyer at the Closing shall be subject to the satisfaction or waiver by Buyer of each of the following conditions:

4.2.1 All representations and warranties of Seller contained herein shall continue to be true and correct at the Closing in all material respects, all covenants and obligations to be performed by Seller prior to the Closing shall have been performed in all material respects and Seller shall have certified the foregoing to Buyer in writing.

4.2.2 Seller shall have executed and delivered to Buyer the Assignment Agreement, the Bill of Sale and each other document reasonably requested by Buyer pursuant to Section 1.3.

4.2.3 No action, suit or other proceedings shall be pending before any court, tribunal or governmental authority seeking or threatening to restrain or prohibit the consummation of the transactions contemplated by this Agreement, or seeking to obtain substantial damages in respect thereof, or involving a claim that consummation thereof would result in the violation of any law, decree or regulation of any governmental authority having appropriate jurisdiction.

4.2.4 The Bankruptcy Court shall have entered the Procedure Order in accordance with Section 8.4.1 below and the Approval Order in accordance with Section 8.4.2 below and the Approval Order shall not have been stayed as of the Closing Date.

4.2.5 All applicable waiting periods relating to the HSR Act shall have expired or been terminated and any proceedings that may have been filed or instituted thereunder shall have been satisfactorily concluded.

4.3 *Termination.* If any of the above conditions is neither satisfied nor waived on or before the date by which the condition is required to be satisfied, the party who is not then in default hereunder may terminate this Agreement by delivering to the other written notice of termination. Any waiver of a condition shall be effective only if such waiver is stated in writing and signed by the waiving party; provided, however, that the consent of a party to the Closing shall constitute a waiver by such party of any conditions to Closing not satisfied as of the Closing Date.

5. *Seller's Representations and Warranties.* Seller hereby makes the following representations and warranties to Buyer:

5.1 *Validity of Agreement.* Upon obtaining the Approval Order, this Agreement shall constitute the valid and binding obligation of Seller enforceable in accordance with its terms.

5.2 *Organization, Standing and Power.* Seller is a corporation duly organized, validly existing and in good standing under the laws of the State of [__________]. Subject to the applicable provisions of bankruptcy law, Seller has all requisite corporate power and authority to own, lease and operate its properties, to carry on its business as now being conducted and, subject to the Seller's obtaining the Approval Order, to execute, deliver and perform this Agreement and all writings relating hereto.

5.3 *No Conflicts or Violations.* Upon obtaining the Approval Order, the execution and delivery of this Agreement, the consummation of the transactions herein contemplated, and the performance of, fulfillment of and compliance with the terms and conditions hereof by Seller do not and will not: (i) conflict with or result in a breach of the articles of incorporation or the by-laws of Seller; (ii) violate any statute, law, rule or regulation, or any order, writ, injunction or decree of any court or governmental authority; or (iii) violate or conflict with or constitute a default under any agreement, instrument or writing of any nature to which Seller is a party or by which Seller or its assets or properties may be bound.

5.4 *Title to Property.* To the Seller's knowledge (which consists of matters actually known to Seller's senior management), Seller has good and marketable title to the Property; provided, however, Seller makes no representation whatsoever as the title to the Intangible Property. At the Closing, Buyer will acquire all of Seller's right, title and interest in and to all the Property, free and clear of any liens, claims or encumbrances, subject to Sections 2.2 and 3.5 hereof.

6. *Buyer's Representations and Warranties.* Buyer hereby makes the following representations and warranties to Seller:

6.1 *Validity of Agreement.* All action on the part of Buyer necessary for the authorization, execution, delivery and performance of this Agreement by Buyer, including, but not limited to, the performance of Buyer's obligations hereunder, has been duly taken. This Agreement, when executed and delivered by Buyer, shall constitute the valid and binding obligation of Buyer enforceable in accordance with its terms.

6.2 *Organization, Standing and Power.* Buyer is a corporation duly organized, validly existing and in good standing under the laws of the State of [__________]. Buyer has all requisite corporate power and authority to own, lease and operate its properties, to carry on its business as now being conducted and to execute, deliver and perform this Agreement and all writings relating hereto.

6.3 *No Conflicts or Violations.* The execution and delivery of this Agreement, the consummation of the transactions herein contemplated, and the performance of, fulfillment of and compliance with the terms and conditions hereof by Buyer do not and will not: (i) conflict with or result in a breach of the articles of incorporation or by-laws of Buyer; (ii) violate any statute, law, rule or regulation, or any order, writ, injunction or decree of any court or governmental authority; or (iii) violate or conflict with or constitute a default under any agreement, instrument or writing of any nature to which Buyer is a party or by which Buyer or its assets or properties may be bound.

6.4 *Financing.* Buyer has sufficient funds available to consummate the transactions contemplated hereby.

7. *"AS IS" Transaction.* BUYER HEREBY ACKNOWLEDGES AND AGREES THAT, EXCEPT AS OTHERWISE EXPRESSLY PROVIDED IN SECTION 5 ABOVE, THE SELLER MAKES NO REPRESENTATIONS OR WARRANTIES WHATSOEVER, EXPRESS OR IMPLIED, WITH RESPECT TO ANY MATTER RELATING TO THE PROPERTY INCLUDING, WITHOUT LIMITATION, INCOME TO BE DERIVED OR EXPENSES TO BE INCURRED IN CONNECTION WITH THE PROPERTY, THE PHYSICAL CONDITION OF ANY PERSONAL PROPERTY COMPRISING A PART OF THE PROPERTY OR WHICH IS THE SUBJECT OF ANY OTHER LEASE OR CONTRACT TO BE ASSUMED BY BUYER AT THE CLOSING, THE ENVIRONMENTAL CONDITION OR OTHER MATTER RELATING TO THE PHYSICAL CONDITION OF ANY REAL PROPERTY OR IMPROVEMENTS WHICH ARE THE SUBJECT OF ANY REAL PROPERTY LEASE TO BE ASSUMED BY BUYER AT THE CLOSING, THE ZONING OF ANY SUCH REAL PROPERTY OR IMPROVEMENTS, THE VALUE OF THE PROPERTY (OR ANY PORTION THEREOF), THE TRANSFERABILITY OF PROPERTY, THE TERMS, AMOUNT, VALIDITY OR ENFORCEABILITY OF ANY ASSUMED LIABILITIES, THE TITLE OF THE PROPERTY (OR ANY PORTION THEREOF) THE MERCHANTABILITY OR FITNESS OF THE PERSONAL PROPERTY OR ANY OTHER PORTION OF THE PROPERTY FOR ANY PARTICULAR PURPOSE, OR ANY OTHER MATTER OR THING RELATING TO THE PROPERTY OR ANY PORTION THEREOF. WITHOUT IN ANY WAY LIMITING THE FOREGOING, SELLER HEREBY DISCLAIMS ANY

WARRANTY, EXPRESS OR IMPLIED, OF MERCHANTABILITY OR FITNESS FOR ANY PARTICULAR PURPOSE AS TO ANY PORTION OF THE PROPERTY. BUYER FURTHER ACKNOWLEDGES THAT BUYER HAS CONDUCTED AN INDEPENDENT INSPECTION AND INVESTIGATION OF THE PHYSICAL CONDITION OF THE PROPERTY AND ALL SUCH OTHER MATTERS RELATING TO OR AFFECTING THE PROPERTY AS BUYER DEEMED NECESSARY OR APPROPRIATE AND THAT IN PROCEEDING WITH ITS ACQUISITION OF THE PROPERTY, EXCEPT FOR ANY REPRESENTATIONS AND WARRANTIES EXPRESSLY SET FORTH IN SECTION 5, BUYER IS DOING SO BASED SOLELY UPON SUCH INDEPENDENT INSPECTIONS AND INVESTIGATIONS. ACCORDINGLY, BUYER WILL ACCEPT THE PROPERTY AT THE CLOSING "AS IS," "WHERE IS," AND "WITH ALL FAULTS."

8. *Covenants Prior to Closing.*

8.1 *Access to Records and Properties of Seller.* From and after the date of this Agreement until the Closing Date, Seller shall, upon reasonable advance notice, afford to Buyer's officers, independent public accountants, counsel, lenders, consultants and other representatives, reasonable access during normal business hours of the Property and all records pertaining to the Property or the Business. Buyer, however, shall not be entitled to access to any materials containing information in respect of any items excluded from the Intangible Property under Section 1.1.4. Buyer shall have no right hereunder to conduct any environmental or other assessment of the Property other than visual inspection and document review; provided, however, that Buyer may have a Phase I environmental assessment of the Real Property and the property subject to the Real Property Leases conducted by an environmental consultant of Buyer's choice. Buyer expressly acknowledges that nothing in this Section 8.1 is intended to give rise to any contingency to Buyer's obligations to proceed with the transactions contemplated herein.

8.2 *Operation of Seller's Business Pending Closing.* Unless Buyer otherwise consents, during the period prior to the Closing Date, Seller shall use commercially reasonable efforts to operate the Business as currently operated and only in the ordinary course and, consistent with such operation, shall use commercially reasonable efforts to preserve intact the Business and its relationships with employees and persons having dealings with it.

8.3 *Hart-Scott-Rodino Cooperation.* Buyer and Seller shall cooperate with each other (at their respective sole cost and expense) to comply with, and provide the information required by, the pre-merger notification and waiting period rules of the HSR Act (codified in Section 18(a) of Title 15, U.S. Code), in any Federal Trade Commission regulations, and in any provisions or regulations of or relating to the Clayton Act. In that connection, Buyer and Seller shall use diligent efforts to make applicable pre-merger notification filings under the HSR Act with the Federal Trade Commission and the U. S.

Department of Justice no later than five (5) days following the Execution Date. The parties will use commercially reasonable efforts to comply as promptly as is practical with any request by governmental authorities for additional information concerning the purchase and sale of the Property to the end that the waiting period specified in the HSR Act with respect to the transactions provided herein will expire on the earliest possible date.

8.4 *Bankruptcy Court Approvals.*

8.4.1 *Bankruptcy Court Approval of Sale Procedures.* Promptly following the Execution Date (and in no event later than five (5) business days thereafter), the Seller will file a motion (the "Sale Procedure Motion") with the Bankruptcy Court requesting the entry of an order (the "Procedure Order") (i) fixing the time, date, and location of a hearing (the "Approval Hearing") to approve Seller's consummation of this agreement, (ii) fixing the time and date of an auction (the "Auction") to be held at the offices of Houlihan Lokey Howard & Zukin Capital at which higher and better offers may be presented to the Seller, (iii) providing that if Seller receives from a third party a higher and better offer at the Auction, and such third party offer is subsequently approved by the Bankruptcy Court and closes as provided by its terms, then Buyer will be entitled to receive from the Seller a flat fee payment (not dependent on amounts actually expended or incurred by Buyer) in cash or other immediately available good funds in the amount of $[________________] (the "Break-Up Fee") which payment shall be made to the Buyer concurrently with the consummation of such third party sale, (iv) no prospective purchaser will be permitted to bid at the Auction unless such party has been deemed "financially qualified" by Houlihan Lokey Howard & Zukin Capital ("HLHZ"), Seller's investment banker, (v) no prospective purchaser who bids for the Property at Auction shall be entitled to purchase the Property unless such prospective purchaser offers to purchase the Property for consideration which is at least $[________________] greater than the consideration set forth in this Agreement (including all cash, non-cash consideration and assumed liabilities) and otherwise on terms at least as favorable to the Seller as those set forth in this Agreement, and (v) after any initial overbid, all further overbids must be in increments of at least $[____________]. Should overbidding take place, the Buyer shall have the right, but not the obligation, to participate in the overbidding and to be approved as the overbidder at the Approval Hearing based upon any such overbid. Should an overbidder be approved at the hearing on the Sale Motion, Buyer shall deliver to such approved overbidder all third party reports, studies and the like resulting from Buyer's Due Diligence investigations. Following the filing of the Sale Procedure Motion, the Seller shall use reasonable efforts to obtain the Procedure Order (the date on which the Procedure Order is entered and becomes final is referred to herein as the "Sale Procedure Date").

8.4.2 *Bankruptcy Court's Approval of Sale.* Promptly following the Execution Date, and contemporaneously with the filing of the Sale Procedure Motion, Seller shall file a motion with the Bankruptcy Court (the "Sale Motion") requesting entry of an order (the "Approval Order") which (i) approves the sale of the Property to Buyer on the terms and conditions set forth in this Agreement and authorizes the Seller to proceed with this transaction, (ii) includes a specific finding that Buyer is a good faith purchaser of the Property, (iii) states that the sale of the Property to Buyer shall be free and clear of all liens, claims, interests and encumbrances whatsoever (except as expressly provided in this Agreement), and (iv) approves the Seller's assumption and assignment of the prepetition Real Property Leases and Other Leases and Contracts (collectively, the "Section 365 Contracts") pursuant to Section 365 of the United States Bankruptcy Code and orders the Buyer to pay any cure amounts payable to the other parties to the Section 365 Contracts as a condition to such assumption and assignment. In no event shall Buyer have the right to terminate this transaction by reason of the failure to assign all of the Section 365 Contracts so long as the Approval Order authorizes the Seller to assume and assign not less than ninety five percent (95%) of the Section 365 Contracts. Following the filing of the Sale Motion, the Seller shall use reasonable efforts to obtain entry of the Approval Order. Both Buyer's and Seller's obligations to consummate the transactions contemplated in this Agreement which the Buyer and Seller may hereafter enter into shall be conditioned upon the Bankruptcy Court's entry of the Approval Order.

8.5 *Further Actions.* The Parties each agree to use all reasonable efforts to take all actions and to do all things necessary, proper or advisable to consummate the transactions contemplated hereby by the expected Closing Date.

9. *Post Closing Covenants.*

9.1 *Post-Closing Maintenance of and Access to Information.* Without limiting Seller's rights under Section 10.2 with respect to the Case, the parties will also comply with the following provisions:

(a) The parties acknowledge that after Closing the parties or their successors may need access to information or documents in the control or possession of the other party for the purposes of concluding the transactions herein contemplated, preparing or filing tax returns or responding to audits, Contracts and to satisfy other legal requirements, and to prosecute or defend third party claims.

(b) The parties shall not dispose of or destroy any of the records and files of the Business prior to the fourth anniversary of the Closing Date. If the party wishes to dispose of or destroy such records and files after that time, it shall first give sixty (60) days' prior written notice to the other party, and such other party shall have the right, at its option and expense, upon prior written notice within such sixty-day period, to take possession of the records and files within ninety (90) days after the date of the notice.

(c) Buyer shall cooperate fully in connection with, and make available for inspection and copying by, Seller, its successors, and their respective employees, agents, counsel and accountants and/or governmental authorities, upon written request, such books, records documents and other information to the extent reasonably necessary to facilitate the purposes set forth in subsection (a) above and for other legitimate corporate purposes. In addition, Buyer shall cooperate with, and shall permit and use its best efforts to cause, its former and present directors, officers and employees to cooperate with, Seller on and after Closing in furnishing information, evidence, testimony and other assistance in connection with any action, proceeding, arrangement or dispute of any nature with respect to the Business or the Property and pertaining to periods prior to the Closing Date.

(d) Seller shall be entitled to retain any records that relate to events or periods prior to Closing for purposes of pending litigation involving matters to which such records refer.

9.2 *WARN Act and Employment Matters.* [It is the intent of Buyer to make offers of employment to substantially all or Seller's employees, other than those identified on Exhibit __; *provided, however,* that Buyer intends to conduct customary employee background checks prior to offering employment to any such employee.] Buyer shall be responsible for and shall pay any and all liabilities or obligations arising under the WARN Act, if any, arising out of or resulting from layoffs of employees or any termination of their employment in the Business in connection with the transactions provided herein. Buyer shall further be liable for any obligation imposed on either Seller or Buyer to provide employees with continued health, disability, life or other retirement benefits (whether covered by insurance or not). Buyer agrees to indemnify, and hold Seller and its successors harmless from or against, any and all claims, losses, damages, expenses, obligations and liabilities (including costs of collection, attorney's fees and other costs of defense) which Seller may incur in connection with any suit or claim of violation brought against the Seller under the WARN Act or any similar state or foreign law, which relates to transactions effected in connection with the transactions provided herein or any other action taken by Buyer after the Closing Date with regard to any site of employment or one or more facilities or operating units within any site of employment of the Business. [Section 9.2 remains subject to review by D'Arcinoff counsel.]

10. *Miscellaneous.*

10.1 *Attorneys' Fees.* In the event that either party hereto brings an action or other proceeding to enforce or interpret the terms and provisions of this Agreement, the prevailing party in that action or proceeding shall be entitled to have and recover from the non-prevailing party all such fees, costs and expenses (including, without limitation, all court costs and reasonable attorneys' fees) as the prevailing party may suffer or incur in the pursuit or defense of such action or proceeding.

10.2 *Reasonable Access to Records and Certain Personnel.* So long as the Case is pending, (i) the Buyer shall permit Seller's counsel and other professionals employed in the Case reasonable access to the financial and other books and records relating to the Property or the Business (whether in documentary or data form) for the purpose of the continuing administration of the Case (including, without limitation, the pursuit of any avoidance, preference or similar action), which access shall include (a) the right of such professionals to copy, at the Seller's expense, such documents and records as they may request in furtherance of the purposes described above, and (b) Buyer's copying and delivering to Seller or its professionals such documents or records as they may request, but only to the extent Seller or its professionals furnishes Buyer with reasonably detailed written descriptions of the materials to be so copied and Seller reimburses the Buyer for the reasonable costs and expenses thereof), and (ii) Buyer shall provide the Seller and such professionals (at no cost to the Seller) with reasonable access to [Note: Seller to insert Name(s) of personnel to whom the Seller will need continued access post-closing] during regular business hours to assist the Seller in the continuing administration of the Case, provided that such access does not unreasonably interfere with the Buyer's business operations.

10.3 *Notices.* Unless otherwise provided herein, any notice, tender, or delivery to be given hereunder by either party to the other may be effected by personal delivery in writing, or by registered or certified mail, postage prepaid, return receipt requested, and shall be deemed communicated as of the date of mailing. Mailed notices shall be addressed as set forth below, but each party may change his address by written notice in accordance with this paragraph.

To Seller: [______________________

____

____

Attn: __________, __________]

With a copy to: [Debtor's Counsel]

[______________________

____

Attn: __________, __________]

To Buyer: [______________________

____

____

Attn: __________, __________]

With a copy to: [______________________

____

____

Attn: __________, __________]

10.4 *Entire Agreement.* This instrument and the documents to be executed pursuant hereto contain the entire agreement between the parties relating to the sale of the Property. Any oral representations or modifications concerning this Agreement or any such other document shall be of no force and effect excepting a subsequent modification in writing, signed by the party to be charged.

10.5 *Modification.* This Agreement may be modified, amended or supplemented only by a written instrument duly executed by all the parties hereto.

10.6 *Closing Date.* All actions to be taken on the Closing pursuant to this Agreement shall be deemed to have occurred simultaneously, and no act, document or transaction shall be deemed to have been taken, delivered or effected until all such actions, documents and transactions have been taken, delivered or effected.

10.7 *Severability.* Should any term, provision or paragraph of this Agreement be determined to be illegal or void or of no force and effect, the balance of the Agreement shall survive except that, if Buyer cannot acquire and Seller cannot sell substantially all of the Property, either party may terminate this Agreement, and it shall be of no further force and effect, unless both parties agree in writing to the contrary.

10.8 *Captions.* All captions and headings contained in this Agreement are for convenience of reference only and shall not be construed to limit or extend the terms or conditions of this Agreement.

10.9 *Further Assurances.* Each party hereto will execute, acknowledge and deliver any further assurance, documents and instruments reasonably requested by any other party hereto for the purpose of giving effect to the transactions contemplated herein or the intentions of the parties with respect thereto.

10.10 *Waiver.* No waiver of any of the provisions of this Agreement shall be deemed, or shall constitute, a waiver of other provisions, whether or not similar, nor shall any waiver constitute a continuing waiver. No waiver shall be binding unless executed in writing by the party making the waiver.

10.11 *Brokerage Obligations.* Seller is represented by HLHZ as its exclusive sale agent with respect to the transactions contemplated herein pursuant that certain order entered by the Bankruptcy Court on _________________, 20___ and HLHZ's commission, fees and expenses are to be paid by the Seller directly out of the proceeds of the transactions contemplated herein as a cost of sale at Closing in accordance with the terms and provisions of such order. The Seller and the Buyer each represent and warrant to the other that, except for HLHZ, such party has incurred no liability to any real estate broker or agent with respect to the payment of any commission regarding the consummation of the transaction contemplated hereby. Except for any claims of HLHZ (which are to be handled and satisfied by Seller in accordance with the above referenced order), it is agreed that if any claims for commissions, fees or other compensation, including, without limitation, brokerage fees, finder's fees, or commissions are ever asserted against Buyer or the Seller in connection with this transaction, all such claims shall be handled and paid by the party whose actions form the basis of such claim and such party shall indemnify, defend (with counsel reasonably satisfactory to the party entitled to indemnification), protect, and save and hold the other harmless from and against any and all such claims or demands asserted by any person, firm or corporation in connection with the transaction contemplated hereby.

10.12 *Payment of Fees and Expenses.* Except as provided in Section 9.2 above, each party to this Agreement shall be responsible for, and shall pay, all of its own fees and expenses, including those of its counsel, incurred in the negotiation, preparation and consummation of the Agreement and the transaction described herein.

10.13 *Survival.* Except for the covenants and agreements that are expressly provided to be performed after the Closing Date, none of the respective representations, warranties, covenants and agreements of Seller and Buyer herein, or in any certificates or other documents delivered prior to or at the Closing, shall survive the Closing.

10.14 *Assignments.* This Agreement shall not be assigned by either party hereto without the prior written consent of the other party hereto.

10.15 *Binding Effect.* Subject to the provisions of Section 9.15 above, this Agreement shall bind and inure to the benefit of the respective heirs, personal representatives, successors, and assigns of the parties hereto.

10.16 *Applicable Law.* This Agreement shall be governed by and construed in accordance with the laws of Mississippi.

10.17 *Good Faith.* All parties hereto agree to do all acts and execute all documents required to carry out the terms of this Agreement and to act in good faith with respect to the terms and conditions contained herein before and after Closing.

10.18 *Construction.* In the interpretation and construction of this Agreement, the parties acknowledge that the terms hereof reflect extensive negotiations between the parties and that this Agreement shall not be deemed, for the purpose of construction and interpretation, drafted by either party hereto.

10.19 *Counterparts.* This Agreement may be signed in counterparts. The parties further agree that this Agreement may be executed by the exchange of facsimile signature pages.

10.20 *Time is of the Essence.* Time is of the essence in this Agreement, and all of the terms, covenants and conditions hereof.

10.21 *Tax Effect.* None of the parties (nor such parties' counsel or accountants) has made or is making in this Agreement any representation to any other party (or such party's counsel or accountants) concerning any of the Tax effects or consequences on the other party of the transactions provided for in this Agreement. Each party represents that it has obtained, or may obtain, independent Tax advice with respect thereto and upon which it, if so obtained, has solely relied.

10.22 *Employee Withholding.* The parties agree that, pursuant to the "Alternative Procedure" provided in Section 5 of Revenue Procedure 96–60, 1996–2 C.B. 399, with respect to filing and furnishing IRS Forms W-2, W-3, and 941, (a) Seller shall report on a "predecessor-successor" basis, as set forth therein, (b) Seller shall be relieved from furnishing Forms W-2 to any of the employees of Seller who become employees of Buyer, and (c) Buyer shall assume the obligations of Seller to furnish such Forms W-2 to such employees for the year in which the Closing occurs.

10.23 *Bankruptcy Court Jurisdiction.* BUYER AND SELLER AGREE THAT THE BANKRUPTCY COURT SHALL HAVE EXCLUSIVE JURISDICTION OVER ALL DISPUTES AND OTHER MATTERS RELATING; TO (i) THE INTERPRETATION AND ENFORCEMENT OF THIS AGREEMENT OR ANY ANCILLARY DOCUMENT EXECUTED PURSUANT HERETO; AND/OR (ii) THE PROPERTY AND/OR ASSUMED LIABILITIES, AND BUYER EXPRESSLY CONSENTS TO AND AGREES NOT TO CONTEST SUCH EXCLUSIVE JURISDICTION.

10.24 *Confidentiality Agreement.* The Confidentiality Agreement dated as of ___________, 20___ between Buyer and Seller (the "Confidentiality Agreement") shall remain in full force and effect during the term specified therein.

IN WITNESS WHEREOF, the parties hereto have executed this Asset Purchase Agreement as of the day and year first above written.

[Buyer], a

____

By: _______________________
Name: ____________________
Its: ___________________________

[Seller]

____

Debtor and Debtor-In-Possession

By: _______________________
Name: ____________________
Its: _______________________

Exhibits "A-1" through "E"
[TO BE DELIVERED]

Appendix 11

State-by-State Receivership and Assignment for the Benefit of Creditors Laws

Appendix Table 11.1

State	Receivership Statutes	Assignment for the Benefit of Creditors Statutes
Alabama	Ala. Code §§ 6-6-620 to -623, 10-2B-14.32 (2005)	Common Law
Alaska	Alaska Stat. §§ 09.40.240–.250, 10.06.643 (2005)	Common Law
Arizona	Ariz. Rev. Stat. Ann. §§ 10-1432, 12-1241 to -1242 (2005)	Ariz. Rev. Stat. Ann. §§ 44-1031 to -1047 (2005)
Arkansas	Ark. Code Ann. §§ 4-27-1432, 16-117-205 (2005); Ark. R. Civ P. 66	Ark. Code Ann §§ 16-117-401 to -407 (2005)
California	Cal. Civ. P. Code §§ 564–570 (2005); Cal. Corp. Code § 1803 (2005)	Cal. Civ. Proc. Code §§ 493.010, 1800–1802
Colorado	Colo. Rev. Stat. Ann. § 7-114-301 (2005); Colo. R. Civ. P. 66	Colo. Rev. Stat. Ann. §§ 6-10-101 to-154 (2005)
Connecticut	Conn. Gen. Stat. §§ 33-898, 52-504 to-514 (2005)	Common Law
Delaware	Del. Code. Ann. Tit. 8, § 8-291 to -302 (2005); Del. Ch. Ct. R. 148-168	Common Law
District of Columbia	D.C. Code §§ 29-101.91–.94 (2005); D.C. Super. Ct. R. 66	D.C. Code §§ 28-2101 to -2110 (2005)
Florida	Fla. Stat. Ann. § 607.1432 (2005); Fla. R. Civ. P. 1.620	Fla. Stat. Ann. §§ 727.101–.116 (2005)
Georgia	Ga. Code. Ann. §§ 9-8-1 to-14, 14-2-1432 (2005)	Ga. Code Ann. §§ 18-2-40 to -59 (2005)
Hawaii	Haw. Rev. Stat. § 414-413 (2005)	Common Law
Idaho	Idaho Code Ann. §§ 8-601 to -606, 30-1-1432 (2005)	Idaho Code Ann. § 68-201 (2005) and Common Law

Appendix Table 11.1 (*continued*)

State	Receivership Statutes	Assignment for the Benefit of Creditors Statutes
Illinois	735 Ill. Comp. Stat. Ann. 5/2-415 (2005); 805 Ill. Comp. Stat. Ann. 5/12.60 (2005)	Common Law
Indiana	Ind. Code Ann. §§ 23-1-47-3, 32-30-5-1 to -22 (2005)	Ind. Code Ann. §§ 22-2-10-1, 32-18-1-22 (2005)
Iowa	Iowa Code Ann. §§ 680.1, 490.1432 (2005)	Iowa Code Ann. 681.1–.30 (2005)
Kansas	Kan. Stat. Ann. §§ 17-6808, 60-1301 to -1305 (2005)	Common Law
Kentucky	Ky. Rev. Stat. Ann. §§ 271B.14-320, 425.600 (2005)	Ky. Rev. Stat. Ann. §§ 379.010–.170 (2005)
Louisiana	La. Rev. Stat. Ann. §§ 12:151–:152 (2005)	Common Law
Maine	Me. Rev. Stat. Ann. Tit. 13-C, § 1432 (2005)	Me. Rev. Stat. Ann. tit. 36, § 607 (2005) and Common Law
Maryland	Md. Code Ann., Corps. & Ass'ns §§ 3-411 to -418, 13-101 to -107 (2005)	Md. Code Ann. §§ 13-101 to -107, 15-101 to-103 (2005)
Massachusetts	Mass. Gen. Laws Ann. ch. 156B, §§ 104–106, Ch. 156D, § 14.32 (2005); Mass R. Civ. P. 66; Mass. Super. Ct. R. 51	Mass. Gen. Laws Ann. Ch. 203 §§ 40–42 (2005)
Michigan	Mich. Comp. Laws Ann. §§ 600.2926, 600.3610 (2005)	Mich. Comp. Laws Ann. §§ 600.5201–.5265 (2005)
Minnesota	Minn. Stat Ann. §§ 302A.753–.755, 576.01 (2005)	Minn. Stat. Ann §§ 577.01–.10 (2005)
Mississippi	Miss. Code Ann. §§ 11-5-151 to -167, 79-4-14.32 (2005); Miss R. Civ. P. 66	Miss. Code Ann. §§ 85-1-1 to -19 (2005)
Missouri	Mo. Rev. Stat. Ann. § 351.498 (2005); Mo. Sup. Ct. R. 68.02	Mo. Rev. Stat. Ann. §§ 426.010–.410 (2005)
Montana	Mont. Code Ann. §§ 27-20-101 to -304, 35-1-941 (2005)	Mont. Code Ann. §§ 31-2-201 to -230 (2005)
Nebraska	Neb. Rev. Stat. Ann. §§ 21-20,164; 25-1081 to -1092 (2005)	Common Law
Nevada	Nev. Rev. Stat. Ann. §§ 32.010–.020, 78.630–.720 (2005)	Common Law
New Hampshire	N.H. Rev. Stat. Ann. § 293-A:14.32 (2005); N.H. Super Ct. R. 165	N.H. Rev. Stat. Ann. §§ 568:1–:42 (2005)
New Jersey	N.J. Stat. Ann. §§ 14A:14-1 to -22 (2005); N.J. Super. Ct. R. 4:53	N.J. Stat. Ann. §§ 2A:19-1 to -47 (2005)
New Mexico	N.M. Stat. Ann. §§ 44-8-1 to -10, 53-16-17 to -18 (2005)	N.M. Stat. Ann. §§ 56-9-1 to -55 (2005)
New York	N.Y. Bus. Corp. Law §§ 1201–1218 (2005); N.Y. C.L.P.R. 6401-05, 8004 (2005)	N.Y. Debt. & Cred. Law §§ 2–29 (2005)

Appendix Table 11.1 (*continued*)

State	Receivership Statutes	Assignment for the Benefit of Creditors Statutes
North Carolina	N.C. Gen. Stat. Ann. §§ 1-507.1–.11, 55-14-32 (2005)	N.C. Gen. Stat. Ann. §§ 23-1 to -17 (2005)
North Dakota	N.D. Cent. Code §§ 10-19.1-117, 32-10-01 to -05 (2005)	N.D. Cent. Code §§ 32-26-01 to -06 (2005) and Common Law
Ohio	Ohio Rev. Code Ann. §§ 1701.90–.91, 2735.01–.06 (2005)	Ohio Rev. Code Ann. §§ 1313.01–.59 (2005)
Oklahoma	Okla. Stat. tit. 12, §§ 1551–1559, tit. 18, §§ 1106–1118 (2005)	Okla. Stat. tit. 24, §§ 31–50 (2005)
Oregon	Or. Rev. Stat. § 60.667 (2005); Or. r. civ. p. 80	Common Law
Pennsylvania	15 Pa. Stat. Ann. §§ 1984–1986 (2005); 39 Pa. Stat. Ann. §§ 1-154 (2005); Pa. R. Civ. p. 1533	39 Pa. Stat. Ann. §§ 1–154 (2005)
Rhode Island	R.I. Gen Laws §§ 7-1.2-1316 to -1317 (2006); R.I.R. Civ. P. 66	R.I. Gen. Laws §§ 10-4-1 to -13 (2006)
South Carolina	S.C. Code Ann. §§ 15-65-10 to -130, 33-14-320 (2005)	S.C. Code Ann.§§ 27-25-10 to -160 (2005)
South Dakota	S.D. Codified Laws §§ 21-21-1 To -10, 47-1A-1432 (2006)	S.D. Codified Laws §§ 54-9-1 to -22 (2006)
Tennessee	Tenn. Code Ann. §§ 17-1-205, 48-24-302 To -304 (2005)	Tenn. Code Ann. §§ 47-13-101 to -120 (2005)
Texas	Tex. Civ. Prac. & Rem. § 64.001–.004 (2005); Tex. Bus. & Com. §§ 7.04–.08 (2005)	Tex. Bus. & Com. §§ 23.01–.33 (2005)
Utah	Utah Code Ann. § 16-10A-1432 (2005); Utah R. Civ. P. 66	Utah Code Ann. §§ 6-1-1 to -20 (2005)
Vermont	Vt. Stat. Ann. Tit. 11A, § 14.32 (2005)	Vt. Stat. Ann tit. 9, §§ 2151–58 (2005)
Virginia	Va. Code Ann. §§ 8.01-582 to -590, 13.1-748 (2005)	Common Law
Washington	Wash. Rev. Code Ann. §§ 7.60.005–.300, 23B.14.320 (2005); Wash. Super. Ct. Civ. R. 66	Wash. Rev. Code Ann. §§ 7.08.010–.200 (2005)
West Virginia	W. Va. Code Ann. § 31D-14-1432 (2005)	W. Va. Code Ann. §§ 38-13-1 to -16 (2005)
Wisconsin	Wis. Stat. Ann. §§ 128.01–.25, 180.1432 (2005)	Wis. Stat. Ann. §§ 128.01–.25 (2005)
Wyoming	Wyo. Stat. Ann. §§ 1-33-101 to -110, 17-16-1432 (2005)	Common Law

Appendix 12

Document Retention Policy

Scope

This Policy is applicable to the [_________] Liquidating Trust (hereinafter the "Trust").

General Objective

The objective of the Trust's Document Retention Policy (the "Retention Policy") is twofold:

- To maintain complete and accurate records necessary to effectively carry out the Trust's legal and business responsibilities; and
- To do so in the most cost-effective, efficient, and productive manner.

Accordingly, it is the practice of the Trust to create and retain only those documents which are accurate and essential to its daily business operations. Unless specific federal or state requirements dictate otherwise, all documents are to be retained only during the period of their immediate usefulness, and then appropriately disposed of in accordance with this Policy.

Specific Goals

By establishing a systematic and accessible procedure for maintaining only those documents necessary to conduct the Trustee's business, this Policy is intended to accomplish the following specific goals:

- to ensure clear and concise Trust records which accurately reflect the Trust's business and ethical practices;

- to avoid unnecessary and costly duplication, and the onerous expense of storing irrelevant and obsolete documents;
- to increase productivity by eliminating redundant circulation of business information;
- to ensure proper identification and classification of documents in order to preserve their confidentiality and privilege, where appropriate; and
- to streamline each employee's filing system, making it easier to locate truly important and useful documents; most employees should experience a reduction of at least one-third of their office records through strict adherence to this Policy.

Application

This Policy applies to any documentary material, regardless of physical form, that is generated or received by the Trust in connection with transacting its business. This includes originals, copies, finals, drafts, typed and handwritten documents, and information stored on microfiche or other such mediums.

The procedures and retention periods set forth in this Policy are equally applicable to electronic records. Documents generated and maintained in Trust information systems or equipment (including mainframe, PCs, laptops, or storage tapes or diskettes) are to be reviewed by their custodians on the same

Exhibit A. Record Retention Guidelines Chart

Type of Record	Retention Period
Audit reports	Permanent
Bank deposit slips	6 years*
Bank statements	6 years*
Cancelled checks	3 years*
Expired contracts and leases	6 years*
Corporate stock records and minutes	Permanent
Daily sales records and journals	6 years*
Depreciation schedules	Life of asset, +3 years
Employee records	Period of employment, +3 years
Entertainment records	6 years*
Expense records	6 years**
Financial statements	6 years*
General ledger and journals	6 years*
Inventory records	3 years***
Paid vendor invoices	3 years*
Real estate records	Permanent
Tax and legal correspondence	6 years*
Tax returns and supporting documentation	6 years**

*From the date of the creation of the document
**From the tax return due date or filing date, plus any amended returns; whichever is later
***Longer if the LIFO method is used

periodic basis as all other documentary material to ensure complete compliance with this Policy.

Documents received, generated or maintained by the Trust shall be kept for the periods on the attached Exhibit A for the time periods set forth in Exhibit A. After such time period, the documents shall be destroyed.

Adopted this ____ day of ______________, 20___.

_______________ Liquidating Trust

By:_________________________________

__________________, Trustee

Appendix 13

Distribution Letter and Questionnaire

[Trustee's Letterhead]

[Date]

All Parties on the

Attached Distribution List

Re: *In re [case caption and number]*, In the United States Bankruptcy Court for the District of ("Debtor")

Dear Former Employee, Nonqualified Pensioner or Supplier:

On _____, 20___ the Trustee of _____ intends to make the initial distribution from the bankruptcy estate. You are scheduled to receive a distribution. Because your distribution represents employee benefits or delivery of services, the Trustee cannot mail you your distribution check until you complete and return the enclosed U.S. Federal tax withholding forms. You must also complete and return the enclosed Distribution Questionnaire form.

You should return the completed forms to:
[Trustee's Name]
[Address]

A pre-addressed envelope is enclosed for your convenience.

The Trustee anticipates making additional distributions. Therefore, you must notify me if your address changes in the future or any of your answers on the enclosed forms change. If you fail to notify me and your check(s) are returned to the Trustee as undeliverable, you may lose your distribution. Failing to provide correct information on the enclosed U.S. Federal tax withholding forms could subject you to penalties imposed by the taxing authorities.

Please telephone _____ at _____ if you have any questions.

Very truly yours,

____

Trustee

Enclosures: IRS Form W 4
IRS Form W4P
IRS Form W9

Distribution Questionnaire

Name:____

Source of Claim: ☐ Wages (including deferred compensation)
☐ Nonqualified retirement
☐ Provider of Services
☐ Provider of Products

Address for Delivery of Distribution Check:

____

____

____

Entity Form: ☐ Individual ☐ LLC
☐ Sole Proprietor ☐ LLP
☐ Corporation ☐ Other (list)
☐ Partnership ____________________

Telephone Number: ______________________________

Social Security Number: ____________________________

Federal Identification Number: ________________________

What state do you currently claim as your legal residence? __________

What state did you claim as your legal residence when you worked for or provided service or product to the Debtor or an affiliate? ____________

____

____

If you were a resident of several states during the years you worked for or provided service or product to Debtor or an affiliate, list each state and the years you were a resident of such state.

____

____

____

____

____

____

____

____

Index

Page numbers in bold indicate figures or tables.